THE FORESTPORT BREAKS

The Forestport Feeder canal breaks, ca. 1899. On the morning of the third consecutive feeder break, officials can only watch as water rushes away. C. Dayton, photographer. *Courtesy of New York State Archives.*

The FORESTPORT Breaks

A NINETEENTH-CENTURY CONSPIRACY ALONG THE BLACK RIVER CANAL

MICHAEL DOYLE

Syracuse University Press

First Edition 2004
04 05 06 07 08 09 6 5 4 3 2 1

The paper used in this publication meets the minimum requirements of American National Standard for Information Sciences—Permanence of Paper for Printed Library Materials, ANSI Z39.48–1984.∞™

Library of Congress Cataloging-in-Publication Data

Doyle, Michael, 1956–
The Forestport breaks : a nineteenth century conspiracy along the Black River Canal / Michael Doyle.
p. cm.
Includes bibliographical references and index.
ISBN 0-8156-0772-5 (alk. paper)
1. Forestport (N.Y.)—History. 2. Conspiracies—New York (State)—Forestport—History. 3. Black River Canal (N.Y.) I. Title.
F129.F686 D69 2004
974.7'62—dc22
2003020472

Manufactured in the United States of America

To Dad, a son of Forestport

Michael Doyle has worked as a reporter in the Washington bureau of McClatchy newspapers since 1988, writing primarily for the Modesto, Fresno, and Sacramento *Bee* papers. He also writes freelance magazine articles for publications including *California Journal* and teaches college journalism classes.

Contents

Illustrations	ix
Acknowledgments	xi
Introduction	xiii
The Forestport Breaks	1
References	225
Index	229

Illustrations

The Forestport Feeder canal breaks, ca. 1899 — *frontispiece*

Oneida County map, ca. 1906 — 2

The Forestport Feeder canal breaks, ca. 1899 — 6

The Forestport Feeder canal under repair, ca. 1899 — 19

Thomas Wheeler, assistant superintendent of the New York Department of Public Works — 21

Repair crews on the Forestport Feeder, ca. 1899 — 34

Below the Forestport state dam — 37

The Forestport state pond, crowded with logs — 41

George Aldridge, superintendent of the New York Department of Public Works — 49

Pinkerton detective Herbert W. Bearce — 107

Pinkerton detective John J. Pender — 111

River Street, Forestport, ca. 1911 — 157

The first lock on the Forestport Feeder, ca. 1920 — 216

Acknowledgments

MANY HANDS HELPED CONSTRUCT THIS BOOK.

All hail the librarians! The Boonville, Utica, and Rochester public libraries were immensely helpful, as was the Yale University Library. These provided invaluable old newspapers, guidance, and inspiration.

Town clerks in Boonville, Rome, and Utica deserve thanks for the way they keep their public records; many blessings go out to the anonymous clerk at the Oneida County Courthouse who found the transcript of Richard Manahan's second trial.

The Oneida County Historical Society and its curator, Richard Aust, made a rich treasure trove available. Ann Salter at the Rochester Historical Society likewise helped open the doors to the past, as did the Rome Historical Society.

Craig Williams, senior historian at the New York State Museum, doggedly pursued archival material and candidly reviewed an early version of the manuscript. Mark Koziol, curator of the wonderful Erie Canal Museum, tracked down some precious documents and helped me understand the canal's history.

Jane Adler, a detective in her own right through her work in the Pinkerton archives, offered insight, documents, and good-humored candor.

Boonville resident Judy Routson repeatedly waded through old microfilm copies of the *Boonville Herald;* what she found proved crucial.

I am particularly grateful for the persistent work of Ellen S. Goodman, assistant to the director of Syracuse University Press; her steady presence throughout a long process helped keep everything on track.

Carol Sheriff, at the College of William and Mary, took time from her own busy schedule to review portions of the manuscript.

Special thanks to Forestport resident Dorothy Mooney, who has tracked the town's history for decades and who generously opened up her collection and her fascinating memory.

My wife, Beth, has provided her boon companionship and acutely intelligent perspective throughout. She helped steer the manuscript in the right direction, she offered keen suggestions, and she's never faltered. My children, Matthew, Brendan, and Margaret, have helped in many ways.

My mom, Joy Doyle, gave me a leg up at the starting gate with her infectious love of reading and writing. My dad, William Doyle, instigated this whole business; he offered some crucial critiques, he was my partner on a memorable upstate research trip, and he provided something priceless: a family mystery to explore.

Introduction

I FINALLY FOUND MY FAMILY PLOT.

Beyond Oneida's Lansing Kill, buried amid the woods and water. Not what I was looking for, but something altogether more intriguing. The facts are these: I went searching for my name, and found instead what one New York lawman called the most damnable conspiracy ever hatched up in the state. I found a town I had never known, and a century-turning world of political rot and plotting men. I found the rise and rousing times and the ultimate sliding into history's backwaters of a village called Forestport.

Forestport is in Oneida County, part of what once was called the burned-over district of New York's upstate. Burned over, some said, in the metaphoric flames of nineteenth-century religious zealotry. Forestport, too, burned over, in a succession of nonmetaphorical fires. Now it is placid, a village with a mist-shrouded past astride a delicate lake. Once it was a town altogether on the edge. It was where the woods and water met, the boundary between Adirondack forests and Erie Canal water; the boundary, too, between aspiring Utica and the North Country wilds.

"There is a bad gang in the village of Forestport," a Colonel John N. Partridge said in the *Rochester Post-Express* on 19 January 1900. "The people seem to be afraid of it. Robberies, assaults and even worse have been laid, by rumor, at its door. There were three deaths in the village, I am told, which took place under suspicious circumstances."

Nor was Colonel Partridge the town's only accuser. He enlisted, in time, the world's most famous detective agency, which raised such questions that, as a turn-of-the-century Forestport man complained in the *Utica Observer* on 12 January 1900, "one would think that this community is outside the pale of civilization and that it is controlled by thieves and murderers." These suspicions were raised by estimable men who knew life's darker edges. But did they really know Forestport, the character of the place?

Partridge wanted justice, and the orderly operation of the Erie Canal. He was, in 1900, the superintendent of public works for the State of New York. Governor Theodore Roosevelt had appointed him to root out problems accreted over many decades, the very problems, it happened, that had undermined Roosevelt's Republican predecessor. Already sensitive to past canal depredations, Partridge believed Forestport men had disrupted his canal several years running. He undertook a secret reconnaissance, but the truth resisted disclosure. Forestport men clammed up, like members of a secret society asked about their fraternal codes. "It ain't healthy to talk about that matter," one man told him, as the *Brooklyn Eagle* reported on 21 January 1900. "When Hiram was talking about that, he disappeared and turned up dead," another said.

And so Colonel Partridge returned from his reconnaissance and unleashed the Pinkerton National Detective Agency. The Pinkertons found in Forestport, one prosecutor said, a unique conspiracy, one for which there was no parallel in viciousness and wantonness. Indeed, the prosecutor would declare in the *Utica Observer* on 28 May 1900 that the Pinkertons unearthed "one of the most gigantic conspiracies that was ever concocted" in New York State.

The town's plotting was undeniably peculiar. It marked the only time in the Erie Canal's history that men were charged with conspiring to destroy canal property. But the conspiring was also emblematic, redolent, many believed, of a broader corruption encrusting the Erie Canal. "It was," one Oneida County observer sadly summed up in the *Brooklyn Eagle* on 21 January 1900, "but natural that the countrymen hanging around the barrooms and stables of Forestport should seek a means whereby they, too, could share in the pickings from the state treasury. The Forestport men did not have the position that enabled them to make the raid on the treasury in a polite and genteel manner, and so they went at it brutally." Nor was it, the *Utica Observer* stated on May 28, 1900, "only the rough characters of the woods" who conspired in Forestport, "but men of means, and men of influence," the kind of men, that is, who had long benefited on other stretches of the Erie Canal.

As the *Observer* noted, "the Forestport gang had been taught by bad examples that men much higher in the political world than they could ever hope to be did not hesitate to filch from the State treasury by various subterfuges." The men who prosecuted the Forestport conspirators—and, certainly, the conspirators themselves, as well as those who loved and protected them—well understood the nature of those bad examples. The canal was overripe with them. Partridge would eventually explain that by investigating Forestport and bringing the town to justice, state officials sent a wholesome warning to the lawless classes, who in the past had made free with the state's property.

Mine is a different case.

I longed, in time, to know my blood's character and the circumstances of its arising. I started with simply wanting a name, my own in full, but one fact led to another until I had apprehended Forestport. Finally, like Colonel Partridge and his agents nearly a century before, I came to Michael Doyle's place. Michael Doyle was my namesake and great-grandfather, the man I was after.

Michael Doyle was a Forestport man. Once upon a time, I was told, my father, when he was a boy, lay upon the second floor of Michael Doyle's Forestport hotel and eavesdropped on the men downstairs. That is what I am about. I am a boy, my ear to the splintered floor. I am a son, tracking back my father's footsteps. I am a spy, eavesdropping on the ever-cryptic past.

THE FORESTPORT BREAKS

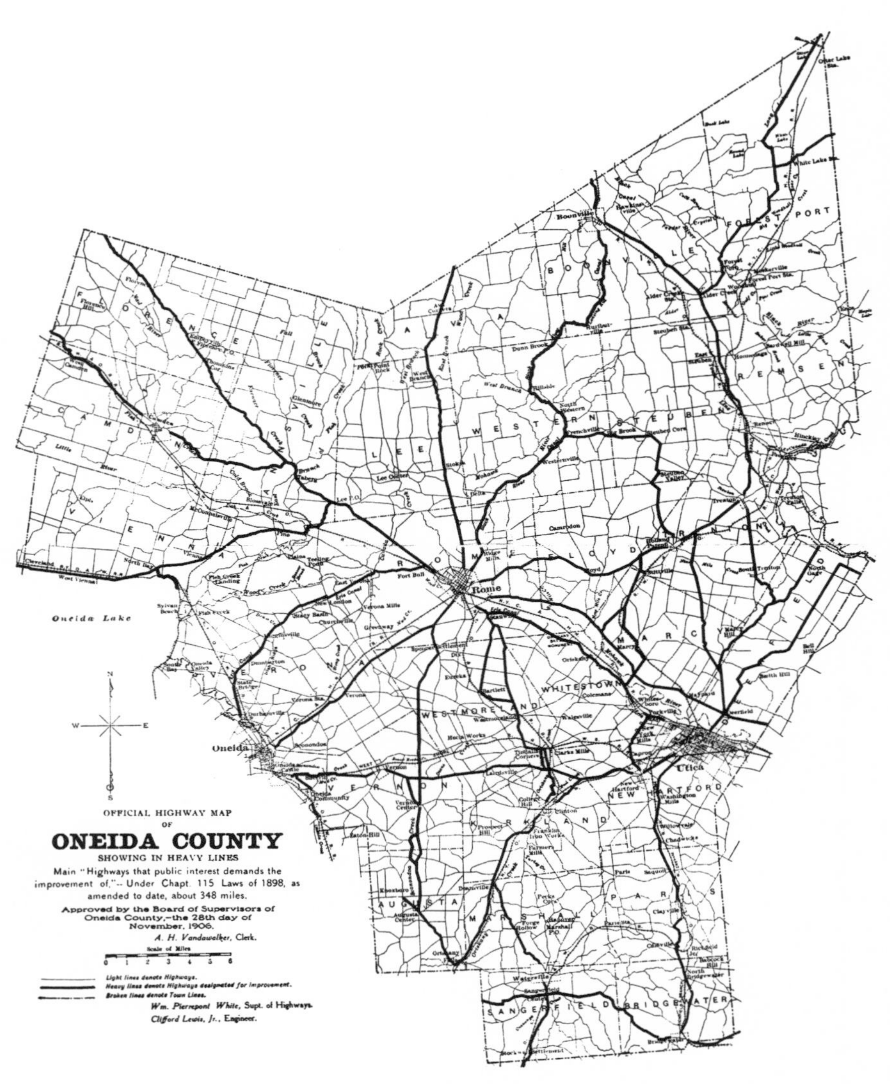

Oneida County map, ca. 1906. *Courtesy of Oneida County Historical Society.*

Chapter 1

THE WATER MYSTIFIES.

At five o'clock on a May morning, 1898, a predawn fog obscures the course of New York's Black River, but the time of revealing approaches. The outlines of spared trees become apparent branch by branch until their patterns are as distinctive as fingerprints.

Al Schoonmaker suspects nothing. The forty-five-year-old farmer and his boy, Robert, are collecting the farm animals from their night wanderings. Their neighbors, the other good people of Forestport, New York, likewise are arising this Monday morning, but the town's sawmills have not yet begun their screaming, the saloons and lively houses are yet dormant. At most, a cowbell tinkles, a word passes from father to son as they walk the damp pasture. It had rained hard the night before, and the grass underfoot is slick.

Al sees something in the distance.

He is mystified, at first, as he peers down toward the Black River that cuts along by his pasture. Al's farm sits on the northwestern edge of Forestport, just beyond the several-block squat of hotels, saloons, and markets that make up the village's business district. All those businesses depend, ultimately, upon the Black River, a northward-bound, often willful waterway that runs 115 miles from its Herkimer County sources to its dispersal in Lake Ontario. Forestport residents are accustomed to taking the measure of the river that sidles alongside. It was the river, the power and transport of it, that drew the first settlers, and it holds them still. By diverting part of the Black River into a canal, Forestport became a town of two parts: a place, the residents liked to say, where the woods met the water.

There are a half-dozen sawmills in the town's immediate vicinity. The Black River brings them Adirondack logs each spring and drives the steam-powered mills that make Forestport one of the busiest lumber-producing centers in late-nineteenth-century New York. In this year, 1898, just three Forestport mills will saw through 10.8 million board feet of spruce and hardwood. Few Adirondack towns can boast higher numbers. The Forestport Lumber Company and Denton & Waterbury mills, the town's two most prominent, will produce 8.2 million pieces of lath in 1898—almost one-fifth the state's total (New York State Commissioners of Fisheries, Game and Forests 1899).

When Al Schoonmaker looks beyond the Black River and up a clear-cut hill on the river's far side, he is seeing the bank of the Forestport Feeder canal, several hundred feet away. The Forestport Feeder channels Black River water, enabling the town's sawmills to ship their shingles and lath. It is the town's lifeblood, but it is anemic. It was barely two weeks earlier that the feeder and the larger Erie Canal system of which it is a part opened for the shipping season following a long winter. There are boats again, traveling the Forestport Feeder down to the Black River Canal ten miles away, and then down through the Lansing Kill to Rome and the Erie Canal and destinations beyond. The boats are relatively scarce; they are old and in poor repair. The canal's best days are behind it, though it remains capable of surprise.

The mist breaks. Al Schoonmaker can recognize, beyond the Black River, that a sheet of water about eight feet wide is flowing over the top of the Forestport Feeder levee. Curious, Al and his boy, Robert, head down to the banks of the river by an old pulp mill (*People v. Manahan* 1900, 149). From there, they can see clearly the unbound waters slushing down the treeless hillside. The canal has broken, Al recognizes, close to the levee bend where it burst the year before. Such breaks are all too common; the Erie Canal is an old man with salty yarns and brittle bones. There are many instigators of disaster, and Al has seen his share of them. Gophers and muskrats, for instance. They chew at canal banks so much that the state for years paid a 25-cent bounty for every muskrat hide brought in. Burrowing crabs were once blamed for an 1888 canal break near Rochester that wiped out bridges and nearby potato fields. Sometimes heavy rains strip unrooted berm-side hills that slump into canals to dam up the water. Men, too, cause problems. Schoonmaker can remember back to 15 May 1890, when the *Boonville Herald* reported that a shovel was found on the Forestport towpath about a mile from town, abandoned next to a hastily dug ditch through which the feeder water was running. Coincidentally, a break had occurred near that very spot just a few years before. Forestport men wondered what that might have been about.

On 4 May, just three weeks before, the *Rochester Herald* had reported that sixty-eight feet of towpath had washed away near the town of Amsterdam, close to Schenectady. On 12 May, the same paper reported that three hundred yards of canal bank near Eagle Harbor had broken open. The very next night, a canal break in the heart of Syracuse had flooded the floors of Greenway's brewery, destroying thousands of bushels of malt. Every break rendered another delay. It was not until 20 May that the first pair of boats set out from Rochester to start the 1898 season. All along the canal, from Buffalo to Albany, there are broken-down locks to fix, bridges to replace, walls to shore up, and not enough money for any of it.

But Al also knows canal breaks can prove beneficial. Well-connected contractors can pocket fat profits, while the contractors' political allies take their surreptitious share. Rochester men had been doing it for years. Back when Schoonmaker was a young man, Rochester's Lord family became notorious for turning disastrous breaks into perfect bonanzas for themselves. Closer to home, the Utica contractor who had run the 1897 Forestport repairs had been denounced for having engaged in one long revel in spoils. Forestport men, too, could always turn a profit when the state shored up the feeder.

Schoonmaker cannot yet fathom the causes or beneficiaries, but he is seeing the direr implications plunk and plain. If the new break is bad enough, it will shut down feeder traffic to Boonville and strand any boats up on the Forestport state pond. Cities like Rome could go dry. The whole Black River Canal might close while the feeder is repaired, depriving the Erie Canal of needed replenishment. The canal cannot afford such

The Forestport Feeder canal breaks, ca. 1899. C. Dayton, photographer. *Courtesy of New York State Archives.*

losses. With the rail competition from the New York Central, there has been talk of closing down portions of the Black River Canal. This closure would be catastrophic for canal towns like Forestport, which are already struggling.

Al resolves himself. He is going to have to run to Forestport's far side, through town and across the Black River to where the lock tenders can shut down the feeder and avoid further damage. He climbs back up the riverbank and starts off across the dampened field toward Forestport's wakening main street. He passes the whitewashed St. Patrick's Catholic Church and the Forestport Social and Literary Union. They suffice for the town's higher aspirations. In another twenty yards Al Schoonmaker is running through the fundament of Forestport, a logging and canal town on the border between the wilderness and civilization.

"They've got more saloons than houses," one prosecutor declares later in the *Utica Observer* of 26 May 1900, "and that is the way the town is ruled."

It is not, literally, true. There are no more than a half-dozen saloons along River Street, and this in a town of about 1,500 souls. Admittedly, come Friday and Saturday night, particularly when the rowdy river drivers are back from the Big Moose River and West Canada Creek, the saloons define Forestport. They have made Forestport a town of uncertain reputation.

"The citizens," a turn-of-the-century Utica visitor wrote in the *Brooklyn Eagle* of 12 January 1900, "are a hardy class of men, honest in the main, but having among them just the reckless daredevil class which makes its living away from humanity and modern civilization in general."

The reputation adorns the known facts like an Adirondack guide's story about a black bear's snatching the guide's flapjack batter and then returning for the frying pan. But, undeniably, Forestport can mean trouble. The *Boonville Herald* would report on 4 August 1898 that the Boonville baseball team once refused to visit because the players feared for their physical safety. The town has its share of other fights, and for a time endured a series of suspicious fires. One Friday night in 1898, someone crept aboard the little steamboat *Ollie,* docked in the Forestport state pond, poured oil all about, set it on fire, and then set the burning boat adrift. From such events, reputations grow. Once, around the turn of the century, a cardsharp named Hugh McDonald was asked if he would be shocked to learn his Forestport acquaintances plotted an enormous crime.

"I wouldn't be surprised," McDonald replied, according to the *Rome Daily Sentinel* of 24 May 1900, "at anything up there." A Forestport correspondent added in the *Boonville Herald* of 27 October 1898 that "a detective could be brought here, who would soon locate some of the lawless characters who infest our town."

The detectives would come, in time. But that was still a year away, and Al Schoonmaker has his more immediate concern. He must call the alert, so the lock tenders can shut off the feeder water and prevent further damage. Running down River Street, he passes by Walt Bynon's saloon and the livery stable run by William Clark, and by the three-story lumberjack's hotel known as Doyle's. Al runs by the Getman House, another three-story place, bought just one month earlier by Dick Manahan. With its second-story porch wrapping around and its corner tower, it is the town's noblest hotel, and Manahan runs it like he is the town's host. He is a big man in Forestport, with his hand in a little bit of everything. Like Michael Doyle, he cultivates big plans. Across the street from the Getman is Jimmy Rudolph's place, where a man can stake his future on pool or cards. Jimmy himself is not one to tangle with, but when circumstances demand, he can be a man of action.

On Al Schoonmaker moves, past the town's cash store, and the market, and the tiny Forestport jail, until he is crossing the twin bridges over the Black River tumble. The bridges cross the river immediately downstream of the dam that binds the Black River water and channels it into the Forestport Feeder. To Al's left, about a hundred yards away, is the dam. To his right, the river calms and settles into its northward course on toward Alder Creek and Boonville. The road forks on the far side, across the bridge. To the right is Dutch Hill, atop of which is the start of the Forestport Feeder towpath. He heads left, along the shore of the state pond. In another two hundred yards, he is at the lockhouse. He is breathing hard by now, sweating.

"I was running pretty fast, and was pretty nearly winded," Schoonmaker recalled much later (*People v. Manahan* 1900, 180).

It is approaching six o'clock when Schoonmaker reaches the lockhouse on the edge of the several-acre state pond. Thirteen-foot logs are jumbled on it like giant matchsticks, though it is not as crowded as it gets later in the year. These logs are just the carryover from the previous year, the logs that according to the *Boonville Herald* of 28 April 1898 had allowed the Denton & Waterbury and Forestport Lumber Company mills to fire up for the season back in late April.

Garrett Nichols, the Forestport lock tender, is already up and about when Schoonmaker arrives. Even with business slow, lock tenders are on duty twelve hours a day. They are indispensable to the workings of the canal. They also have, in some upstate places, a reputation for cussedness. They can offend the sensibilities of proper men and ladies, as when Syracuse University Chancellor James R. Day took a party on an 1898 cruise through the Champlain Canal. At one lock, Day complained to Superintendent of Public Works George Washington Aldridge Jr. that "this man [was] rough and brutal. He seemed to think the whole thing of letting in the water a coarse joke, and his language before the ladies of my party was ungentlemanly and rough" (George Washington Aldridge Papers). Other travelers complained about lock tenders' being too old, or too feeble, or too drunk to do the work required. They could, at times, demand criminal exactions.

Lockport was notorious for extortion in the 1890s; for example, the boat owner J. H. Webster advised public works superintendent Aldridge that "we were obliged to pay from twenty-five to fifty cents each (according to the humor of the lock-tender) under penalty of having our boats damaged for not promptly complying with their requests" (George Washington Aldridge Papers). But George Aldridge, the boss of all the canals, had been endeavoring to clean up the more troublesome locks. "The locks are," he had declared in the *Boonville Herald* of 1 January 1897, "no longer lounging places for toughs and loafers [and] the boatmen no longer fear to pass the locks at all points on the Canals at all hours of the day or night." And Garrett Nichols is, besides, a man of the town who has retained his job amidst the state's political fluctuations. Lock-tending is proper work for this Episcopalian elder and native of Holland, and he is not hindered by his small disfigurement. Six years earlier, while running a saw at one of the Forestport mills, the *Boonville Herald* of 18 August 1892 had reported that Nichols had cut off three fingers of his left hand below the first joint. He is not the only Forestport man to have lost part of himself to the mills.

Nichols and his helper, George Klinck, a fifty-seven-year-old war veteran, have already checked the water in the feeder. It appears to be at its proper level, six inches below the high mark. There is no evidence anything is amiss until Al Schoonmaker comes running.

"I was out after the cows with my boy, and saw the water in the river rolling," Schoonmaker tells them. "I think something's the matter" (*People v. Manahan* 1900, 148).

Much later, questions will arise again about the specifics of what Schoonmaker says. There will be questions, indeed, as to whether Al

Schoonmaker revised under prosecutorial pressure his recollection of what he saw and what he said. But whatever the particulars, the gist of what is reported is plain: there is a break, again, in the Forestport Feeder.

Nichols and Klinck take action.

The lock they tend guards the sluice that channels dammed-up Black River water into the feeder. If there is a break downstream and the lock is open, the water will keep flowing through the rupture, worrying the wound. Nichols closes the lock and stops the flow of water. When he is done, he, Klinck, and Schoonmaker start up Dutch Hill toward where the towpath starts. It is a hill steep enough to cause trouble if a man is imprudent. Two years before, Al and Dan Grinno had been whooping it up when for a thrill they whipped their wagon as fast as they could down Dutch Hill and toward the Black River bridge. They ended up in a ditch, and the *Boonville Herald* of 17 June 1896 reported that a chastened Al ended up with a broken jaw.

Nichols, Klinck, and Schoonmaker are as sober as the sunrise when they climb Dutch Hill and then strike right, down the packed clay and gravel towpath (Garrity 1977, 25). They still cannot detect anything unusual. The dark green water still is contained within the banks to the left of the towpath. On the feeder's far side, the berm-side, a denuded hill rises, its trees cut down the year before for shoring up the towpath banks. After walking several hundred feet, the three men reach the waste weir. This is a safety valve, a sluice cut into the towpath. Gates, four big wooden ones and two small iron ones, are closed at the moment. When the gates of the waste weir are opened, the feeder water will drain into the Black River one hundred feet or so below. It takes the men about twenty minutes to lift all the heavy gates. Once the water is rushing out, the men set out back along the towpath to see what has transpired.

It is a well-trodden path they are on. Countless boys have walked its length, barefoot and daydreaming, keeping the mules hauling the fifty-ton boats ten miles to Boonville and the Black River Canal there. The feeder is surprisingly modest for the burden it carries, only about forty feet wide and four feet deep. But a world can change in shallow water. The boats can float along at four miles per hour, their hulls stuffed with potatoes, hops, and wheat and their decks stacked with lath, shingles, and milled lumber.

The cribs of thirteen-foot-long spars, bound together like makeshift boats themselves, can likewise be eased down the waterway, and a beloved little steamboat can transport Forestport picnickers while the town's brass band plays and the women hold on to their wide-brimmed hats in the breeze (O'Donnell 1949, 99, 60).

Al Schoonmaker the farmer, George Klinck the helper, and Garrett Nichols the lock tender walk on down the towpath, not yet sure what they will find. There is a turbulence in the feeder, and a definite lowering of its depth. The men walk around a final bend, and then they are upon it.

The towpath wound is grotesque, and worsening by the minute.

Schoonmaker, Klinck, and Nichols approach the collapsing lip of a chasm that is already at least thirty feet across the towpath's length. Water is rushing out the break, tearing off, every few minutes, another crumbly towpath chunk. Fissures split the treeless berm-side hill on the feeder's far side, as rootless soil slides into the water. The canal bottom, too, is being sucked down the hillside, and Schoonmaker can see its muddy crawl down toward the Black River and his modest farm below. The men cannot fathom what caused the break, nor envision how big it will become. But having shut off the lock and opened up the waste weir, Nichols knows he has done everything he can to minimize the damage. When the rest of the world awakens, he will alert Mr. Dayton, the Forestport telegrapher, so the canal authorities can learn of this latest catastrophe. The engineers will start arriving, and the politically connected contractors, and then there will surely be a mob of workmen, shovelers and pickmen, Irish and Italians. It is going to get lively again in old Forestport.

Canal watchman Warner Yeomans is among the first to arrive. He had already noticed something out of the ordinary that morning when he struck the towpath and crossed the waste weir where the water was running. He hurried along until he came upon Nichols and the others, watching the break growing larger. Yeomans observes there is only about three feet of water left in the canal; it is down a foot and subsiding further by the minute (*People v. Manahan* 1900, 152).

Back in town, the good people of Forestport are awakening to the realization that there has been another break in the routine of their lives. Soon boys in short pants and girls in sturdy dresses are skaddling out along the towpath. Men and women, too, flow to the break. The men cross arms across their chests and point fingers, calculating causes and consequences. Some men think it is obvious that the Saturday rain caused the berm-side hill to slump. All that muck just dammed up the water and forced it over the towpath; once the water started washing over the towpath, there was no stopping it.

"There was a large amount of dirt out of the bank, and it had slid down into the canal . . . in a kind of half-moon shape," a Forestport man named Henry Cascum, a neighbor of Al Schoonmaker's, tells interrogators later. "It was opposite the hole in the towpath; it was solid dirt half way in the canal from the other side" (*People v. Manahan* 1900, 166).

But not everyone remembers it precisely the same way. Charley Pratt drives his rig all the way from Boonville and arrives before noon. By then, the towpath has gone out a length of about one hundred feet, eaten away by the continuing outflow of water.

"There was a regular hole worked into the bottom of the canal 30 or 40 feet deep, and that was working back towards the berm bank and up and down the canal in both directions," Pratt recalled about two years later. "Dirt was caving into the bottom of the canal and big chunks of earth was dropping into this hole as the water undermined it" (*People v. Manahan* 1900, 81).

Pratt is as observant as a detective. Everyone is saying the berm-side hill slumped off in the rain and dammed up the feeder so that the backed-up water washed over the towpath. But if that is the case, then where are the signs of any impromptu dam? Pratt sees none. There are others who make their own skeptical observations. One man, John Scanlon, comes right out and disputes the crowd's conventional wisdom:

"I've known this bank a good many years," he says. "There was no slide on the berm bank" (*People v. Manahan* 1900, 66).

Scanlon should know. He was in charge of the Forestport Feeder in the 1860s and 1870s and has seen his share of breaks, but the crowd's adopted theory remains the slumping berm bank. All day, curious Forestport residents visit the break. When it is still relatively early, the liveryman William Clark arrives with an occasional Forestport visitor by the name of Howard M. Fordham. Clark is a trim thirty-four-year-old former saloonkeeper who now runs a River Street livery. Fordham is forty-eight and much-traveled. He is a man of diverse and chancy commercial interests, in real estate no one has seen, in timberland that is full of scars and stumps.

This morning Fordham had been awakened at Dick Manahan's Getman House hotel by shouting out on the street. When he dressed and went downstairs, he hooked up with Clark and together the men proceeded to the break. After they regard it a while, the two men return to town, engaged in a conversation that they will later come to remember very differently.

The proper authorities are already on the way, alerted by telegraph. Edgar Hughes sets out for the latest catastrophe from Boonville. Hughes is the superintendent of the Black River Canal, in charge of some seventy-eight miles of waterway and the attendant locks. Another break now is the last thing he needs. The Black River Canal is doing poorly enough these days—the portions north of Boonville to Port Leyden are already under consideration for closing—and Hughes has his hands full with other repairs. The latest break is an even worse aggravation for State Engineer and Surveyor Campbell W. Adams. Adams, by happenstance, is in his hometown of Utica the morning of 24 May. Word of the fresh disaster arrives just in time to sour his breakfast. He is there with Thomas Wheeler, the state's deputy superintendent of public works, who is in charge of the entire Middle Division of the Erie Canal. Adams is a self-trained engineer, while Wheeler is a politician through and through, a former mayor and a blunt, determined, pinochle-playing man of fifty-two years. Boss Wheeler, as some inevitably call him, is not a trifling man. He stands a solid six feet tall, with broad shoulders and a stern face. He is not particularly eloquent, but men attend to his every word (Bielby 1890b, 4).

Tom Wheeler, in truth, knows far more about politics than about canal engineering, though politics is not all he knows. He knows what a crime scene looks like, and where the Oneida County crime scenes are. He once served as chief detective for a stretch of the New York Central and Hudson River Railroad Company and, despite unsettling whispers about his own past, he served a four-year term as county sheriff. Wheeler will need all his old detecting skills to plumb the bottom of the latest Forestport break. In the end, another kind of lawman will finish the job.

Neither Adams nor Wheeler need more bad news. They are both already coping with a mess of crumbling locks and leaking levees. There is not enough money or manpower as it is to handle what has already gone wrong, and they are having to defend how they have spent the repair monies they have been given. Their own reputations are slumping like a hillside under rain, and investigators are swarming all over the canal.

Wheeler and Adams and their unhappy retinue board a New York Central line at the station near Utica's bustling Baggs Square. In less than half an hour they reach the tidy hub town of Remsen, atop a hill overlooking parts of the Kuyahoora and Steuven valleys. Into the Remsen station poke the various lines that have been absorbed by the Central. The Mohawk & Malone strikes north through the newly created Adirondack forest preserve all the way, eventually, to Canada (Harter 1979, 29). Adams knows that rail line well. Before he became a canal man, he helped engineer the Mohawk & Malone tracks through the swampy bogs, dense forest, and steep grades of the Adirondacks. The two state authorities are not going nearly that far, but they are going, some believe, to a world markedly different from the orderly bustle of Utica.

"There is no law," people whisper, "north of Remsen."

From Remsen, Adams and the others pass through dense banks of uncut forest, on up through the Honnedaga and Black River Siding stops and then over the tail end of what is grandly called Kayuta Lake. It is really just the tamed leftover from the Black River, impounded by the Forestport dam. In not quite twenty minutes of traveling time from Remsen, the engineers reach Forestport's Buffalo Head station, a little more than a mile outside Forestport proper. From Buffalo Head, a stagecoach ferries the disembarked Mohawk & Malone passengers to their destination. By late afternoon, the state's contingent has arrived in force. The resident engineer of the Erie Canal's Middle Division, George Morris, makes his observations alongside his chief assistant. Edgar Hughes, the superintendent from Boonville, briefs the newcomers. And by nightfall Monday, as the *Utica Press* reported on 24 May 1898, certain facts had become clear.

The repair will require hundreds of men working day and night. It will be expensive. It cost the state $62,781.78 to repair the 1897 Forestport break, and that figure did not really capture the full burden of shutting down the entire Black River Canal for nearly a month. This new break, like the last, will seize the region, the way an engine's pistons jam in the cylinders when deprived of oil. Stranded boats will remain tied to snubbing posts in Boonville and Port Leyden. The shingles and lath cut by the Forestport mills will remain stacked up in town. In water-starved Rome, fountains will be shut down and fire engines will be secured to pump reserve supplies through the city's pipes.

If there is any good news for Wheeler and Morris, as they finally settle into their room that night in Jimmy Rudolph's place, it is that the break was discovered so early. Al Schoonmaker did everyone a service when he peered through the morning's lifting mist and detected water breaking out of the feeder to the Black River below. By his run through town, his quick alert to the lock tenders, Schoonmaker helped save the state considerable aggravation and no little amount of money. Yes, Al Schoonmaker is a modest state hero on this 24th of May 1898. But if that is the case, then why are there Forestport men this very evening who are wishing him dead?

Chapter 2

SOME LAWS CANNOT BE BROKEN, EVEN NORTH OF REMSEN.

The natural laws are inviolable: where water will flow, and how, and at what speed. An experienced state inspector based out of Schenectady, Peter Minders knew the water laws like a sheriff knows his city code. That is what puzzled him as he began inspecting the blown-out Forestport Feeder two days after the 1898 break. When Minders received the telegram about the latest feeder mishap, he was repairing another bad break that had forced several hundred westbound boats to tie up between Cohoes and Schenectady. He reached Forestport on Wednesday.

"When I arrived, I found the towpath had gone out to a depth at that time from 60 to 65 feet, extending back nearly the entire width of the canal about 40 feet," Minders reported later. "The prism of the canal had gone out into the river, and I estimated the opening at the top across the towpath about 300 feet" (*People v. Manahan* 1900, 55).

The prism was the packed clay canal bed, swept away and deposited down the hillside toward the Black River below. It was a mess everywhere he looked, but Minders had an eye for the critical detail. He noted the exposed wooden piles jutting from the ruptured earth like so many snapped bones. They were the remnants of levee strengthening done the year before, following the last break. He noted as well the condition of the berm bank opposite the towpath. Unlike some Forestport men, Minders saw no evidence the berm bank might have slid into the canal during a rainy night.

"We examined anything we could see," Minders recounted later, describing his search for natural causes. "We could not find anything whatever" (*People v. Manahan* 1900, 58).

Minders and Charles Tuttle, the Black River Canal's general foreman, walked carefully over the surviving towpath. Tuttle had arrived by train the Tuesday after the break. Like Minders, he knew the Forestport towpath well from the 1897 repairs. Minders saw that about three hundred feet closer to Forestport, where the levee had broken out the year before, the towpath had settled from about fifteen inches lower than the original bank. Minders thought it strange that the latest break did not occur at the low spots. If the berm bank had slid down and dammed up the feeder water, as Forestport men were saying, then the backed-up water should have pushed first over the towpath's lowest spots. That would have been the water's lawful course.

The essential engineering questions were answered quickly. Wooden piles would be pounded into the chasm and the space filled up with a puddled gravel and clay core. Over all would be layered packed-down dirt taken from the nearby hillsides. Done right, the wooden piles should hold the levee against any insult. The repair scheme resembled the plan used the previous year. The same contractor, James J. Dwyer of Utica, would again be employed. County Tipperary-born, James Dwyer and his brother Thomas were a familiar pair around the canal, having proven themselves remarkably adept at securing contracts. They were cronies, many believed, of Tom Wheeler, and auditors had taken to nitpicking at some of the Dwyers' practices. The tens of thousands of dollars the Dwyer firm had charged for recent canal improvement work were giving auditors fits. It all seemed, some thought, all too cozy, and emblematic of the canal's inner workings.

"A contractor can make money nearly every time that he becomes a friend of some assistant engineer," Darwin James, a prominent Republican New Yorker, told the *New York Times* on 5 August 1898. "All this system works in the favor of the contractors. I lay the whole blame to politics and to the system."

Nor was it only the private contractors like Dwyer who benefited through their personal acquaintances. Canal breaks could be more an opportunity than a disaster for the well prepared. The patronage carnival was exemplified several years earlier following a break in the Erie Canal near Montezuma that caused some three hundred boats to tie up:

"It is exceedingly amusing," the *New York Times* observed on 30 July 1891, "to see assistant superintendents, sub-superintendents, section superintendents and super-superintendents, with a flock of other useless, salary-drawing, honorary canal officials gather around . . . to be told what to do . . . the whole shooting match don't appear to know a canal from a bale of hay."

The Forestport break would likewise attract platoons of state workers and draw questions about how the money was being spent. The auditors, though, could straighten out the money later. The main goal was to get the feeder opened again, and that meant hiring workers. The state needed shovelers, carpenters, teamsters, watchmen, timekeepers, water boys. There was call for blacksmiths, pile-driver operators, mechanics, steam pump engineers, woodchoppers. Forestport men could not nearly fill all the jobs, and the town soon swelled like a North Country river in springtime. Men from nearby Alder Creek and Hawkinsville and Boonville rode hitches or walked in. As word spread, men came from further away, by train to Buffalo Head station and then by stage. In just a few days, some 1,800 men had been hired on to work the break, nearly doubling the town's population.

In the initial days following the break, work crews followed much the same course as they had the year before. They grubbed out the stumps and debris scattered down the hillside toward the Black River. They tamped out paths so that horse-drawn wagons could draw near the repair site, and they squared away the disheveled feeder prism. Engineers identified several nearby quarry pits from which they could extract the fill they would need, and the men scraped away rudimentary roads after the fashion of a figure eight, connecting two pits on the far side of the berm-side hill. As horse-drawn wagons passed by the pits, lines of about fifty men tossed into the boxes several shovelsful of sand each; by the time the wagons reached the end of the line at each pit, their boxes were full. The teamsters drove the wagons down the slope, across a temporary wooden bridge to the towpath side, and into position for emptying.

The Forestport Feeder canal under repair, ca. 1899. C. Dayton, photographer. *Courtesy of New York State Archives.*

The prevailing sounds, for a time, were the slam and clatter of the steam-driven pile-driving machines set up to pound piles into the soft soil. There were two of them, wooden A-frames about twenty feet tall. Once a trench had been cleared away, the men set in the wooden piling: planks two inches wide tongue-and-grooved into lumber poles between sixteen and twenty-two feet long. The men wrapped chains around the poles and centered them in the middle of the A-frames, while heavy barrels were lifted and let fall down their tracks. The pounding lasted until the piles were about fifteen feet deep and would go no further; then men chopped off with an axe whatever was excess at the level of the towpath. These piles, wooden frames with their core filled by gravel and clay, were laid in for a distance of about two thousand feet along the towpath (*People v. Manahan* 1900, 56).

The work rarely stopped. Workers rigged large kerosene lights so they could labor past midnight, and one foreman asserted later that he worked twenty-two hours a day for the nine days he was in Forestport. The repair scene reminded one observer of a military camp, with the men speaking only in low, civil tones. Loud swearing, either at their fellow men or at the obstinate teams of horses, was supposedly forbidden. There was time enough for pent-up rowdiness when the shifts were done.

The Forestport hotels filled up several men to a room, several men, sometimes, to a bed. Some temporary shanties were thrown up, camps for the transitory men, and some impromptu hotels were established. Jimmy Rudolph, who had already opened his place for the state engineers, cleared away space in his pool hall so he could put more men up. Conveniently, he rented office space to Tom Wheeler for the administration of the repairs.

"We employed whoever we could get," Wheeler later recalled. "A large majority were people that came right there from different places, to Forestport, and stayed during the break. The hotel where I was was crowded with boarders and lodgers" (*People v. Manahan* 1900, 99).

Everyone in town seemed to be profiting. The liveryman William Clark, for one, was getting $1.60 an hour for each of his single rigs and $2.80 an hour for each of his double rigs. He kept them running throughout the day and night, bringing timekeepers, shovelers, messengers, and supplies past the River Street hotels and saloons. His rigs were clattering across the Black River bridges, up Dutch Hill, and then down the winding towpath until the breaks were reached, the wagons hauling, foreman Peter Minders later recalled, as many as thirty foremen each time.

"For God's sake, how many foremen were there?" a Utica lawyer would later ask Minders, according to the *Utica Observer* of 23 May 1900.

The workers were hungry for distraction in their scant free time, and Forestport tended to all their myriad appetites. A man could lose his shirt playing cards with the sharp-eyed Frank Murray or Hugh McDonald, or pursuing a fevered moment with a local adventuress, one of the sporting gals whose names were passed along like counterfeit currency. The town was accustomed to men of high spirits, though sometimes they could get too rambunctious.

William Barlow was an Alder Creek man, hired on for the repairs. One

Thomas Wheeler, assistant superintendent of the New York Department of Public Works. Photographer and date unknown. *Courtesy of Oneida County Historical Society.*

Wednesday evening, the *Boonville Herald* of 16 June 1898 would report, he was making his way home from Boonville. As he neared a bridge over the Black River Canal, two toughs sprang from the shadows and demanded his money. Barlow recognized the men from their work on the breaks; they looked dangerous, but he was not easily cowed. He had earned his money and would fight to keep it. The two highwaymen advanced; Barlow hit back. The men swore and shuffled, fists tangling; something sharp nicked Barlow above the eye. He bled, but kept fighting until the robbers disengaged and, swearing at their ill fortune, slipped back into the night. They were still out there, in the dark, awaiting some easier victim.

Some fretted about the flush of two-fisted new workers, particularly the Italian gangs come up from Utica. The Forestport Irishmen considered the Italians dangerously exotic. An immigrant wave had recently increased Utica's Italian population to nearly six thousand, and polite society considered the newcomers a race apart from the "white" folk (Schiro 1940, 90). Their brute strength was welcomed, so long as it was properly harnessed.

"As diggers, they stand supreme," the *Rochester Post and Express* stated on 6 September 1897. "Nobody can touch them when it comes to swinging a shovel or driving a pick. [But, the Italian] is dirty, and he will drink beer, and gets stabbed with regularity."

As late as 1894, the Italians were still exotic enough to cause the *Boonville Herald* to note "the sight of Italians on the line of the Black River Canal" on 16 June 1898 and to explain "the cheapness of the dagos, and their ability to excavate for the new locks to be built with neatness and dispatch . . . [and] their few wants above bread, cheese and tobacco." The Italian workers were making a similar impression on Forestport observers:

"Those who watched the Italians at work on the break came to the conclusion that they can do more labor on less sleep and less food than any other class of men," the *Herald* approvingly noted on 30 June 1898. "They are satisfied with a loaf of bread and a cup of water for each meal."

Italians up from Utica, hybrid farmers out from Alder Creek, first- and second-generation Irish Americans from all around: all together, Forestport in late May and early June of 1898 was more vibrant with workingmen than it had been anytime since . . . well, since the last breaks in 1897.

The breaks brought booming business to Forestport's saloons. Men would lean on the walnut- or mahogany-front counters, their passing images reflected by the large framed mirror behind. There were cuspidors distributed about the floor, but no bar stools. Bartenders poured nickel shots of Golden Wedding rye and Jas. E. Pepper's bourbon. Salty foods—crackers and dried fish—were set out at one end. The cigars smoking up the room were locally rolled down at John Weikert's or at one of the other Utica cigar manufacturers. The saloon floors could be pockmarked by years of calked lumberjacks' boots. Sensible bartenders armed themselves with saloon peacekeepers. A good Spalding Black End baseball bat, solid ash or willow, cost only twenty cents and could be stocked beneath the bar for when the boys got too rowdy.

The workers paid for room and board both. In the mornings, they tromped downstairs to the common dining rooms for lumberjack-style replenishments thick with starch and gravy: baked beans, flapjacks, potatoes, ham, bread. Traditionally, Adirondack loggers ate in silence while in camp; the bull cook did not want the men wasting time (Welsh 1995, 71). The

Forestport hotel dining halls lacked such discipline, and the workers had plenty to gab about that late May.

Far away, in the Klondike, there were new gold finds below Dawson, a good break for the men who survived. Reports circulated about Spanish and American warships engaging in West Indian waters. The news was imprecise and prone to error, but the war drumbeats were unmistakable. Just the Saturday before the Forestport levee burst, the battle cruiser *Charlestown* set sail from San Francisco Bay for the Philippines and the edges of a new empire. The rumors of war were joined by rumors of spies. The Pinkerton National Detective Agency, despised already by laboring men, was confronting suggestions it had provided secret information to the Spanish. Spanish operatives were being detected in Key West on their way to scout out the defenses of New York Harbor. The newspapers were tracking the fate of a man named Jiminez, who had been nabbed with a sword in his steamer trunk and a key to coastal charts. His capture was a reminder that men are not always what they seem.

So the men talked and drank and fought, but mostly they worked. All the while, the Forestport businessmen exploited the good break. Jimmy Rudolph, for one, catered to men's chancier interests. Rudolph was forty years old and a hard man, not easily shaken. He had been a partner once in the Forestport undertaking business, before selling out his grave interests in 1893 in favor of a livelier gang of customers. At three o'clock on a Sunday morning, a half-dozen men might be found drinking and swearing loudly at his River Street place, prompting one social standard-bearer to wonder in the *Boonville Herald* of 31 August 1893 "why a legitimate restaurant should keep its doors open at all hours, knowing either night nor Sabbath."

One of Rudolph's regulars was a carnival-wise twenty-five-year-old character named Hugh McDonald. McDonald had a barker's patter smooth enough to lure Rudolph's teenage daughter, Lulu, and he played cards with the cynical artisanship of a bawdy house musician. In 1897, around the time of the first Forestport break, he and Rudolph had established a card-playing partnership that lasted about three months. They played to win, no matter how.

"The cards that I bought I marked, or caused to be marked, and I sent another person back to the store to exchange the cards for another pack," McDonald admitted later (*People v. Manahan* 1900, 78.)

It was a cunning little con. The marked decks returned to the store were bought innocently, seventeen cents a pack, and brought to the game by the dupe, who would then be foreclosed from accusing other men of playing with marked cards. The scheme lasted until Hugh and Jimmy broke up their 1897 partnership, but Hugh was still gambling in May 1898. There were always men around for a game.

"I don't know as I had any friends there," McDonald said later. "I played with whoever I could get to play with" (*People v. Manahan* 1900, 78).

Jimmy's pal Frank Murray likewise relished the new marks. Frank was a mason by trade and had lived in town for more than a decade. He was thirty-three years old in 1898, and he made his living as he could, earning about $3 a day for his bricklaying, or twenty cents an hour loading boats on the state pond. He had worked nights as a sub-foreman during the 1897 feeder repairs, but he preferred gambling. Sometimes he would anger men with his uncanny luck, like the time he had taken a substantial pot from a fellow named Ike Daniels.

"He played poker and lost a large sum of money," Murray recalled. "I went to him and offered him two dollars. He refused the two dollars because he claimed he had lost a much larger sum. [But] he was so drunk he didn't know what he was about" (*People v. Manahan* 1900, 122).

Even more than the drinkers and the gamblers, the Forestport hotel owners were doing well serving all the new workers. And no man was doing better than Dick Manahan.

Dick was a big man in Forestport. Owner of the town's largest hotel, keeper of its most popular saloon, organizer of some of its most beloved dances, builder of the area's newest Black River bridge, forty-five-year-old Dick Manahan kept his hands in all the pots around town. He could host a party or bounce a troublemaker with equal vigor. At five feet ten inches, and about 227 pounds, he was not a man to be pushed about. Once when Forestport was recovering from the 1897 break, some rambunctious Utica toughs had challenged Dick on the gaslit streets.

"Teddy McMahon came to Dick's assistance, and when the Utica fellows regained consciousness, they found they had run up against the wrong men," the *Boonville Herald*'s admiring correspondent reported on 2 September 1897.

Dick Manahan's had always been a terribly practical world. At thirteen he was working down in Utica. By fifteen, he was cutting Adirondack timber in the winters and working boats in the summers (Wager 1896b, 208). A man learned to take care of himself in the logging camps, and along the towpath, and at the locks where the more determined fighter got through first. He learned men had to make their own order. Twice, after he entered the Forestport hotel and saloon business, he had pleaded guilty to selling liquor without having paid his $200 for a license (*People v. Manahan* 1900, 206).

But if he were a hard case, Dick also kept his eyes open for opportunities. He would run, for a time, the stage route connecting Forestport and the Buffalo Head rail station. When winter froze the Forestport state pond, he tried making money by cutting fourteen-inch-thick blocks of ice for storing and shipping south. When he was thirty-one, Dick had erected the first of his hotels, next to the Buffalo Head railroad station that served Forestport. He ran a livery, a grocery store, and a feed store, while his wife, Ida, cooked up juicy trout dinners for the sporting visitors. Dick and Ida hosted well-attended platform dances and ice cream parties, with the *Boonville Herald* of 10 June 1895 noting that cut roses adorned each table and that the guests stayed until the early morning, while the schoolteacher, Miss Lang, played popular songs on the buoyant little organ. Dick Manahan was a Forestport leader, an instigator of events.

By the spring of 1898, Dick had purchased the three-story Getman House hotel, Forestport's best. It was an authoritative structure, the one chosen by Thomas Wheeler as his headquarters during the 1897 break repairs. Though Dick and Ida Manahan had only bought the Getman House on 20 April 1898, they happened to be well stocked and prepared to exploit the crush of business following the May 1898 canal break. Immediately after taking over the Getman House, Dick had bought 130 pounds of crackers for the men who would be drinking in his saloon, and he bought ginger beer, ale, and a half-barrel of wine to go along. In the weeks following his hotel purchase, Dick kept up a steady supply of orders: a seventy-pound case of tomatoes, ninety pounds of corn, a forty-pound case of salmon, a one hundred-pound case of pickles, a seventy-pound case of peaches, a fifty-pound case of beans, a thirty-pound pail of jelly, a forty-pound case of cherries. The mundane commercial transactions were memorialized in the flimsy manifests and documents filed at the Buffalo Head rail station, where eventually men with an eye for patterns and telling details would be asking for them.

Dick Manahan's was one place a working man could be sure of getting what he needed. Drinking men did have other choices. They could frequent Charley O'Connor's new place, or the River Street saloon run by twenty-seven-year-old Walt Bynon, a cigar-smoking, 220-pound man prone to rheumatic attacks. Across River Street from Bynon's stood one of the village's other hotel-and-saloon combinations, the one known alternatively as The American, or The New American, or simply as Doyle's.

Like Dick Manahan, Michael Doyle took a rutted route to the hotel and saloon trade. Born in 1856, the son of Irish immigrants and farmers named Ellen and Cornelius Doyle, Michael was one of six children raised on a small farm about midway between Alder Creek and Forestport. Cornelius and Ellen had lived in the area since the early 1840s, even before the Forestport Feeder, and they had accumulated some property by the time Michael was born in their modest log house. The 1870 census recorded that the farm, the year before Michael's birth, included a half-acre of buckwheat, one and one-half acres of corn, two acres of the inevitable potatoes, and thirty-eight acres of unimproved rolling land not far from Black River. They had two horses, two cows, and one pig.

The children of Cornelius Doyle scattered like buckwheat chaff in wind. None seemed to stick about the farm. Michael took the basic schooling, enough to read and write, before becoming one of the North Country's common teenage laborers. There were boats to be loaded with lumber around the Forestport state pond, buildings to be hammered together in the summer, cribs of timber to be floated to the cities of industry. He took such work as was necessary, taking his chances as they came, until he married Jenny Donovan.

The Donovans were a prototypical Forestport family. The patriarch,

Michael Donovan, had arrived from County Cork as a hungry teenager fleeing the Great Famine, one of about five thousand Irish immigrants to reach Oneida County between the years 1850 and 1855. Michael Donovan and many of the others gravitated to Forestport, where strong backs were needed to finish the new feeder. Michael Donovan worked as a boatman, and in time took as his bride Catherine. Sons followed fathers: John, William, and Michael Jr. all worked the Forestport Feeder and Black River Canal through their teenage years. Michael Doyle duly courted young Jenny, and in a springtime ceremony in 1888 they married. Jenny was petite, a bride of eighteen in her home-tailored white dress.

Their first child lived. She was Grace. Their second child died: Edward Vincent was born in 1892 and lived not quite a year. He died in a fever, initiating Jenny into the town's bleak sorority; sometimes it seemed as if every Forestport woman had lost at least one child. Ida Manahan, Dick's wife, had likewise lost one baby. Jenny's brother William and sister-in-law Margaret lost the infant Grace, the toddler Helen, and the baby James. Whooping cough, pneumonia, croup: all worked their way through the village's young. Of some 293 Forestport mothers recorded in the 1900 census, 146 were recorded as having lost at least one child.

By the time little Edward died, Michael Doyle had elevated himself a step from the laboring life, to run The American. This was a rough-hewn lumberjack's place, a good base for small-town political plotting. Michael was a Democrat, as all the saloon men were. In September 1897, shortly after the last feeder break, Michael's fellow Forestport Democrats selected him as a delegate to the state assembly convention. Though plagued by periodic illness that confined him to his hotel during the bitter winter of 1895–96, Michael involved himself thoroughly in town doings. A good hotel man and saloonkeeper was like a priest in that way. He would hear the drunken confessions, the threats, and the promises. He would hear the talk, when it arose, of Al Schoonmaker.

Among state officials, in May 1898, Schoonmaker was a man to be thanked. Bad as the Forestport break was, his prompt alert had saved the state from worse. If the lock on the state pond had not been shut and the waste weir opened, even more water would have ripped through the towpath levee. Forestport men, nonetheless, calculated matters differently.

They reckoned the break an opportunity, something good for the town at long last. There were men with cash to spend, and work for those who wanted it. The feeder break had breathed some life back into struggling Forestport. Save for Schoonmaker, the break would have been luckier still.

On the sidewalk near Michael Doyle's hotel, Forestport postmaster Enos Crandall heard the talk about Schoonmaker. There were several men milling about, Crandall recalled later.

"I heard them say something about Schoonmaker's giving the report too soon," Crandall recalled. "I can't tell which one I heard . . . [saying] that Schoonmaker ought to be damned, or something of that kind, for reporting the break too soon . . . a good many people said the same thing" (*People v. Manahan* 1900, 83, 85).

The talk grew murderous, or so investigators later believed. Howard Fordham, the visiting salesman who had ventured down to the canal on the first morning after the break, would recall several such conversations.

"The God-damned son-of-a-bitch Schoonmaker ought to be kicked for reporting it so early; he ought not to have a stroke of work," Fordham recalled one Forestport man's muttering. There were still darker intimations. A Forestport man, one of the town's most prominent, was said to be overheard saying he "wished somebody would kill" the blabbermouth Schoonmaker (*People v. Manahan* 1900, 89).

However it happened, by act of God, muskrat, or man, the break was a lick of good luck for Forestport. Who could be blamed for wanting it to last just a little bit longer? Because what could not be denied even in the busiest of weeks for this tough little canal and logging town, with all the men about, the hotel beds filled, and the saloons lively, was that Forestport's canal-centered world was dying, and not even the luckiest break could save it for long.

Chapter 3

MICHAEL DOYLE HAD BEEN BORN in a good year for the Erie Canal. By the time of the Forestport Feeder breaks, in the seasons immediately preceding the century's turning, the good years were gone.

"There is no longer any reason why the people of the state of New York should bear the burden of maintaining a free waterway from the lakes to the ocean," former New York City mayor Abe Hewitt declared in the 3 August 1899 *Boonville Herald*. "My knowledge of the subject inclines me to believe that we have reached a permanent era of low cost of transportation by rail."

No new boats were registered in 1898, because the canal system no longer merited the investment. The waterways themselves were clogged and in ill repair. Miles of canal bank leaked more or less permanently. Rubbish and debris so filled feeder canals near Oriskany, Chittenango, Fayetteville, and Orville that the *Boonville Herald* of 17 June 1897 reported that most were only three feet deep instead of six. Near Port Jackson, silt and rubbish piled so high that the *Rochester Union & Advertiser* of 21 October 1898 found that only one boat could pass through at a time. Slithering eel grass so thickened the canal's stretch through Wayne County that boats could hardly crawl through. Locks built of locally quarried stone a half-century before were melting back to dust. The waste weirs meant to shunt off excess water were shattered and leaky. Rocks and boulders, boatman said, had been left in the bottom of some of the canals, a jutting and constant hazard to their trade. Timber piles driven into the towpaths and berms for strengthening had been indifferently sawed off, so that vulnerable boats passed by them like barefoot boys in a field of rusty nails. The refuse from tanneries, soap factories, and other industrial plants gunked the waterways. Near one Monroe County canal feeder, the county's board of supervisors reported to public works superintendent Aldridge, "[A] thick, nasty, ill-smelling scum is rapidly covering the surface" (Aldridge Papers). Three Buffalo maritime insurance companies simply stopped insuring eastbound canal traffic, the *Buffalo Express* had reported on 11 December 1897.

"They were," Public Works Superintendent George W. Aldridge lamented, "in a dilapidated condition in every particular" (New York State Canal Investigating Commission 1898b, 383).

William Gere knew well the canal's deterioration in Oneida County. He had worked on the Erie Canal for some fifty years, starting as a rod-and-chain man and rising by 1898 to Middle Division engineer. The stone walls along the canal had crumbled to loose rock, he said. The culverts and bridges were falling apart, masonry was cracked, silt had risen so high that the canals could barely be filled to seven feet, and the worn-down towpaths were in constant danger of being swamped.

"Whenever steamboats swept by, the water would flow clear over the towpath," Gere complained (New York State Canal Investigating Commission 1898b, 3429).

Political and moral encrustations, too, hindered canal commerce. For years the rough-and-ready lock tenders near Albany were infamous for demanding a payoff before letting boats pass. But the soft-handed office crews, too, demanded their share. In September 1898, Buffalo businessman and canal champion G. H. Raymond set out his complaints to Aldridge. "The Forwarders here," Raymond advised, "say that it is impossible to get a boat cleared without giving some clerk in the office not less than 50 cents . . . one man said he would not go to the office for a clearance and take the abuse usually meted out for a $5 bill" (Aldridge Papers).

Aldridge himself, though he cleaned up some problems among the lock tenders, aggressively squeezed the canal for political advantage. Public works superintendent Aldridge, Theodore Roosevelt would later con-fide to his friend C. Grant Lafarge, "appointed men and removed them for political reasons, and this inevitably meant that the welfare of the canals was sacrificed to party exigencies at primaries, conventions and elections" (Roosevelt Papers). For simple boatmen and others outside the canal world, there sometimes seemed to be little difference among the different classes of canal exploiters.

"I tell you," an irate reader wrote the *Buffalo Express* on 16 January 1898, "in these days of steam and electricity, the Canal is past its usefulness, except to rob the state treasury by a gang of thieves."

The Erie Canal suited a passing century. Once it had been a great leap forward over turnpikes impeded by mud, dust, and felled trees. Its construction had been an engineering wonder, manned, perhaps, by morally suspect boatmen, but servicing the vital economy (Sheriff 1996, 138). Now only scattered outposts like Forestport fully relied on the canal. However artfully constructed, the canal in its operations remained tethered to the archaic pace of mules and horses. The railroad had long since bypassed both turnpike and canal (Ellis 1948, 269).

In the year of Michael Doyle's birth, 1856, boats on the Erie Canal system carried 4,116,082 tons of products—lumber, wheat, potatoes, dry goods, ice (New York State Department of Public Works 1899, 369). That same year, the combined shipping total for the New York Central and the New York & Erie railroads came to 1,719,327 tons. But by 1869, when Michael Doyle and Dick Manahan were entering the world of laboring men, the New York railroads for the first time surpassed the canal. By 1898, the competition was well over. That year, the New York canals carried 3,360,063 tons; the New York railroads carried 45,950,968 tons.

"The rail competition is killing the Canal business," the *Buffalo Courier* lamented on 22 July 1897. "The boats are scattered all along the line of the canal. Some of them are doing something, but as a rule they are waiting for something to do that will earn them a cent."

During the summer, when the waterways were open, the New York Central would lower its shipment rates. But when the canal froze up over the winter, the railroads would raise those same rates (Ellis 1948, 289). Sometimes it was a political season that inspired railway rate changes. During the commercially ruinous season of 1895, just as politicians were considering whether to spend additional millions of dollars on canal improvements, the railroads abruptly cut rates nearly in half. The rates charged were unprofitable, but, as canal historian Noble E. Whitford noted, the railroads' true bottom line was to see if the canals and their usefulness could be discredited by a reduction in tonnage before the election (Whitford 1906, chapter 5). It cost the railroads an estimated seven cents per bushel to haul wheat from Buffalo to New York City, the 3 November 1898 *Rochester Democrat & Chronicle* reported. They were charging about two cents per bushel.

Boatmen dropped prices, but they could never outlast the railroads in a price-cutting competition. The state prohibited corporations with stock worth greater than $50,000 from owning canal boats. Small, undercapitalized boatmen could not prevail in a protracted price war, a war in which the railroads enjoyed all the technological advantages.

The freight lines of the New York Central & Hudson River Railroad averaged a speed of eighteen to twenty miles per hour. Canal boats plodded at four miles per hour. The rails delivered grain from Buffalo to New York City in three or four days. It took a canal boat twelve to fifteen days to make the same delivery, assuming that the canals actually remained open. Canals were, after all, reliant on fair weather. The Erie Canal system froze up and had to close on 1 December 1897 and did not reopen until 7 May 1898. That was a typical season. The rail lines, meanwhile, stayed open year around even if hindered by heavy upstate snows.

Even when the canals were ostensibly open, traffic dragged. A certain Captain West, in charge of the steam canal boat *Richard K. Fox,* reported in the 22 July 1897 *Buffalo Courier* that constant canal breaks caused him to take forty-three days to make the round trip from Buffalo to New York and back. It was a trip that should have taken only about twenty-two days. The delays were so bad that a load of Fourth of July fireworks bound for Ohio had to be removed from the stalled boats and repacked onto the more reliable railways. The situation perfectly symbolized the canal's degradation. It had been a cannon-booming Fourth of July morning in 1817 that the first spadeful of Erie Canal dirt had been turned near Rome. Eighty years later, the canal could no longer deliver the sparkle.

"Never before have I known of the unloading of boats on their way to

Buffalo or New York and the reshipment of their cargos by rail because of the uncertainty of their arrival in time," West grumbled to the *Buffalo Courier.*

The canal's repair crews were forever chasing after emergencies in their horse-drawn square-bowed scows, called, without irony, "hurry-up boats." Tom Wheeler, who oversaw the Black River Canal and Forestport Feeder, reported in 1898 that the year "has been one of ceaseless labor and activity . . . a large number of repairs were made to the banks, culverts and locks before the opening of the canals" (New York State Department of Public Works 1898, 142). All the spring and summer of 1898, an intermittently malfunctioning double lock in the city of Syracuse caused canallers and lock tenders problems. The lock finally broke altogether in July, not long after the Forestport repairs were finished. Boat traffic stopped for five days until engineers had replaced parts badly undermined by time and the elements. In June, an old wooden culvert south of Montezuma collapsed. Canal traffic again stopped for five days as engineers unearthed and replaced the old structure, which, they found, was thoroughly decayed and built on a shifting foundation of quicksand. Boats too were decaying irrevocably. With the Erie Canal's future so bleak, there was little motivation to maintain boats beyond the bare floatable minimum. In just a seven-day period in May 1898, shortly before the breaks in the Forestport Feeder, three boats sank in the Black River Canal or in the feeder itself, with each sinking's delaying other boat traffic by anywhere from six to forty-eight hours (New York State Department of Public Works 1898, 143).

"Of the whole number, the great majority are old and rotten and only require a slight accident to sink them to the bottom," Aldridge complained in 1897 (New York State Department of Public Works 1897, 7).

Even the innocent bicycle, the most benign of modern inventions, was kicking up towpath trouble. On the towpaths, the boatmen were complaining that boisterous bike riders spooked the mules. At least one mule team was reported drowned, scared off into the water by the pedaling onrush of the new era. The bicyclists, too, had their concerns, about whether, for instance, they were required to fix lamps to their bikes while using towpaths. The problem, wheelman J. L. Fitzgerald advised Aldridge

Repair crews on the Forestport Feeder, ca. 1899. C. Dayton, photographer. *Courtesy of New York State Archives.*

in 1897, was that "they frighten the mules and excite the wrath of their drivers" (Aldridge Papers).

The Erie Canal's deterioration was most obvious along the so-called laterals. Between 1877 and 1880, the state had abandoned the Crooked Lake, Chemung, Genesee Valley, Oneida Lake, and Chenango lateral canals to the Erie. None had ever been of more than marginal economic value.

The Black River Canal survived in part because its water was still needed to replenish the Erie Canal. Replenishment had long been one of the canal's requirements. Shallow water in the main canal slowed traffic because of hydraulic drag on the boats, or because the boats had to wait longer to proceed through the locks. Considerable water was lost during locking operations. Engineers soon calculated that major portions of the

Erie Canal lost an average of ten inches of water per day to seepage and evaporation (Langbein 1976, 2).

Beyond replenishment, the lateral canals were meant to extend the reach of commerce. Even as other laterals closed, the Black River Canal and associated Forestport Feeder were kept open as viable routes for transporting lumber from the remote and lavishly endowed Adirondack North Country. The commercial potential, though, was constrained by the locks, a tight fifteen feet wide by ninety feet long. Black River Canal boats could carry only about seventy-five tons—about one-third the amount carried on the enlarged Erie Canal. The limitations impeded the Black River Canal from fulfilling its economic promise. Black River Canal boats carried just about as many goods in the year of Michael Doyle's birth as in the year of the second Forestport Feeder break. In 1856, a total of 68,126 tons of goods had shipped on the Black River Canal: milled North Country lumber, or potatoes dug from the Tug Hill plateau north of Boonville, or wheat, or ice cut and stored over the previous winter. In 1898, a remarkably similar amount shipped along the canal: 69,803 tons. Lumber, shingles, flour, bran, apples, furniture, nails, limestone, coal, sugar, and hay, among other products, filled the 1898 boats. The 1898 shipping total was less than half of the Black River Canal's commercial high point, reached in 1889, and all trends were downward.

The potential had seemed so much grander at the Black River Canal's beginnings. On the edges of the North Country timberlands, little settlements like Boonville and Port Leyden had been jealously watching the east-to-west pulsing of economic life along the Erie. Without a canal, the area's wheat farmers and sawmill operators had to route their grain and lumber laboriously by Black River boat to Lake Ontario and through the lake to the St. Lawrence River, or by wagon through the rugged confines of the Lansing Kill gorge down to Rome, where the goods would have to be reloaded onto canal boats for shipment east. As early as 1825, Black River area residents began petitioning the state legislature for a new lateral canal (Larkin 1964, 8).

Following the failure of two private canal-building attempts, legislators authorized the Black River Canal and Forestport Feeder in 1836 as part of the state system. The Forestport Feeder was replenishment for the Black River Canal, but it was also navigable to accommodate the boat traffic from sawmills springing up by the banks of the Black River (O'Donnell 1952, 39).

Construction proceeded fitfully from 1837 onward. Many civil engineering problems became quickly apparent as the Irish workers dug through the ravine of the Lansing Kill between Rome and Boonville, and along the steep, sandy hillside above the Black River near Forestport. Some of their solutions set the foundation for later decay. The lock walls, for instance, were sometimes built from stone quarried directly from the lock pit excavation. This convenient, porous stone softened so by the 1890s that many of the Black River Canal locks needed rebuilding. Other problems, more immediately apparent, beset the Black River Canal construction. The state's money, at times, seemed to be leaking away too liberally.

By 1846 the state assembly had appointed an investigative panel to probe the evaporation of state funds. The canal commissioners subsequently advised the Assembly that, despite some irregularities, "no frauds, to any extent, were proved in the construction of the work" along the Black River Canal (New York State Legislature 1847, 289). In May 1850, some intervening breaks having been repaired, the first boat was locked up from Rome to Boonville.

Together, the Black River and Forestport Feeder canals were a considerable achievement, a triumph of politics and engineering both. Indeed, the state investigators who had found serious problems elsewhere along the Erie Canal in 1846 praised the generally "well-executed" work along the Black River Canal. But the Black River Canal and Forestport Feeder were also subject to misuse even during their construction. When work stopped and state engineers left loads of lumber and iron lying about unguarded, Boonville and Forestport men scooped it up and made use of what they found. The 1846 team of investigators who uncovered the Boonville-area thefts concluded that "an entirely different morality seems to prevail in this and other communities; with regard to public property, from that which prevails with regard to the property of private individuals" (New York State Legislature 1847, 297). The state, some feared, had become a public goose, ready for the plucking.

Below the Forestport state dam. Photographer and date unknown. *Courtesy of Dorothy Mooney.*

Fear of theft helped shape, among other decisions, the location of a crucial Forestport dam. In 1883 officials determined that another reservoir was needed to store Black River water. Workers built a boarding house and blacksmith shop near Forestport. The workers scraped out roads and quarried six hundred cubic yards of stone, and at night they enlivened the town. The Forestport men worked until the money ran out, and then they waited until state legislators in 1889 authorized an additional $45,000. That authorization was a victory for the state engineer and surveyor, who had used every argument possible to promote revival of the Forestport dam construction. Among its advantages, he had assured state legislators, was the fact that its proximity to human habitation meant it could be "readily guarded from surreptitious uses" (New York State Engineer and Surveyor 1896, 5).

Such uses were no trivial concern. Upstate water, whether running free or channeled through the Erie Canal system, always posed a temptation. Everyone wanted it for their own sometimes incompatible purposes. The lumbermen wanted roiling rivers for the springtime drives, so the Adirondack logs would not be left stranded up in the North Country. The sawmill operators wanted river flows strong enough to drive the steam engines powering their saws. The Erie Canal engineers wanted river water as replenishment, at least sixteen thousand cubic feet per minute flowing through the Forestport Feeder. Whether through political influence or brute force or covert infiltrations, men found ways to make the state's water work for them.

For some time, state engineers in the early 1880s wondered about the shortfall of water flowing into the Erie Canal. The shortfall was odd. The state had built reservoirs specifically to ensure an adequate water supply, but the shortfalls continued until engineers investigated the reservoirs in May 1882.

"The gatehouse had been broken into," investigators reported, "the valves opened and water used to float logs down the stream; and we were told that each spring when the natural flow in the streams was not sufficient to float their logs, the lumbermen helped themselves to the water in the reservoirs, in violation of the protests and strict orders of State officials, and in utter disregard of the State's rights and interests in the matter" (New York State Engineer and Surveyor 1896, 523).

The locks were rebuilt, only to be broken again. The state engineer and surveyor lamented the "constant use of the water surreptitiously by lumbermen for the purpose of floating logs down the stream," and observed that "the funds at the disposal of the superintendent of public works are not large enough for the employment of sufficient guards to prevent this surreptitious use of the water." Forestport lumbermen resented the recurring accusations, proclaiming in the *Boonville Herald* of 6 April 1899 that it was "entirely immaterial to us how many men are employed at these places, or who they are . . . but we most emphatically protest against being branded as thieves."

The Forestport dam, begun in 1883 and then stalled for seven years, was supposed to help keep the state's water safe and secure. The town thrived when construction resumed in the spring of 1890. Dam building was a big undertaking. It was muddy and messy, and noisy with the steam engines grinding, the teams of horses clattering their loads across the

Black River bridges, the blacksmiths forging, and the carpenters sawing. At night the laborers tramped back to the River Street hotels and saloons. Forestport appreciated the benefits of the state's spending money through a stop-and-start process that lasted several years. In the rainy first week of September 1892, for instance, a state engineer recorded that there were 18 foremen, 152 laborers, 36 quarrymen, 28 woodchoppers, 12 water boys, 10 carpenters, 6 blacksmiths, 6 steam-pump operators, and 2 pile-driver operators at work in and around the new dam. These men needed hotels to live in, saloons to drink in, general stores to buy their supplies in, and fancy women to dally with.

The boom was unsustainable. When the Forestport dam construction was finished in 1894, the flow of state money trickled off and Forestport quieted down. The canal business resumed its customary declining pace, a pace that had, for Forestport and other upstate towns, always been both provoked and bedeviled by politics.

Chapter 4

NO ONE COULD STOP THE COMING FLOOD.

Galloping into Forestport, the breathless messenger shouted out the news. The North Lake Dam had failed, twenty-three miles away, and now a half-million cubic feet of water was roaring down the Black River channel, sweeping away everything in its path on the cloudy afternoon of 21 April 1869 (Thomas 1985, 137).

The water was coming twice as fast as any canal boat, uncountable tons at eight miles per hour. That speed gave Forestport men several hours to prepare furiously. They could move wagons and animals to higher ground, get the women and children away, save some possessions, and throw up some barricades. The crisis inspired some heroic efforts. One-armed General Jonathan Hill, operator of the Proctor and Hull tannery near town, directed fifty men to strengthen a small dam near the tannery. But the Forestport state pond was congested with logs waiting for the sawmills, and there was only so much anyone could do before the flood swell reached Forestport. Not everyone, moreover, pitched in properly, even as the water rose.

"Other lazy drones stood with hands in their pockets, watching those working and the angry waters pouring over the dam, and whenever a quantity of water would go down they would hurrah! and send up a shout of joy as though they enjoyed the wholesale destruction going on before them," a dismayed Forestport correspondent noted in the 6 April 1869 *Black River Herald*.

The Forestport state pond, crowded with logs. Photographer and date unknown. *Courtesy of Dorothy Mooney.*

At about 7 P.M. the flood hit the hardworking and the lazy alike. The water bullied through the state pond and snapped logs like matchsticks. It punched straight through the 130-foot-long and 30-foot-deep packed-dirt dam, carrying away the remains. The water swept over what had once been the dam's east side and rushed on, shoving an immense jam of logs against L. R. Clark's grist mill downstream. The grist mill shuddered and collapsed and joined the downriver rush, north toward Lyons Falls. The next morning, thousands of logs, piles, and spars littered every bend and crook of the blown-out river. Forestport men found the shattered remains of Clark's grist mill as part of a driftwood pile a mile downstream from town. Every bridge across the Black River was gone, cutting off all communication to Boonville save by boat. The town stank of mud and drowned animals.

The April 1869 flood ultimately caused an estimated $700,000 worth of damages. Forestport alone tallied losses in buildings and lumber estimated at between $30,000 and $40,000, and more than two thousand people sued for restitution. The state settled with many, and the subsequent rebuilding of the Forestport dam brought workers flush with the state's cash. There remained, nonetheless, some unsettled questions, most notably why the North Lake dam broke in the first place. Rumors began sprouting in the North Country and were finally given voice in the *Utica Morning Herald.*

"This winter, for political consideration, Mr. Dawson, who had been in charge of the reservoirs for several years, was removed and a new man placed in charge who knew nothing of the importance of protecting this work against spring floods," the paper reported.

State appraisers began investigating. They noted the North Lake dam was compacted earth, cheap and easy to build but prone to undermining by the elements and the workings of burrowing muskrats. The dam was only half as wide as it should have been to restrain the 423-acre reservoir. The spillway was insufficient to carry away surplus water. The dam, therefore, was vulnerable to the pressures whipped up in the 1869 storms. But beyond these technical limitations, the appraisers had pinpointed another truth behind the ugly rumors.

"Nor does it appear," the appraisers concluded, "that the person in charge at the time of the rupture was a competent and faithful officer" (New York State Canal Appraisers 1869).

A political hack, in short, had fallen asleep at the switch. He had won through patronage a job that he lacked the ability to perform, and the result was a catastrophic flood. It was not the first time the competence or fidelity of a canal appointee had been questioned. Certainly the role of politics in assigning canal workers was well understood even by those who lamented the consequences. The Erie Canal was a creature of politics. Its envisioning and construction had been political acts, as were, most assuredly, its ongoing operation and maintenance. The politicians wrote the bond acts that paid for the work, pushed for their approval by state voters, and rewarded their friends with the fruits. Sometimes, as the North Lake Dam failure showed, such politics conflicted with proper administration.

The spoils system was present from the start. Premier canal champion DeWitt Clinton, even before construction began in 1817, had earned a reputation in New York as an aggressive proponent of the spoils system. A patronage innovator, Clinton was the spiritual godfather for the system of displacement, reward, and favor that ruled along the canal by the time of the North Lake dam break. The rules were well established, though only rarely written down (McBain 1967, 13).

An inherent tension defined the Erie Canal. As a public work, it was to be operated for the greater good. Individual benefit and self-interest were to be subsumed. But as a public work, it was administered by public men, those reliant on polls and voters. Usually the harms committed by men more politically than technically adept were not so catastrophic in and of themselves. They were small nicks and tears, as modest as a muskrat's nibbling. Only over time were the harms compounded enough to cause a bad break.

Though unusually abrupt, the North Lake Dam failure was not unique in Erie Canal annals. Shortly after the newly elected Whigs took power in 1839 and deposed all but one of the experienced canal superintendents, the waterway suffered a series of breaks that the partisan press blamed on a set of clamorous brawlers who were altogether ignorant of their duties. Within years of the canal's opening, moreover, repair costs nearly doubled as contractors and state employees alike started appreciating the potential for skimming and padding. As one irate *Albany Argus* reader recognized in 1846, "no part of the public service furnished greater opportunity for infidelity to the public interest than the present system of canal repairing."

A drifting mist obscured the boundaries between public and private along the Erie Canal. Boundary crossing was easy, and temptations were many. Despite various civil service reforms, politics in the 1890s still regulated much about the canal, from the running of the locks to the granting of the contracts to the fundamental decisions about water use.

In the upstate town of Waterloo, for instance, mill owners learned in the mid-1890s that canal engineers wanted to install a retaining wall across the flume of the waterway. The engineers' decision was hydraulically rational but politically blind. The retaining wall would have meant less water for the mills and the potential loss, some feared, of hundreds of jobs. Into the breach stepped New York's paramount political boss, Thomas Collier Platt. His lieutenant, Tom Wheeler, visited Waterloo with reassurances that the engineers were wrong. The retaining wall would not go forward; indeed, the state would deepen the channel so that canal and mills both could secure adequate water.

"By this action we saved at least 300 votes to the Republican ticket, and secured a liberal contribution to our campaign fund," a Mr. Charles Andrews subsequently reminded Platt (Aldridge Papers).

Often the political system worked well enough. But, like a winter snowpack, small canal exploitations accumulated year by year, the built-up tension releasing, periodically, and scattering both rubble and reputations. Such a release happened in the mid-1840s, when investigators found that the contractors who "obtained large and important contracts were former friends, acquaintances and neighbors of the chief and resident engineers." Construction costs soared by tens of thousands of dollars above the bid amounts. The canal contractors, keeping the system well oiled, "made merry over their profitable iniquity [and] in turn gave champagne suppers for the especial benefit of the engineers" (New York State Legislature 1847, 74). There seemed always to be room for another $1-a-day friend or relative of a state official.

"They were riding about a great deal, apparently for pleasure, and in attending parties," worker Harry Brown testified. "They spent so much of their time in pleasure, and etcetera, that it was the subject of remark among people here" (New York State Legislature 1847, 78).

As in the 1840s, so too in the 1870s, when Forestport was still fixing itself up from the North Lake Dam catastrophe. Forestport's Michael Doyle and Dick Manahan were young working men then, and could overhear the canal talk about how the Rochester-based contractor Jarvis Lord had squeezed undue profit from a contract to repair an April 1870 break in the Chemung Canal feeder. They could read the contemporary papers about Boss Tweed and his Tammany Ring's being shaken by the reform lawyer-turned-governor Samuel Jones Tilden.

"The interest which fattens on abuses of public expenditure is intelligent, energetic and persistent," Tilden declared in the *New York Times* of 20 March 1875. "Acting as a unit, it takes part through its members in the organization and the doings of both political parties; seeks to control nominations, rewards friends and punishes enemies, and begins to operate by every form of seductive and coercive influence upon public officials as soon as they are elected."

The Canal Ring, in short: a conspiratorial term that would recur throughout the decades.

A study commissioned by Tilden found that state funds built canal wharves for the benefit of private parties. Fictitious improvements were contrived to supply profitable jobs. Cost estimates were being broken wide open. Prices paid for materials bore no relation to their real value: hemlock timber used for shoring up canal banks cost $3 per thousand board feet in some contracts, and $30 per thousand board feet in others. Canal breaks and their subsequent repairs were especially lucrative for well-placed contractors. George D. Lord, the son of state senator Jarvis Lord and well connected in his own right through his service in the legislature, had secured the five-year contract to maintain and repair the Chemung Canal between 1867 and 1872. For repairing an April 1870 break, Lord's company took $125,000—about twelve times what critics thought the work was worth. A few years earlier, the Lord firm had billed the state $70,000 for a canal break repair job that should have cost perhaps $11,000.

"The capacity exhibited by the Lord family in turning these disastrous breaks into perfect bonanzas for themselves is apparently inexhaustible," one skeptic marveled in the 5 March 1875 *New York Times.*

Tilden called for systemic reforms, including, fatefully, the establishment of a superintendent of public works to assume control of the New York canals. He called as well for a deeper investigation into how the state canal improvement funds had been spent. The resulting Canal Investigating Commission found an unseemly web of self-dealing manipulators who lavished the Erie Canal improvement funds on themselves and their friends (Flick 1939, 266). An estimated 70 percent of the $8.4 million spent on extraordinary repairs between 1867 and 1875 was "inconsiderate, unwise and unprofitable to the state," the commissioners concluded.

"The interest of the public has been systematically disregarded," the commissioners wrote. "The precautions with which the Legislature has attempted to defend this property from peculation and fraud . . . have been deliberately and persistently disregarded, while the responsibilities of its agents have been so divided and distributed as to leave the State . . . at the mercy of the predatory classes, who have been, if they do not continue to be, a formidable political power" (New York State Canal Investigating Commission 1876, 6).

The problems were exemplified not far from Forestport, by the work done in the city of Utica by the contractor Henry D. Denison. He had been hired to construct a 1,500-foot vertical canal wall near the city's eastern edge. Denison contracted to do the work for $10,617. Neither he nor the state authorities supposedly overseeing the project bothered with surveys, maps, or preliminary estimates. By the time the investigating commission uncovered the Denison project, he had been paid $50,700 and the Utica work was only two-thirds done. The restraining wall was supposed to average fifteen inches in thickness, backed by a bed of gravel. Investigators found the wall averaged about nine inches, backed by nothing at all. The wooden ties were supposed to be sturdy and expensive white oak. Investigators found them to be cheaper beech, birch, and maple. The work was supposed to stand for a generation. Investigators found the walls already bulging and falling apart.

The contractors and the state authorities were in business together, often literally. A Colonel John Yates informed aghast commissioners about the qualifications of some of the canal men he had been forced to work with: "They are generally appointed by political influence, by their friends. That is all the examination they have," Yates said. "[It is] his political relations that control . . . [and] it is sometimes hard work to dispense with them, even if they are incompetent" (New York State Canal Investigating Commission 1876).

The canal investigation helped secure Tilden's national reputation and led to the indictment of ten New York men on charges of fraud, bribery, and conspiracy, including former state assemblyman George D. Lord. There were, however, few convictions. Although a judgment of $387,000 against Denison's company was secured, it, like the conviction of Lord, was eventually overturned. Still, New York legislators sought to fix the canal's systemic problems. They followed Tilden's suggestion for appointment of a superintendent of public works to whom the state engineer would answer.

In theory, the new system might have worked. The theory, however, did not fully account for political imperatives. The public works superintendent, appointed by the governor, inevitably became the top dispenser of patronage. With hundreds of jobs and dozens of contracts to distribute, the public works superintendency offered sore temptations for political operatives.

Canal boatmen, perennially agitated anyway over their declining livelihood, complained in 1889 that public works superintendent James Shanahan's negligence and incompetency allowed breaks that could have been prevented by ordinary precaution.

Shanahan's successor, Edward J. Hannan, seemed during his 1889–94 reign far more concerned with his party's advantage than with the proper administration of the Erie Canal. Under Hannan, it was said, canal officials charged canallers extra fees for pumping out sunken boats because "we must raise money for elections" (Archdeacon 1978, 426). More than once, disgruntled boatmen told the *New York Times,* Hannan's slack-handed reign had allowed canal breaks that any competent man could have prevented. By 1891, critics were contending that the canal was rapidly approaching the point at which it had been when Tilden took over.

"If the state's waterways," the *New York Times* reasoned on 28 September 1890, "are used as means of favoritism, bad appointments, corrupt contracts or extravagance and mismanagement to promote partisan ends at the expense of public service . . . there ought to be exposure, and it ought to have effect upon this year's election." Instead of wholesale exposure, a committee was established whose members included Democrats loyal to General Hill and Republicans loyal to the canal status quo. The committee members, in the words of the bemused *New York Times* on 4 December 1889, were "legislative tailors who are now fabricating a robe of spotless white for the form of Edward Hannan."

But even Hannan was an amateur when it came to real politics. There were other men with greater authority who could exploit aggressively the Erie Canal's annual budget, which by 1898 had reached $863,092.46 a year. There were enough line items, special allocations, and discretionary freedoms in that budget to allow a clever man to reward many friends.

George Washington Aldridge Jr. was a very clever man indeed. "The man," the chaste *New York Times* lamented on 8 August 1898, "was one of the most unscrupulous and notorious spoilsman [*sic*] of the state. He was known to be perfectly shameless in prostituting the public service . . . he was put there to use the canals to strengthen the Republican Party, and he let slip no opportunity for partisan advantage."

Aldridge was a rock. Other men could lean upon him, or, resisting, they could be crushed by him. He knew all the tools of power and patronage. By means of such tools he had risen from the Rochester executive council, a carnation-wearing, whiskey-sipping political prodigy. He was six feet two inches tall, heavily built, with a broad balding forehead and a blunt manner of speech. That he was, in 1898, superintendent of public works and not New York's governor was only a matter of a few maneuvers fallen short two years before. Not that Aldridge let himself lose anything for long.

"Never lose your nerve," Aldridge would advise his son in a 1911 letter. "If at first you fail at any undertaking, shut your teeth and try again with renewed effort" (Aldridge Papers). As a young member of the Rochester executive council, dispensing public contracts to improve Rochester's water, street, and fire systems, the Republican Aldridge traded favors with Democrats so long as the deals were to everyone's mutual advantage.

"Every time Aldridge bestowed a political favor, he made certain that he was repaid in measure," one former Rochester reporter recalled. "All he asked in return was funds to conduct a political campaign, and votes to win his election" (Lanni 1939, 13).

Aldridge's skills brought him to the attention of the man who ran New York State, Thomas Collier Platt. Before his election to the U.S. House of Representatives in 1872, Platt learned politics from Reuben E. Fenton. Fenton, Harold Gosnell related in his magnificently detailed *Boss Platt and His New York Machine,* was one whose "administration of the Canal system of the state furnished many lessons for aspiring young political

George Aldridge, superintendent of the New York Department of Public Works. Photographer and date unknown. *Courtesy of Rochester Historical Society.*

managers" (Gosnell 1924, 135). Platt absorbed those lessons well and became the man to see.

"The Canal officials, from Superintendent Dutcher down to the boat inspector at Syracuse are under obligation to him," the *Syracuse Journal* had noted on 13 January 1881. "And so it is all along the Canals and in the government offices."

Aldridge and Platt had a common understanding of the Erie Canal and its political potential. After he delivered Monroe County for financier Levi Parson Morton in November, Aldridge figured Morton owed him the position of superintendent of public works—the dispenser of canal patronage and the builder of things. But however loyal his Republican service, Aldridge still faced resistance. "Political bosses," the self-described "Canal Defender," Captain M. DePuy, said in the *New York Tribune* on 1 December 1894, "should be forced to keep their hands from the state's waterways."

Aldridge commissioned letters of support from Rochester banks, businessmen, judges, editors, and most members of the state Republican committee. He secured the support of Rochester's clergymen by dutifully ordering closed the city's saloons for three consecutive Sundays. After he had his post secured, the saloons reopened.

The maneuvering finally paid off when on 2 January 1895 the newly inaugurated Morton submitted Aldridge's name to the legislature. With a triumphant Aldridge looking on from the rear of the chambers, the Senate quickly confirmed the new boss of the Forestport Feeder, the Black River Canal, and all the patronage-rich network known as the Erie Canal.

Chapter 5

BY THE NUMBERS, at least, George Aldridge had taken command of an impressive public works empire. The Erie Canal system included, the *New York Times* reported on 7 October 1895, 640 miles of navigable canals, 84 miles of unnavigable feeders, 1,100 bridges, 263 locks, and 33 aqueducts.

But deteriorating conditions were also undermining the system. Aldridge's predecessor as public works superintendent, Edward Hannan, had cautioned in the *New York Times* of 30 December 1894 that "the time is fast approaching when the operations of the canals in a practical manner must cease unless the canals are improved." A vocal canal boat captain named W. C. Clark complained in the 24 October 1895 *Times* that "nothing in the way of improvements have been made since 1862 to the Erie, Oswego and Champlain Canals, except lengthening a portion of locks . . . [and] they have been left to deteriorate to a state bordering on dilapidation."

For years Captain Clark and the Erie Canal's other champions had sought to rally support for canal improvements. They succeeded in 1894, when the state's Constitutional Convention approved by the barest of margins a resolution authorizing an unspecified new debt for canal improvements. The political ambivalence about the new spending was expressed by the Constitutional Convention's presiding officer, New York City lawyer Joseph Choate. Choate had warned—as the *New York Tribune* of 11 February 1898 would later note—that the spending "would inevitably result in schemes of plunder." The canal's reputation preceded it, compelling proponents to limit how much money they could ask for. Canal champions ultimately decided $9 million was sufficient to undertake the most pressing improvements but modest enough to win voter approval. The assembly and senate approved the measure in February 1895, just as Aldridge's reign was beginning.

About the canal itself, Aldridge had much to learn. About its political potential, he proved a quick study. He had some five hundred canal jobs to distribute. There would be the three district superintendents, who would annually be earning $3,000 each, and the nineteen section superintendents, who could expect a $1,000 salary, and the myriad patrolmen, clerks, bridge tenders, and lock tenders. During February and March, as the *Rochester Union & Advertiser* reported on 19 April 1895, scores of Republican politicians and office seekers had trekked through the bitter Rochester cold to Aldridge's Plymouth Avenue house, where he held court and heard their pleadings.

"This much you may be sure of," Aldridge assured one reporter, according to the 21 January 1895 *New York Times.* "All the berths will be filled by Republicans. The Republicans of this state made possible a Republican superintendent of public works, and I believe that the good things that should be disposed of by the superintendent should go to men of his own party. Yes, the canals will be Republican from the locktenders up."

Every town demanded its share. When Boonville resident Edgar Hughes was named local superintendent of the Black River Canal in early 1895, everyone in Forestport was reported to believe that "Forestport should have secured the superintendency." Despite Hughes's admitted qualifications, a Forestport man reported that "one old war horse says that 'we are suffering an overdose of Boonville politics.' " The Forestport murmuring grew more intense a few weeks later, when the sinecure of caring for the North Lake gate was awarded to a Mr. E. A. Klock. Forestport men had come to think of the North Lake spot as one they owned, and its loss irked them.

"No one has a word to say against Mr. Klock personally, but all regard his appointment as a slight, and a total disregard of the claims of the town for recognition," the *Herald*'s Forestport correspondent reported on 20 March 1895. "This feeling of resentment is general and deep-seated, and will surely cause trouble when delegates are wanted this fall."

Playing patronage well meant defusing potential trouble early, but, even for the most adept, solutions sometimes proved comically elusive. In the early spring of 1895, Norman Nelson of tiny Alder Creek, a fifteen-minute horse ride from Forestport, won his desired position as reservoir tender at Woodhull Lake. Some prominent outdoorsmen apparently associated with the Adirondack League Club objected to Nelson's appointment. The canal authorities dutifully revoked Nelson's appointment and assigned the Woodhull Lake job to a Mr. John McBeth. But that appointment proved troublesome as well, as McBeth was accused of being "an out-and-out Democrat." That would not do either, so McBeth's appointment was rescinded and the job given back to Nelson. McBeth, however, had already furnished his Woodhull Lake camp and put in his summer supplies, and he refused to surrender the post. The result: both Nelson and McBeth settled in to tend the simple reservoir.

"Patronage," mused the seasoned old politician Chauncey Depew, "is a boomerang. The appointment of a citizen in a town arouses the anger of many others who think they are more deserving" (Depew 1922, 77).

The reward and patronage opportunities only increased once the state undertook its long-delayed program to upgrade the canal (McCormick 1981, 150). The $9 million approved by state voters in 1895 would pay for scraping the canal prism deeper and raising the berm walls to increase the depth to nine feet. Stone walls would be constructed and locks lengthened to accommodate more boats. The improvements would allow faster travel, bigger boats, fewer breakdowns.

Lengthening locks, for instance, would enable two connected boats to pass through without having to stop, disconnect, lock through, and then reconnect on the far side. Deepening the Erie Canal from seven feet to nine would allow boats to increase the loads carried to four hundred tons from three hundred tons. Engineers developed an impressive if targeted list of goals, and the contracts went far and wide.

For two years the work seemed to go as planned. Contractors like Utica's James Dwyer hired new men for twelve or fifteen cents an hour.

Aldridge and his lieutenants hired dozens of inspectors to oversee the contractors. Surveyors marked out the course of new improvements during the winter. Before the canals opened in the spring, contractors scooped out the accumulated silt and deepened the prism. New stone replaced old.

"The work has been inaugurated in a manner so systematic and comprehensive as to attract but little public notice and nothing but favorable comment as the work progress[es], which it does with commendable speed and at the same time keen supervision of every detail," *Seaboard* newspaper proclaimed on 26 August 1897.

To enhance the point, *Seaboard*'s editors helpfully included a headline stating "No scandal under present management." But in truth, *Seaboard* was not an objective judge of the matter. The weekly newspaper was one of Aldridge's allies, well fed with paid advertising announcing upcoming Erie Canal contracts. Outside the confines of *Seaboard*'s editorial offices, it had already become apparent that the $9 million provided was falling far short. By 1896, the New York Civil Service Reform Association found that about 1,500 men had been hired for the canal improvement, nearly all without being subjected to competitive exams.

Everyone expected patronage play along the canal, but Aldridge had taken the tradition to a new level. The Civil Service Reform Association noted that Aldridge's predecessor had employed twenty-four men as foremen, patrolmen, and special agents for a total of $17,211. After being on the job for but a year, Aldridge was paying seventy-two men a total of $49,829 for the same work. The public works chief had hired more than two hundred additional canal workers to be paid out of a maintenance fund. Their talents tended toward the political (*Good Government* 1896, 115).

"A large number of the department employees have participated actively in county caucuses, or have occupied time for which the state has paid in the performance of other political work," the reformers charged, according to an account in the 24 August 1896 issue of the *New York Times*. "Positions in the labor force have been filled by liquor dealers, farmers, Aldermen, retired lawyers . . . and the entire patronage has been misused in a scandalous manner."

Oneida County alone accounted for a substantial share of the problem.

The son of one of Tom Wheeler's old gambling partners was living easy courtesy of a no-show canal job. Another canal clerk was alleged to be simultaneously employed at Wheeler's private coal business. A Utica alderman held one job, and several ex-convicts and saloonkeepers were foremen. One of the assistant foremen, a saloon owner, spent too much time away from the canal, including one day that he was "in court, attending to the naturalization of a number of Hebrews." The North Lake reservoir—the very dam whose 1869 collapse had been contributed to by inept political appointees—was being kept by a gang of men doing the work formerly done by one. And in Forestport, a canal laborer named Arthur O'Brien was infamous for his election-day service, when he would loom behind the ballot boxes with money in his hand.

The reformers thought some of George Aldridge's chief lieutenants were among the shadiest of appointees. Foremost among these was the Utica man who would oversee the Forestport Feeder repairs in 1898, the man who was in charge of the Erie Canal's entire Middle Division, the two-fisted, impeccably Republican boss of Oneida County, Thomas Wheeler.

. . .

War made Tom Wheeler.

He had been nothing before, just another Utica mill scrapper with no future, until he enlisted in the 146th New York Infantry in September 1862. He was seventeen, and for the next three years he forged his character at Chancellorsville, Gettysburg, the Wilderness Campaign, and bloody but forgotten Five Forks. When the regiment returned to Utica in July 1865, as the *Utica Observer* would recall on 16 October 1916, young Lieutenant Wheeler was one of only 427 soldiers to have finished his three-year tour out of the 1,568 volunteers who had mustered in. Wheeler learned in war the skills he later used to command the ragged battalions that swarmed Forestport during the repairing of the breaks. He was the perfectly ruthless lieutenant in George Aldridge's canal administration.

"He took to politics naturally, for in that arena fighters are always at a premium, and the reward is pleasant for those who succeed," the Utica *Observer* would record on 16 October 1916 following Wheeler's death.

"He believed in the doctrine that 'to the victor goes the spoils' . . . and he did not fail to distribute his favors among the members of his own party. He was very much more a partisan than a statesman. Great questions of state did not concern him, but he had an eye ever open for party advantage, and no man on earth was ever quicker to see and accept a play in which he could gain a point for his party, and especially to those who stood nearest to him."

Those near him included James Dwyer, the Utica contractor who ran the Forestport Feeder repairs in 1897 and 1898. As regional distributor of canal patronage, Wheeler had placed other friends and allies throughout Oneida County. His fingerprints were everywhere. As it was delicately put in one summary, he did while young "unfortunate things . . . in thoughtless moments of temptation" for which he later had to beg forgiveness while running for office. Of some of these actions, only hints ever became public.

One April day in the 1890s, for instance, a Norwich resident named Abner Culver reported passing by a rail station. He spied there a serious looking man who glared at Culver and then began following him down the street. The man inserted a cartridge into a revolver. The nervous Culver picked up his pace, but the man following him did likewise. Finally, with no place to run, Culver turned to confront his pursuer. The agitated man following him approached and appeared ready to draw his weapon until, startled, he examined Culver's features more closely.

"I beg your pardon, sir," the surprised, mustached man said. "I mistook you for Tom Wheeler of Utica."

Why, Culver asked, was the man stalking Tom Wheeler?

"That is my business," the man replied, according to a later account in the *Utica Daily Press* of 18 April 1899. "But I vowed if I ever caught him outside of Utica, I would kill him. When I saw you pass the depot, I thought you were he."

What Tom Wheeler might have done to deserve vengeance was left unclear. Perhaps his long service with the Oneida County district attorney's office, or as county sheriff, or as detective with the New York Central might have entangled him with desperadoes with long memories. But

Tom Wheeler trampled more than desperadoes in his days of fervent rising. The further back in his career one looked, the darker were the rumors.

In November 1895, the Oneida County Grand Jury called Wheeler in for help settling an odd affair. By then an Aldridge loyalist, Wheeler had been appointed deputy superintendent of public works overseeing the Erie Canal sections including the Forestport Feeder. Somehow he had come into the possession of $500 cash immediately prior to the commencement of the Oneida County Republican Convention the previous August. Wheeler, equally as attentive to county politics as he was to canal administration, was working the 17 August convention in support of some particular candidates. The grand jury wanted to know what the money was for and why it was in Wheeler's hands.

Wheeler testified that the cash bundle from the Utica City National Bank had been provided him "to aid him in his fight" in the convention. Wheeler took the money with him to Rome, but once he arrived, he determined his candidate was past saving and subsequently returned the $500 unspent. He did not explain, though, why the money had come from a Tammany Hall crony named Milton C. Gray. Tammany Hall's chokehold on New York City had been diminishing; still, the old machine retained some authority. It was odd, the *Utica Daily Press* noted on 9 November 1895, that a Tammany Hall Democrat would be wiring cash to the Republican chief of Oneida County.

But answers were elusive. Gray ignored a subpoena. The Oneida County sheriff, a partisan Republican and Wheeler ally, showed little enthusiasm for tracking down witnesses. Wheeler's own testimony was inconclusive. Reluctantly the Oneida County Grand Jury had to admit it could not resolve the mystery. The coming and going of the Tammany Hall money would remain one more ambiguous shadows trailing Tom Wheeler.

The Civil Service Reform Association report issued in the summer of 1896 added other Tom Wheeler stories. In the old days, the association reported, Tom Wheeler had lent out money to faro players in Utica, and for three years he ran a gambling hall himself. The Utica authorities, it was said, feared to interfere with Wheeler's business because of his political influence. He allegedly assaulted one clergyman in the streets, records showed, and at another time he was said to have been fined for larceny. He had even done time in prison, according to the report summarized in the 24 August 1896 *New York Times*: he was "sentenced to the penitentiary for six months, [and] was subsequently indicted for petit larceny and fined, [and] was indicted for a burglary committed in Albany."

The Civil Service Reform Association timed the August 1896 report to appear on the eve of the Republicans' convention in Saratoga Springs. Aldridge was seeking the gubernatorial nomination, and he had prepared the ground well. Oneida County observers had discovered in early August that anywhere between sixty and two hundred additional men had joined the state's canal employment rolls. Cooks, watchmen, inspectors, messengers, reservoir tenders, the additional men swarmed about Oneida County's stretch of the canal. Aldridge's new Oneida County hires seemed an unusual lot. They included three Utica city aldermen and, according to the *Good Government* magazine (15 June 1896), "many . . . criminals or semi-criminals."

But the appearance of the Civic Service Reform Association report undercut Aldridge's work. In some New York City Republican clubhouses, as a political reporter noted in the 24 August 1896 *New York Tribune*, the report was "read with surprise, and the prevailing opinion in Brooklyn was that the statement practically removed Mr. Aldridge from the list of possibilities in the contest for the first place on the ticket." Aldridge fought on and led the first round of balloting, but ultimately lost out to a spare, clean-shaven Dartmouth graduate named Frank Black.

A lawyer and one-time reporter, Black had fought an entrenched Democratic rule in Troy and served a quiet, backbench term in the House of Representatives before coming to Saratoga. He was neither an intimate of the Thomas Platt organization nor a good-government freelancer. He seemed a politically suitable combination of independence and reliability. But the problematic way of business along the Erie Canal, which had helped undermine Black's rival in 1896, would eventually turn on the governor himself. Among the problems would be Forestport, where canal reliability was proving increasingly elusive.

Chapter 6

THE CANAL COULD STEAL BOTH LIVES AND MONEY.

So many men and children were drowning in 1897 that public works chief Aldridge ordered the issuing of cards detailing proper resuscitation techniques. The canal itself was breaking open with disconcerting regularity. Summer breaks at Utica and Syracuse forced exasperated canallers to tie up and wait out the repairs, grumbling all the while that canal officials had done nothing about deteriorating locks.

But by early July 1897, the Forestport Feeder had been open two months and the town's lumber mills were running at full steam. Twelve million board feet of uncut logs jammed the state pond, and the Black River water supply was for once sufficient to power the mills at their full capacity. More than one hundred Forestport men were in the mills by summertime. The men had little time for relaxation, though the mills did shut down on a suffocatingly hot Monday, July 4, for Independence Day. Most everyone in the town had pitched in with the preparations, and Michael Doyle took time out from his saloon to post handbills about town. The Reverend Prendergast of St. Patrick's Church, who a decade earlier had presided over the marriage of Michael Doyle and Jenny Donovan, orated at length on God and country, after which the Forestport cornet band and the Remsen brass band and drum corps played and the village cheered the town's baseball players as they beat Boonville in an afternoon game. In the evening, as the *Boonville Herald* recorded on 8 July, the fireworks burst like promises in the evening sky.

The good ladies of the Forestport Social and Literary Union were likewise convening on Fridays or Saturdays in early July to sell ice cream and strawberries, raising the money needed to summon the light of culture. The literary union was the ladies' retort to those who whispered about Forestport's rough and unsanded ways. It was a season for libraries in many cities, thanks to the munificence of steel magnate Andrew Carnegie. Some in Oneida County, though, considered Carnegie's handouts the equivalent of blood money. They would not forget the 1892 trauma at Homestead, Carnegie's Pennsylvania steel complex, where two boatloads of Pinkerton guards had fought a pitched battle with union strikers. Carnegie could keep his money, some felt, and Forestport built its own library, modest as it was, from the ground up.

The $1,300 needed had come dollar by dollar from the entire community once the idea had first been broached the previous Fourth of July by a politically influential lawyer who summered in Forestport. The town's sawmill owners pitched in with contributions. Dick Manahan offered some wood, the lock tender Garrett Nichols and the undertaker Hiram Whiter helped hammer it together, and the Utica newspapers offered free one-year subscriptions. The *Boonville Herald* of 4 February 1897 reported its opening, a two-story building near St. Patrick's Church with a sunny reading room downstairs lit by three large windows and warmed in the winter by a fireplace. No one would confuse it with one of Carnegie's pillared endowments, but it was proof of Forestport's higher aspirations.

Forestport's ladies cultivated the literary union like a flowerpot in winter. But in a town where most book learning had stopped by the eighth grade, where the men worked ten hours a day or more, and where there was still no electricity to ease the women's daily chores, there was precious little time available for literary grace notes. It took too many hours a day just to feed—and sometimes restrain—the necessary fires.

Fire was the essential if dangerously insubordinate servant at the time. Wood had to be chopped and fires fed to boil the family laundry. Every day, fires were stoked in the iron-clawed stoves that dominated each kitchen. Wood or coal stoves glowed throughout the fall, winter, and spring in the common areas of country stores and in the blacksmith and harness shops. Kerosene lamps provided their odiferous, sooty light. Firemen fed boilers in the town's sawmills and shoveled coal into the boxes of the New York Central steam engines passing through the Buffalo Head station. Fire made life possible, but also followed its own rules. Sparks thrown off by New York Central engines ignited forest fires that annually destroyed swaths of Adirondack timberland. In 1897, about 20,000 acres of Adirondack forest, much of it previously cut, burned in forest fires, with railroads identified as the primary cause (McMartin 1994, 139).

The North Country's sawmills and local factories, with their furnaces firing and their stacks of dried lumber, caught fire with frightening regularity. Back on a snowy April night in 1891, fire had destroyed four barns, a blacksmith shop, thirteen houses, and a hotel in downtown Forestport. The cause was never satisfactorily determined, though a rumor spread about a vengeful lumberjack who had lost one too many hands of cards. Forestport men thereafter formed their first volunteer fire company, a spirited band whose efforts sometimes fell one hose-length short. In June 1893, a fire broke out of control at Bill Stanburgh's Forestport sawmill along Big Woodhull Creek. The shrill, prolonged whistle from Stanburgh's mill cut through the air at about six fifteen on a Friday night, drawing more than one hundred spectators and the bustling volunteer fire crew. The mill was already past saving by the time the Forestport men dragged up their Howe pump and its eight hundred feet of hose. It was all the volunteers could do to save the neighboring buildings and the boats tied up at the mill's dock. The fire reduced Stanburgh's mill to charred wood and twisted metal, and according to the *Boonville Herald* of 29 June 1893 stole the jobs of more than one hundred mill workers.

Forestport men knew fire. So when the fire calls clattered once more at three thirty in the morning of 21 July 1897, the villagers sprang to. This time the alarm came from the Nichols and Curran pulp mill built a decade before by Phil McGuire. In the predawn hours men hurriedly harnessed horses and rigged the Howe chemical and water pump, but they were too late. By the time they arrived, the fire had already taken the mill and thirty tons of wood pulp inside. The 22 July *Boonville Herald* reported that all the firefighters could do was train their modest stream of water on the pulp piled outside.

As with the April 1891 fire that destroyed Bill Stanburgh's mill, there was little hope of an economical recovery from the July 1897 mill fire. And, as with the 1891 mill fire, questions lingered about causes. The mill's machinery had been shut down the previous day, so it could not have been residual sparks from boilers or mechanical friction. Lightning was one possibility, but it was also said publicly that "an incendiary" might have caused the blaze as well. But why would anyone cast havoc on a mill that offered honest work for the local men?

Forestport men were still raking through the ashes of the Nichols and Curran mill fire when, two days later, another alarm ripped down River Street. It was the canal this time. The Forestport Feeder had burst open.

The 1897 Forestport break came at a bad time for Tom Wheeler. He already had enough to deal with, including an 18 July canal break right in the center of Utica. The Forestport break was worse. Wheeler learned the Forestport Feeder bank had ripped open about a mile and half outside of town. He knew the site. Several years before, another break had caused some problems in the same vicinity. It would take Wheeler a day to clear his Utica obligations and get up to Forestport. In the meantime, the state's representatives would include an engineer named David Whitford.

Whitford was a chess-playing, book-devouring, deer-hunting man who had been working on the Erie Canal since before the Civil War. In the days prior to the Forestport break, Whitford recorded in his diary that he had been staying up until near midnight compiling his account of North Country water storage (Whitford 1897). A meticulous record keeper, Whitford was asked by resident engineer George Morris on the morning of 23 July to reconnoiter the latest Forestport break. Reaching the Alder Creek train depot in the mid-afternoon, Whitford rode by horse and wagon to the break. It was, he saw, like a gulch in the towpath. He and Edgar Hughes, the local division superintendent, clambered down into the muddy ravine and made their estimations. The gulch they figured to be about forty feet deep and four hundred feet long. There, within the upheaved muck, Whitford and Hughes looked for clues.

"We found a small portion of the stone box culvert which was carried away, and its failure doubtless caused the break," Whitford recorded in his diary on 23 July 1897 (Whitford 1897).

The water had run riot toward the Black River about three hundred feet below, ripping stones from a nearby culvert, tossing boulders willy-nilly, and uprooting small trees. The hillside between the canal and the river resembled the flanks of a volcano, covered with congealing brown-clay lava. Whitford advised Hughes to clear away the wasted trees and brush lying in the breach and then await further instruction. They considered themselves fortunate that no boat had been plying the feeder at the time of the break. They did not yet know, however, how best to repair the damage.

Whitford, after staying overnight locally, returned to the break Saturday morning. It was a warm, moist day, leavened with summer showers. Up from Utica, Tom Wheeler arrived to examine this latest canal insult. One inspector recommended building an aqueduct to replace the broken feeder section. It would cost an estimated $35,000 and would provide the most secure fix, Whitford recorded in his diary on 24 July 1897. Wheeler, though, was not sure. After tramping through the gulch and consulting with his engineers, Wheeler concluded he needed to consult higher authorities. He and Whitford returned to Alder Creek to use one of the area's few telephones.

By Monday morning, the state's full contingent arrived, led by George Aldridge himself. It took a major event to lure the canal chief to an outlying town like Forestport, and men treated him as a visiting potentate. Aldridge allowed that he was impressed.

"[He] said that the nearest he ever remembered of a break in any way to be compared with this was at Ox-Bow, near Rochester, some years ago, but it was not so large or ugly," the *Boonville Herald* correspondent reported on 29 July 1897.

Aldridge's entourage concluded that some combination of a failed culvert and the heavy rains on the night before the break had mortally pressured an already weakened stretch of the towpath. They considered rebuilding the canal south of its present location, but dismissed that as impractically expensive. They considered erecting a timber culvert, but threw that idea out as well. Finally the engineers decided to fill in the break and restore the towpath to its previous state, a task, they figured, that would require at least 100,000 cubic yards of fill earth.

The scope of work was becoming clear. Crews would work day and night, for the feeder was too crucial to the Erie Canal's overall operations to be allowed to remain idle for very long. The niceties like competitive bidding were set aside, and Wheeler's favorite Utica contractor Thomas J. Dwyer, whose brother James would be the lead contractor on the 1898 repairs, quickly secured the job of preparing wood pilings to set into the new towpath, as well as the hauling, loading, and dumping of the fill earth itself. Dwyer talked of laying in rail tracks on the berm side of the feeder canal, opposite the towpath, so that horses could haul trains of five or six cars each from borrow pits where workers would toss in shovelsful of clay and gravel.

George Aldridge stayed but the day in Forestport. He had the rest of his empire to tend to, and engineers would handle the technical details. David Whitford stayed through Wednesday, setting angle stakes, laying the groundwork in an intermittent rain for the rebuilding. Whitford, for one, objected to another engineer's plans for placing sheet piling into the rebuilt canal bank. The piling was to serve as a barrier to water seepage, and Whitford eventually lost that dispute. He had, in any event, other problems to resolve. When he returned to Syracuse on Thursday, he learned of fresh trouble at an important lock elsewhere on the main Erie Canal.

Word of the Forestport break spread quickly. The town became a magnet for hungry men. Some five hundred men had been taken on within a week. By horse and wagon and foot they pulled into Forestport, drawn by the prospect of work at state wages, fifteen cents an hour and all the hours they could handle. Within three weeks the number of workers had swelled to nearly one thousand. Michael Doyle and all the other hotel owners jammed as many boarders into their rooms as they could manage, the liveryman William Clark was renting out his rigs for thirty-five cents an hour, and the saloon boys sold drinks as fast as they could pour them.

"Thousands of dollars will be expended in Forestport this year, and the break will prove a God-send to the community," the *Boonville Herald* predicted on 12 August 1897.

Approvingly, the *Herald* correspondent asserted that the politics and religion of no man had been asked by the hiring bosses. The patronage system, however, was still alive and well. An Albany attorney named W. W.

Mead, one of Aldridge's lieutenants, endorsed the employment applications of three gents named Henry Hughes, Lawrence Collins, and John McMullen. John Burke, one of the state men running the Forestport repairs, dutifully reported back to Mead that all three men were hired; though Hughes was "quite an elderly man," Burke was able to "place him as a scrub foreman, where he will be treated properly, at same time earn his money." The three men, in turn, were appropriately grateful to their benefactors. From the crowded Buckley House hotel, McMullen wrote Mead to say he was "very thankful to you and the superintendent, [and] will you please keep me on as long as you can" (Aldridge Papers).

Patronage alone, however, could not fill all the hundreds of positions needed to complete the Forestport repairs. More hardy backs were needed, and so officials called upon Mr. Vincenzo Marrone of Utica, an influential man within the city's Italian community. Marrone brought up about 185 Italians, immigrants and first-generation sons who settled into a rough boarding house on the outskirts of Forestport. They worked at night and slept briefly during the day in their three-tiered bunks. They were restricted from leaving quarters in daytime, when they might clash with the local Irishmen. Inevitably the confinement grew irksome.

One Sunday well into the repairs, a deputy sheriff named Owens and one of his colleagues were called out to the big boarding house where Marrone's Italians lived along with other men. Many of these workers on the Forestport break were said by the *Boonville Herald* to be overly boisterous, spending much of their spare time drinking and carousing. On this Sunday they had turned irritable and ugly. They had been drinking in close quarters and feeling their confinement. By the time Deputy Owens arrived, nearly fifty men were jostling about, many with knives drawn, and eighteen-year-old Joe Scatto was bleeding from a cut under the eye. The *Boonville Herald* of 19 August 1897 reported that Owens and his deputy waded into the crowd and hauled away five men, including Scatto.

For all the roistering, however, the work proceeded apace. The crews spent the first week clearing away trees and dense underbrush. They denuded the hillside between the feeder and the Black River below, stripping away a zone two hundred feet wide and nearly one mile long. They reduced to simple soil and stumps five acres of the berm-side hill opposite the towpath, and poured dirt into the feeder bottom to form a temporary coffer dam. They cut roads in to haul supplies and hammered together quick buildings. As they would the following year, work crews dug two sand pits at the opposite ends of a road, cut in the form of a figure eight. The men tossed sand into the backs of wagons slowly rolling past; the sand was then dumped into the chasm at the bottom of the feeder. Some 100,000 yards of dirt would eventually be required to fill the hole. Dwyer's crews cut the timber for the rows of sheet piling pile-driven into the ground at eight-foot intervals. This so-called triple-lap sheet piling was basically a wall, 450 feet in length, that would undergird the rebuilt towpath. With the sheet piling as the skeleton, a puddle of clay and stabilizing gravel was poured in between and dirt tamped down over all. It was not easy securing all the dirt and gravel needed, nor was it easy to drive the timber posts into the uneven ground.

"There were some places in the bank that were pretty soft, and the water would fly up every time they struck it," recalled Billy Gorman, a one-time bartender who worked driving piles following the 1897 break. "There were more or less obstructions all the way through. They would get a plank started and drive two or three maybe, and then the next two or three would not go off" (*People v. Manahan* 1900, 173).

With the feeder shut down, the Black River Canal started choking. Rome stopped sprinkling its dusty streets, and residents were advised to forego their lawn sprinklers. The public watering troughs set out for teams of horses dried up. By 11 August 1897, the *Rome Daily Sentinel* had reported that Rome's three fire engines were pumping water from a spring into the city's main supply pipes. The Erie Canal, too, could ill afford to lose its Forestport replenishment. The canal was a sieve already, losing water through unlined beds, evaporation, and the locking operations. By early August, canal water levels had fallen six inches lower than normal. Canallers were potentially facing big trouble, and so were lumbermen whose North Country logs were now bottled up at Forestport without a way to reach market.

"A big jam of logs on the dam and in the river below the dam as far as we can see," David Whitford reported when he revisited Forestport in late August (Whitford 1897).

Intensely motivated engineers pressed on day and night. By late August, after more than a month of steady work, the end was closely in sight and some of the work crews were starting to get paid off. Flush with cash, the laid-off workers did not always return quietly to the farms or city wards. On 26 August a teamster who had been driving for Forestport liveryman George Williams pocketed his pay and promptly got boozed up at one of the town's saloons. When he was stinking drunk, the teamster weaved belligerently down to Williams' house and began loudly demanding the horse team he had been using. Williams told the man to leave. The teamster stayed, and shouted again for horses. Williams repeated his order to leave. The teamster said he would take the horses now, or else he would kill Williams and burn his house down.

Forestport men took fire seriously, and the thirty-eight-year-old Williams was not one to let murderous threats lie. He had lost three children to disease already, according to census records; he knew loss, and would not take any more. Inflamed, Williams grabbed a club and started swinging. The teamster was partly subdued by the time that Deputy Sheriff Shanks arrived. But the teamster, once handcuffed and brought to the Getman House hotel, broke free and swung at the deputy. The *Rome Daily Sentinel* reported on 27 August 1897 that the furious Shanks thumped the obstinate teamster with his billy club "very severely before the [man] was conquered."

By Saturday, 29 August, engineers opened up the Forestport state pond lock to allow the first test flow of water through the repaired canal. That same morning the night crews and most of the day crews were laid off and given their pay. On Wednesday, 1 September, the state reopened the Black River Canal for navigation and replenishment to the Erie Canal. The state had spent, all told, $62,781.78 in repairing the Forestport Feeder in 1897. It was money much appreciated among those who picked up a piece of it: the contractors with Dwyer, the hotel owners and saloonkeepers, the liverymen and carpenters, the shovelers and timekeepers who flocked to town. One by one, and then in groups, the men drifted away from Forestport in early September, until there was only one man who had failed to call for his pay from the state's paymasters. That man was named Joseph Daily, and the mystery of why he failed to collect his earnings may have been resolved on Saturday, 4 September, when the body of a thirty-five-year-old laborer was pulled from the Forestport state pond.

The drowned man had twenty cents in the pockets of his striped cotton trousers, a plug of tobacco, and a soggy scrap of paper on which was written "George, Port Leyden, N.Y." He was five feet eleven inches tall, with light brown hair and a mustache. He was, in all respects, an ordinary man. He had been dead, investigators determined, about two weeks. That meant he had died at the very busiest time of the repairs, when Forestport was at its most boisterous. There was one unusual aspect: The coroner identified a bruise on the corpse's chest, possibly evidence of a fight. But the coroner considered it nothing conclusive, and the *Boonville Herald* reported on 9 September 1897 that the inquest jury determined the man had died by accidental drowning. Joseph Daily, or whoever it might have been, could easily have drunk his mind away one night down at Doyle's or Manahan's or Bynon's saloon and then wandered off the deep end into the Forestport state pond. No one could conceive a motive for murder.

Joseph Daily's disappearance and the surfacing of the drowned man were two of the last loose ends left over from the repairs of 1897. Soon there was only the memory left of what the breaks had done—the memory and the one fundamental unanswered question of what, exactly, had happened along the Forestport towpath.

Chapter 7

CANAL BREAKS did not usually have to bear much scrutiny. They were altogether commonplace, and their probable causes manifold. Officials could blame the 1897 Forestport break on some unfortunate combination of rain, slumping earth, and broken culverts and leave it at that. Considered on its own, the 1898 Forestport break could likewise be vaguely attributed to misfortune and nature's way. Two days before the 1898 break, men reminded each other, a sustained cloudburst had swamped the North Country. The rain so filled the Forestport Feeder that it put unbearable pressure on a silent flaw in the towpath bank. Men had found, after the towpath had burst, pieces of broken timber right in the middle of where the break occurred. The timber had been part of a culvert designed to carry an underground spring beneath the canal. At some point, men reasoned, the timber must have broken so that the spring began seeping into the sandy soil of the towpath bank, undermining it one grain at a time until the bank burst beneath the unusual pressure of the July storm.

It was a reasonable theory, considering the 1898 break in isolation. But the two consecutive Forestport breaks in 1897 and 1898 invited other kinds of speculation as well. There grew by June 1898 a feeling among the authorities, in the words of the *Boonville Herald* on 30 June 1898, that "breaks in the feeder banks are of altogether too frequent occurrence." The engineers began talking of installing telephone lines so that future breaks along the Forestport Feeder might be reported quickly.

Thomas Wheeler's men began patrolling the towpath at night with special vigilance.

On the night of 25 June 1898, a lively Saturday evening in Forestport, watchmen D. Bryan Brown and George Barber slowly walked their posts, talking quietly until, as they subsequently reported, they stumbled upon a man digging at the towpath with a shovel. Caught in the act, it seemed, of attempting to cause another break, the man dropped his shovel and ran toward Brown. The diligent watchman unholstered his revolver and fired four errant shots. Untouched, the unidentified towpath digger ran off into the night. The next morning the canal authorities found the beginnings of a ditch dug about sixteen inches deep through the towpath. It was not far from the freshly repaired May break.

"It is sufficient to say that if the right man is caught, it will go hard with him," the *Herald* vowed on 30 June 1898.

Watchman Brown's close call sparked fresh speculation about the most recent canal break. The state authorities began openly voicing their suspicions, so much so that an otherwise unidentified "reputable resident of Forestport" complained that authorities "have insinuated that the break was caused by some Forestport man and not by natural causes." Forestport men, in turn, questioned the actions of watchman Brown himself.

The "reputable resident" of Forestport suggested Brown had concocted the story to justify his continued employment. Just consider the incident. What kind of foolhardy ne'er-do-well would attempt a canal break while watchmen patrolled the banks? And wasn't gunfire a little excessive to stop an alleged ditchdigger? Adding it up, the reputable Forestport man concluded that someone was seeking to cast more bad light on the town.

"There is no question that a break, the magnitude of that of this summer, or that of last summer, proves very remunerative to any place in the locality where it occurs," Forestport's defender in the *Herald* acknowledged on 30 June 1898. Still, "it seems incredible that any person would be so evilly disposed as to attempt to create a break simply for the advantages a town or a set of men would enjoy from that source."

Everyone knew how Forestport had profited. The lumbermen who had sold the wood, the saloonkeepers who had sold the drinks, the hotel owners, the dry goods merchants, the liverymen, and the common laborer all made money in the course of the Forestport Feeder repairs. But the good people of the town knew as well that malign motives could be found just as easily among the patronage bosses and big city canal contractors. These were the men who had profited unduly from the lavishing of canal improvement contracts, where millions of dollars had been spent to little effect. Indeed, some of the politically connected contractors who had benefited so garishly from their Erie Canal work had also been at the center of the Forestport Feeder repairs. The stories about these contractors and their political patrons had long circulated upstate, but never with greater force than in the summer and fall of 1898 amidst the most searching canal investigation in a generation.

The investigation had started in search of how the $9 million in canal improvement funds had been spent. Questions had been accumulating like so much canal silt ever since New York voters approved the $9 million in 1895. The patronage workers were being hired and the contractors were getting their fill, but the improvements themselves seemed altogether elusive. The normally reticent state engineer, Campbell Adams, finally admitted that he had had doubts all along that the $9 million was going to be sufficient.

"I did, finally, consent to the $9 million figure, not without misgivings, but on the idea that if we asked for much in excess of that amount, we would get nothing. Perhaps in that I had it wrong; it might have been better judgment to have insisted on the higher figure," Adams confessed, according to the *New York Times* of 8 January 1898.

Political insistence was not necessarily Adams' way. Though himself elected to statewide office, Campbell Adams remained at heart a self-educated engineer, a reserved man with a black mustache and a receding hairline. The *New York Times* of 18 September 1895 noted that the Utica native's formal schooling had ended with his graduation from the Utica Academy. He had worked five years in the family business, traveling about the state as a rope salesman, before returning to Utica for the first of a series of surveying jobs. He went back and forth between appointed positions in Utica's surveying department and worked for various railroads until he first won election in 1893 at the age of forty.

Despite Adams' protestations, Democrats had forced Governor Black to accede to a special investigation of the canal improvements. After some casting about, Governor Black found four Republicans and three Democrats willing to make up the Canal Investigating Commission. The commission invited skepticism. The *New York Times* of 13 February 1898 noted how Black's friends at the *Troy Times* opined that the supposed investigation would be a gentlemanly inquiry "so that the people may know what has been accomplished on the canals thus far, and be prepared to vote on the continuation of the work." One wag suggested the Canal Investigating Commission should be renamed the Commission to Recommend Further Expenditure on the Canals.

Nonetheless, the Canal Investigating Commission had settled into Syracuse in late May 1898, mere days after the second Forestport Feeder break. Syracuse was the headquarters for the Erie Canal's Middle Division, and it was rife with stories told by people like resident engineer George Morris. Morris was a $2,400-a-year engineer who had risen to the number two position in the division. He had been up in Forestport following the 1897 levee break and again following the 1898 Forestport break. He was familiar with improvement contracts and $4-a-day inspectors.

"Some of the inspectors made very good men and did very good work . . . but they were like hen's teeth, few and far between," Morris said. "On some contracts, we had to put our own men on the work . . . because the inspectors didn't know whether the work was being properly done or not" (New York State Canal Investigating Commission 1898b, 3393).

The canal contractors, too, were getting a close look, including the firm responsible for multiple repairs along the Forestport Feeder. The Utica firm of T. J. Dwyer & Company had two of the Erie Canal improvement contracts: Contract No. 1 to deepen a 3.3-mile stretch of the canal from Lock 46 to the Oneida County line, and Contract No. 12 to lengthen and improve Lock 46 so that two tied-together boats could be locked through simultaneously. Even as the canal commissioners were asking their questions in Syracuse that May, it was the Dwyer firm that had secured the back-of-the-envelope contract to run the repairs at the Forestport Feeder break. The year before, too, the Dwyer firm had profited by handling the Forestport Feeder repairs. Sometimes the company's methods seemed unnecessarily extravagant. But if the 1897 Forestport Feeder break repair job was one long revel in spoils, as the newspapers characterized it, the money involved was still petty change compared to the Erie Canal improvements.

For Contract No. 1 on the Middle Division, state engineers had estimated the work would cost $208,420. T. J. Dwyer & Company won the contract in November 1896 with a bid considerably lower than the estimate—but by the time accounts were settled in 1898, the Dwyer firm was billing the state $301,155.15. On Dwyer's second contract, to improve Lock 46, a $16,482 bid grew to an $18,751 payment before the work was done. The commission's attorney voiced particular interest in the classification of materials, a subject that had fast become a top priority for the investigating commission. The contractors were paid depending on the type of material being excavated. Rock, or soil sufficiently hard and compacted to be considered the equivalent of rock, took longer to excavate and therefore the contractors were compensated more. The plow test was one commonly employed. If the earth in question could be plowed up with four good horses, it was dirt; if it was so compacted or rocky that harder methods were required, the contractor would be paid a higher rate. In the disputes over classification, contractors invariably won.

Engineer William Gere, called to testify, recalled how he, his assistant Mr. Diehl, Mr. Morris, and state engineer and surveyor Campbell Adams had met one day in the Dwyers' Utica office.

"Mr. Morris said that there was a good deal of hard material taken out on the contract, but that he had not time to examine it," Gere replied, according to the *Rome Daily Sentinel* of 27 May 1898. "He said that the contractors claimed about 8,000 yards as rock. Mr. Diehl said that he had no measurements of the amount of rock. It was suggested by the state engineer, I think, that he should make his notes show some rock."

Although Gere went on to say that Adams did not order the engineers "to find 8,000 yards or any other arbitrary amount," the implication of what had happened that day in the Dwyers' Utica office was clear. Contractors held sway over state officials.

The Syracuse testimony about patronage and contracting excesses was duplicated in hearings throughout New York's canal region. However sympathetic the investigating commissioners might have been to start with, they could not whitewash all the dark stories they heard. On Saturday, 30 July, the Canal Investigating Commission submitted its report to Governor Black in Albany. It was a boulder heaved into the center of the Republican pond.

The commission's several-hundred-page report was a frustrating piece of work. It criticized sharply some canal practices, but was vague in its assessment of responsibility. It numbingly recounted the particulars of certain contracts, but lacked a clear summary of the commissioners' conclusions. And yet, shining through the muddle, the commission's underlying message could be discerned.

"The conditions as they developed were most unfavorable, and required a high degree of skill and moral strength to meet them," the commissioners pointedly concluded. "Pressure for haste necessarily resulting in disorganized and demoralized execution was exerted from quarters from whence it should not have been expected; influences hereditary in Canal work began to exert itself [*sic*]. The traditions and habits of Canal contractors were a power for evil which required continual watchfulness to oppose; here and there political influences controlling the appointment of subordinates and personal political ambition put its hand on the lever" (New York State Canal Investigating Commission 1898a, 9).

In sum, the investigators found that although all but $25,000 of the $9 million had been spent or obligated, only one-third of the promised work had been done. A total of sixty-five miles of work had been completed; there was no money left to complete the additional 144 miles of work that had been anticipated. "Not less than" $1 million of the total had been improperly spent, the commissioners advised. Ill-qualified political ward heelers had been employed courtesy of the patronage-minded public works superintendent. Proper administration was altogether lacking.

The particulars were illuminating. Aldridge, or his lieutenants, had spent $178,969 on hiring what were termed "superintendent's inspectors." Far too many were kept on when they were not needed during the warm weather season of open canal navigation. In 1898, ninety-six of those inspectors were appointed temporarily without any kind of testing, and, as the commission delicately put it, "apparently, competency and fitness were not the only test of their appointment." Of those ninety-six inspectors, fifteen subsequently failed the required civil service examination and forty-eight failed to show up to take the test.

"Men working for George Aldridge [were] getting $4 a day, and [the] duties were to get out the enrollment in the 18th Ward," businessman Edward Inglehart explained (New York State Canal Investigating Commission 1898b, 4890).

A carpenter named David I. Snell was hired by the state to work on the same two Utica-area contracts held by the Dwyer firm. Snell was, by chance, the brother of Jacob Snell: a section superintendent on the canal's Middle Division, a former Republican state committeeman who had been a strong supporter of Governor Frank Black. David Snell, in addition to being a seasonal canal employee, was also a silent partner in the Dwyer firm, an apparent violation of state law (New York State Canal Investigating Commission 1898a, 22).

To help secure the canal banks, the contractors were supposed to drive spruce piles deep into the earth. The Dwyer men and local state engineers, however, followed the same course in Utica as they did in Forestport. They resorted to the more costly triple-lap sheet piling, composed of three layers of two-inch spruce planks nailed together in a tongue-and-groove and driven into the ground as a barrier against water passage. This was a more elaborate and costly approach than had originally been anticipated. The local engineer fixed it so that Dwyer was, according to the investigating commission, "paid twice for putting the [same] material in the work." That is, the contractor was paid for nailing the planks together at the price originally agreed upon for driving the piles into the earth; then an additional price was paid to drive the new fixtures underground.

Though the commission's report most directly implicated George Aldridge and Campbell Adams, Governor Frank Black was besmirched as well by his association with the two men.

"The people will not renew their license to plunder and destroy," the Democratic *New York Times* declared on 8 August 1898 upon release of the report. "If the Democrats, putting aside rivalries and quarrels, will put before the people honest, capable and tried men as candidates this Fall, it will be many years before the Republicans will have anything further to say about Canal expenditures."

Some advisers urged Black to fire Aldridge, to get it over with. But Aldridge was a party man, and Black felt unable to cut him loose. The governor called for further review, by a one-time Albany judge named Edwin Countryman. This action was insufficient. By the first week of September, the state's Democratic campaign committee began distributing a sixty-four-page pamphlet highlighting the findings of the Canal Investigation Commission. "Millions of the people's dollars lost!" the screed proclaimed, according to the *New York Times* of 4 September 1898. "The people deceived. Their confidence misplaced. One million dollars stolen. Two million dollars more 'unnecessarily,' 'unauthorizedly,' 'injudiciously,' or 'improperly' spent. . . . A great public work irredeemably harmed."

From Long Island, attorney George Wallace lamented to party boss Thomas Platt in August that "as a party, we must lose more or less strength on the Canal muddle" (Platt Papers, box 1, 29 August 1898). New York Supreme Court Judge Alfred Spring of Cattaraugus County predicted to Platt in August that "the renomination of Governor Black will be fraught with disaster for our party . . . if nominated, he must run the gauntlet of the 'Canal scandal'; he must bear the sins of Aldridge and Adams, real and imagined" (Platt Papers, box 1, 16 August 1898).

For the Republicans reporting to Platt in the late summer of 1898, there was but one man thought likely to save the party come November. That man was Theodore Roosevelt. With his good government talk and his reformer's zeal, Roosevelt had been irritating Platt for years. The boss, nonetheless, had assented to Roosevelt's appointment as first assistant secretary of the navy; it was, Platt reasoned, a place where Roosevelt could probably do less harm to the organization. Roosevelt's subsequent heroism in July 1898 as lieutenant colonel and organizer of the First United States Cavalry Volunteers—the Rough Riders—had made his political future the talk of New York (Alexander 1923, 303).

Platt summoned Chauncey Depew in August to meet in Manhattan Beach. Depew, in his carefully burnished memoirs, recalled that he instantly endorsed the Rough Rider. Imagine, he told Platt, what would happen if Governor Black were renominated.

"The heckler in the audience will arise and interrupt me, saying, 'Chauncey, we agree with what you say about the Grand Old Party and all that, but how about the Canal steal?' " Depew said. "I [would] have to explain that the amount stolen was only a million, and that would be fatal."

Whereas, Depew went on, Roosevelt could be introduced as a battlefield hero, a renowned fighter for reform. If he were selected, everyone would know "that every thief will be caught and punished, and every dollar that can be found restored to the public treasury. "Then," Depew said, "I will follow the colonel leading his Rough Riders up San Juan Hill and ask the band to play the Star Spangled Banner" (Depew 1922, 161).

Black was past saving. At the Republican convention of 28 September, the combination of pragmatists and enthusiasts chose Roosevelt over Black by a 753–218 margin and made a perfunctory bow in the direction of canal reform.

"If there are errors in the system and the law we will correct them; if there has been fraud we will expose it and punish the wrongdoers," the platform stated, according to the *New York Times* of 15 September 1898.

Roosevelt struck a consistent tone throughout his flag-waving campaign. He would dismiss the canal business in a sentence or two and then move on to grander matters.

A typical appearance was his brief stop at Boonville, the terminus of the Forestport Feeder, on 19 October. The *Boonville Herald* of 20 October 1898 welcomed Roosevelt as "the brave hero of Santiago, the leader of the Rough Riders, the brilliant writer and statesman, the noblest work of God, an honest man." At 12:45 P.M. this paragon arrived on the New York Central and stepped out onto the platform of the rear car. An estimated 1,500 people, their spirits swelled by the Boonville band, surrounded him. He had brought with him his Rough Rider ensemble, but still he could not entirely avoid the state topic of most pressing concern. When the cheering had settled down, Roosevelt briskly disposed of the matter at hand.

"If the trouble has arisen because of any corruption of any public servant, or because of the failure of any public servant to perform his duty, that man shall assuredly be punished wholly without regard to any personal or political consideration," Roosevelt declared.

Roosevelt's Democratic opponent, Augustus Van Wyck, was a former New York Supreme Court justice who was acceptable to Tammany Hall without being excessively beholden to it. He also had one good issue. Van Wyck stuck to the canal scandal as diligently as Roosevelt stuck to flag-waving.

Utica, the hometown of well-connected Tom Wheeler and the state engineer Campbell Adams and the contractors at T. J. Dwyer & Company, warmly welcomed Van Wyck's Democratic caravan shortly after noon on 31 October. Van Wyck pulled into town on the New York Central's Empire State Express and straightaway rode by horse-drawn carriage from the train station to the Butterfield House hotel at the corner of Genesee and Devereaux streets. The Democratic candidate spent a quiet afternoon in his Butterfield room, preparing his speech and turning away visitors. That evening the ornately uniformed clubs—the St. Vincent's Cadets Drum Corps, the Ninth Ward Sullivan Club, the Eleventh Ward Sullivan Club—led Van Wyck's way toward the city's Opera House. Several hundred up-county residents, from Boonville and Lowville and Forestport, accompanied Van Wyck to the Opera House, where according to the account of the *Utica Observer* on 1 November 1898 he gave them what-for.

When the Opera House cheering and clapping ended after several minutes, Van Wyck was looking out at nearly 3,000 people crammed into a theater made to seat 1,700. Some Forestport men were in the audience, including merchant Johnny Neejer and the liveryman Charley Denslow. Outside, hundreds of other partisans strained to hear from the windy city streets. Van Wyck's Utica speech summed up his campaign.

In a talk spanning thirty-three paragraphs of printed text, fully twenty-two paragraphs dealt directly with the canal scandal, and the remainder touched upon it indirectly. He called the canal matter "one of the most shocking scandals in the recent politics of America." He scornfully dismissed the idea that Republicans, the very men who had let the problem run up, could be trusted to set it right. He summoned up the old phrase "the Canal Ring," redolent of the days of bad Boss Tweed and crusading Samuel Tilden. To illustrate the point, a large portrait of Tilden stood on stage amid the palms and ferns.

"Let the people turn the rascals out," Van Wyck declared, as the *Utica*

Observer recounted on 1 November 1898, "to the end that new accountants may examine the books and correct the evils, that the ill-gotten gains may be recovered for the state treasury and punishment meted out to the offenders as a warning to those who may be tempted in the future to violate a sacred public trust!"

Roosevelt finally hit his reform-minded rhetorical stride in the campaign's final days, while, much more quietly, Platt went about collecting campaign funds from, as he put it, "those abundantly able to give" (Gosnell 1924, 145). In rural upstate counties, farmers pocketed their cash and ushered voters to the polling places, or stood watch, or simply accepted their party payments. Certain expectations developed about how politics worked. In Forestport, five cocky young lumbermen emerged from the woods on election day and demanded $5 each in exchange for their votes. They were refused their money, the *Boonville Herald* reported on 11 November 1898, and so they stomped back into the wild woods, victims of someone's passing sense of good government.

Forestport voters gave Roosevelt a 203–152 victory, a margin considerably narrower than the town customarily provided Republican candidates (Cookinham 1912, 184). Statewide, Roosevelt won by a spare 17,000 votes out of 1.3 million cast. He could savor the victory only briefly before the tough decisions began. Aldridge had finally asked to be relieved following the post-election release of a highly critical report on the canal improvements. Finding the right replacement would tax the newly elected governor.

"In the actual state of affairs, his office was by far the most important office under me," Roosevelt recounted in his autobiography, "and I intended to appoint to it some man of high character and capacity who could be trusted to do the work not merely honestly and efficiently, but without regard to politics" (Roosevelt 1973, 154).

Roosevelt would be vexed for some time before he could find a man acceptable both to Platt and to his own good-government instincts. The matter required delicate handling. Some fundamental decisions would have to be made about the future of the Erie Canal. Other, more focused, decisions would also have to be made. The peculiar circumstances of the consecutive Forestport Feeder breaks, in particular, had been gnawing at some canal officials even as Roosevelt and Van Wyck had gone about their campaigning.

As chief engineer for the Middle Division of the Erie Canal, William Gere supervised the technical aspects of the Black River Canal and Forestport Feeder. Old Man Gere, as some called him, had decades of service on the canal. He knew all about breaks, their prevalence and repair. Gere had supervised some of the repair work on the 1898 Forestport Feeder break, and his account books showed the state had spent $50,764.47 in repairing the Forestport break. As he composed his annual canal report that fall, he was ready to make public an extraordinary accusation.

"The cause of this break is not positively known," Gere advised in September 1898, "but is believed to have been started by some evil disposed person" (New York State Engineer and Surveyor 1898, 144).

Gere did not elaborate. In due time, though, newly elected Governor Roosevelt himself would have reason to take notice of rowdy Forestport. There was one more break to come, one for which the town, at last, would be held to answer.

Chapter 8

ROOSEVELT PROMISED to put his honest mark on the Erie Canal. In replacing Aldridge, he told the *New York Times* of 5 January 1899, he would "disregard politics altogether" in selecting a man with "honesty, energy, courage and executive ability." The Platt machine, however, had not ceased its efforts to guide the young governor, and Roosevelt had to slog through a succession of candidates until he could split the difference between his progressive and his organization instincts (Chessman 1965, 72).

Named on 12 January, Colonel John Partridge seemed a perfectly satisfactory compromise choice for the $6,000-a-year job. The white-mustachioed, sixty-one-year-old Massachusetts native appealed both to independents who wanted reform and to the party organization that wanted its interests protected. He had a Civil War record that attracted young Roosevelt, having fought his way through North Carolina and Virginia before being wounded in September 1864 at Fort Darling. He was cut from a different mold altogether than Aldridge. Aldridge looked like a political boss, a man of appetite. Partridge looked like a soldier, a trim and self-disciplined horseman. He was a firm, reserved man who, it was said, demanded unfailing courtesy from every man under him. Unmarried, he had a reputation for painstaking attentiveness to detail, but the *New York Times* noted on 13 January 1899 that he was not unsympathetic to the working man during his service as president of the Brooklyn City and Newtown Company, a railroad firm.

Roosevelt told him he wanted the bloated public works payroll cut down remorselessly. Partridge saluted and promised to scrape the canal clean. He would select men based on merit and serve the public rather than party interests, just as he had served Brooklyn mayor Seth Low as fire and police commissioner in the early 1880s. Partridge immediately put canal workers on notice that the old ways were changing and executed several high-profile demotions and dismissals to make his point. The district superintendent in charge of the canal's western division, a brother-in-law of former governor Morton, was quickly sacked. But patronage had not retired with George Aldridge. Roosevelt himself weighed in on behalf of a certain canal candidate in a 29 March letter (Roosevelt Papers). Other patronage exemplars were retained including, surprisingly, Utica's Tom Wheeler.

Of all people, Wheeler should have been the first to go. He had been one of Aldridge's chief lieutenants and infamous in his own right for his bare-knuckled Oneida County politics. By 23 January, Roosevelt had heard enough rumors that he asked his Utica friend Fred Fincke for "a little confidential information" concerning Wheeler.

"Is he a rank spoilsman who has used the canal simply for political purpose?" Roosevelt asked (Roosevelt Papers).

To Partridge, that same day, Roosevelt confessed his confusion. The governor had heard from some, including Partridge, that Wheeler was "a good man and ought to be kept." But from others, Roosevelt said, he had heard that Wheeler was "the worst man on the whole canal." Ultimately, Partridge's confidence in Wheeler's efficiency won out, and the Utica boss retained his job as assistant superintendent of public works. It was a decision Partridge would soon enough regret.

. . .

The canal rested in the winter while Governor Roosevelt selected his team. The Adirondack woods, which provided the other half of Forestport's economy, seemed livelier. Lumberjacks were working and trees were falling, as they had for decades. But however furious it seemed,

Adirondack logging in the winter of 1898–99 was nearing a downhill slide from which it would never recover.

The trajectory of Adirondack logging can be traced against the outline of Michael Doyle's life. In 1856, the year of his birth, some 650 million board feet of lumber were produced in New York State. New York was, by then, the nation's leading lumber-producing state. There were in that year an estimated two thousand sawmills in the Adirondacks. In 1868, there were twelve sawmills within about ten miles of the village still known informally as Punkeytown, soon to be renamed Forestport (O'Donnell 1948, 62). By the time Michael Doyle was a teenager, New York was producing more than 1.1 billion board feet of lumber annually. Black Phil McGuire, Irish brogued and thickly bearded, began building mills and shipping long spruce spars down the Forestport Feeder and all the way to Albany (Wager 1896b, 63).

Two-thirds of the Adirondack forest had been logged at least once by 1885, and new railway lines were plunging into the previously unlogged sections. By 1898, the year of the second Forestport break, total New York state lumber production had slackened to about 850 million board feet. From Canada, huge amounts of pulpwood were being imported to serve New York's 1,087 pulp mills, supplanting what once had been supplied by the Adirondacks. It had become, moreover, logging of a different sort. The grandest trees had long since been taken. White pine was no longer the premier species, and by the year of the second Forestport break more Adirondack spruce trees were being cut for the pulp and paper mills than for sawlogs.

In 1890, New York produced 325,690,634 board feet of lumber and the equivalent of 51,966,262 board feet of pulpwood. Seven years later, the year of the first Forestport break, the state produced 284,907,544 board feet of lumber and the equivalent of 229,581,918 board feet of pulpwood. In Michael Doyle's boyhood, jacks cut only floatable softwood, the pines and spruce that could be sectioned into thirteen-foot lengths called "markets" and dropped into the spring-flushed rivers for driving to the mills. Loggers once left standing trees too small to bother with. But the indiscriminately voracious pulp mills were a different matter, and loggers began taking trees as small as five inches in diameter. The hardwood trees of the forest—birch, maple, and beech—were being logged as well, hauled out by new rail lines instead of by the traditional river drive (Bethke 1994, 12).

"The rapidity with which the Adirondack land owners are cutting over their woodlands recalls to mind the old fable of the goose that laid the golden egg, and its untimely fate at the hands of the enterprising owner," state superintendent of forests William Fox warned in January 1899 (New York State Commissioners of Fisheries, Games and Forests, 1899, 306).

Some aspects of Adirondack logging and Forestport industry had faded altogether. When Michael Doyle was a boy, there were at least seven tanneries in the vicinity of Forestport and Boonville. Each needed hemlock bark to provide the tannin-rich soup used for converting cowhides to leather. The hemlock trees were simply stripped of their bark for use in tanning, and the denuded and dying hemlocks left to rot in the thick forest. After the Civil War, a one-armed former general and his partners took over a tannery on the banks of Big Woodhull Creek about a mile from town. Two years after the general arrived, the town split off from Remsen and took as its name Forestport. In due time, General Jonathan Hill and his partner, Thomas E. Proctor, were running Oneida County's largest sole-leather manufacturer. Its 240 vats could go through four thousand cords of hemlock bark, and by 1880 the Forestport tannery was producing fifty thousand sides. In her marvelously detailed *Hides, Hemlocks and Adirondack History,* Barbara McMartin reports that Hill and Proctor employed about sixty Forestport men a year by 1888, and another one hundred were hired during the bark-peeling season (McMartin 1992, 268). The tannery made work coming and going: the raw hides were boated in to Forestport along the feeder canal, tanned, and then shipped back throughout New York State. But by the early 1890s, Proctor and Hill had abruptly shuttered their Forestport tannery, abandoning piles of unused hemlock bark.

New visions, too, were changing the woods upon which Forestport relied. The town stood just outside the Blue Line, the border for a fourteen-county region whose state-owned land was supposed to be "forever kept as wild forest lands." In May 1892, the legislature had strengthened protections by passing the Adirondack Park Enabling Act, which defined the park as a 2.8-million-acre expanse. The park was championed by nature sentimentalists, but also by hard-nosed engineers and businessmen. One of them was a Herkimer County man of some property and foresight, Judge George W. Smith—the original owner of the Forestport hotel operated by Michael Doyle. Smith pressed as early as February 1894 for the preservation of more forest land, for the most practical of reasons. "Here," Smith declared in the *Boonville Herald* of 1 February 1994, "are natural fountains and watersheds that send their waters, not only to all northern New York, but they create the Mohawk and fill the upper channels of the Hudson . . . the navigation of the Hudson to the capital will become impossible unless the supply of its upper waters be maintained." By 1897, the year of the first Forestport break, the three-million-acre Adirondack area included 1 million acres owned by sportsmen's clubs and individuals, about 1.2 million acres owned by lumbermen, and 802,000 acres owned by the state.

Increasing foreign and domestic competition, the depletion of the original Adirondack forest cover, the carving away of state lands ineligible for further logging: piece by piece the upstate timber industry was transforming. The one thing that stayed the same was the danger, and Forestport families knew intimately just how dangerous logging could be.

In late April 1895, lumberjack Dennis Laquay was stepping between the tangled logs on a Woodhull Creek jam when the monster stirred, and several thirteen-foot logs crushed him, injuring him, it was reported, "quite severely." The *Boonville Herald* of 1 May 1895 subsequently reported that his friends hauled Dennis back to his Forestport home for his recuperation. Others came home rheumatic from standing in bitterly cold North Country rivers during the springtime drives, or with lost limbs from the momentarily careless flash of an axe. Forestport saloonkeeper Walt Bynon had only been twenty-two years old in the early spring of 1893 when he had collapsed while in the midst of the annual river drive. Stricken with what the doctor diagnosed as inflammatory rheumatism, Walt was hauled back to Forestport for the start of a lengthy recovery that never really concluded. The attack was, more or less, the end of Walt's logging career and the start of his saloon life. The mills, too, could turn on the men of Forestport. Young Arthur Hoban was barely fifteen when, the *Boonville*

Herald reported on 18 August 1892, he cut his right hand almost completely off while working in one of the Forestport shingle mills. Every year one man or another ran afoul of the machinery. On a May morning in 1894 at the Forestport Lumber Company, for instance, a blast of steam blew Sebastian Fleury off his feet and scalded him waist to toe. Garrett Nichols, the lockkeeper on the Forestport Feeder, had lost some of his fingers in a mill accident.

The chancy work roughened the men who survived it. One was Edward Marshall, a dodgy fellow some called the "Snake Charmer of the Woods." Marshall was an occasional river driver for the Forestport Lumber Company and a veteran of innumerable winter logging camps. He was about forty-four years old at the time of the first Forestport break, a single man and an infamous storyteller. Everyone in Forestport had heard Ed Marshall's tales, spun out around the stove or in the saloons. It would be a gullible man who would believe Ed Marshall for long. Soon, though, strangers would come to Forestport, wanting to know Ed Marshall's tallest tale.

Chapter 9

THE DOG HOWLED PAST MIDNIGHT.

Outside, the bitterest, below-zero cold felt in years gripped Forestport. Gale winds shrieked through town, rattling windows and bullying drifts of snow. It was murderous weather. Outside Rochester, the *Utica Observer* reported, the son of a wealthy farmer had just been found frozen to death beside the railroad tracks he had been following home. In upstate rail yards, cattle stopped shivering and simply died. In the shacks and alleyways of cities, the drunk and homeless fell asleep and never woke up. It was 2:30 in the morning of 9 February 1899.

Again the dog howled, and James Christian stirred in his room.

Dick Manahan's father-in-law, Christian was keeping a downstairs room off the kitchen. He heard the family's faithful Newfoundland dog howling, and then he smelled smoke. Christian rose in the dark and the cold, and went to the door. He opened it, the *Boonville Herald* of 16 February 1899 later reported, and staggered backwards from what he found.

"Fire!"

Flames lit the kitchen, already hopelessly engulfed. Christian's shouts awakened Dick and Ida Manahan and their children, and in seconds the hotel's boarders on the upper two floors were scurrying from their rooms in their nightclothes.

"Fire!"

The Utica and Boonville newspapers, in coming days, would vividly recount what then unfolded over the next few transforming hours. The boarders in Manahan's hotel fled with what they could carry. A traveling Syracuse salesman named C. K. Kelts ran half-clothed from the hotel, leaving behind his suitcase and wares. Kelts reached the street, where the other guests were already huddled while the flames lashed up the hotel's second floor and then the third floor and up the corner tower. Kelts, still half-clothed, watched until he was numb with cold and had to be bundled off to a nearby store for warming.

The Getman House was past saving. Dick Manahan ran quickly back into the hotel to recover some family valuables. He got as far as inside the cellar, down the steps and into the heat and choking black smoke, before being forced to retreat. The Getman House, the hotel Dick Manahan had spent his soul in building up, was gone. The contagion spread. Already flame-licks were catching at H. A. Whiter's undertaking establishment next door. Men who were not too busy saving their own homes rolled out from its storage the Howe hand pump they had bought following an 1891 fire. Rushing in loose-laced boots and unbuttoned jackets, they set the engine up near Manahan's place. Some men furiously pumped up the pressure, while others directed the meager chemical spray at the flames. When the spray was exhausted with no discernible effect, the men rolled the engine downhill to the banks of the icy Black River. Whiter's place was burning, and others had caught, and all the men could draw from their pump was a feeble trickle. Ice clogged the suction hose. While men fiddled with it, a wagon rolled over another section of frozen hose and cut it into pieces. Other hose sections simply burst.

The flames spread and the streets filled with dispossessed people. All the telephone and telegraph wires entering the village were burnt by fire or blown down by storm. There were not enough men about to help. So many were out in their winter logging camps, or busy saving their own homes, that the town's firefighting corps was dangerously shorthanded. John Neejer, who had lost his own slaughterhouse to fire four years earlier, hitched his horses to his sleigh carriage and whipped them toward Boonville, eleven miles away (Thomas 1958, 49). The volunteers remaining had finally given up on drawing water directly from the Black River. They rolled the fire engine back up onto crowded River Street and began supplying it with barrels of water hauled up from the river. Women and boys lined up and passed buckets of water hand to hand.

The houses and carriage barns were catching the wind-driven sparks and passing the flame along like a fever. Walt Bynon's saloon flamed up and was gone. The cash store and barber shop built by the young go-getter Herb Helmer, its barrels of foodstuffs and stock of dry goods, the shoes and apparel, caught like kindling. In a flash, the New American Hotel—Michael Doyle's place—was burning too.

Jenny Doyle had bustled outside with six-year-old Jimmy Curtis and eight-year-old Grace. They joined the throngs of shivering children with thin blankets and the arms of older sisters around their shoulders. One uncomprehending young boy shouted out the most popular song of the day: "It's a Hot Time in the Old Town Tonight." Women hauled out rugs, photographs, possessions to be saved. Rose Bynon, wife of Walt the saloonkeeper, summoned unimagined strength and with a friend carried onto River Street a beloved four-claw bathtub. Men carried out sideboards, stoves, rocking chairs, everything they had labored for.

"For God's sake!" one old man cried, according to the *Utica Saturday Globe* of 11 February 1899, "help get the whiskey out of the way! Here's two barrels of whiskey worth $150, and if you don't move them they're going to burn up!"

The salvaged whiskey was put to use. One spirited man poured the remains of his whiskey bottles into the pot of coffee being distributed by the good church ladies of town (Thomas 1971, 50). It couldn't hurt; prayers were unavailing. Charley O'Connor's new three-story hotel was ablaze, a special pity. Charley and his wife had finished the place nicely, after having sold the Getman House to Dick Manahan. They had equipped the new O'Connor hotel with the most modern conveniences, a big dining room, and a handsome cherry bar, all gone now as flames lunged from the hotel's second-story veranda toward John Helmer's house nearby. If Helmer's house caught, nothing would stop the fire from racing on until the town's whole east end was gone.

Ed Marshall, the dodgy river driver with quick feet and unbelievable tales, saw his opportunity and took it. He grabbed a rope and climbed up one of the O'Connor hotel's posts. It was devilishly hot, flames all over, and while Ed was atop the post and tying the rope around it some of the building crashed down about him. Ed kept his cool. He had been in tight spots before, in the buck and crash of a springtime logjam come suddenly loose, and he stayed at the post until he finished his North Woods knot and jumped to safety. The other men out on the street pulled on the rope and brought down the burning post before it spread the flames to Helmer's house. The *Boonville Herald* reported on 16 February 1899 how the wind-bitten folks cheered Ed Marshall for that singular act.

Tough Jimmy Rudolph, too, showed his mettle. He was a man for a fix like this. His own house had caught a spark the previous year, in January 1898; his quick work then, and the help of an impromptu bucket brigade, had saved his place. He could handle fire. He had run from his gaming place at the sound of the alarm and pitched in at the hand pump. When Charley O'Connor's place was burning at its hottest and still threatening John Helmer's house, Rudolph and Henri Utley hefted the hose and hauled it up to Helmer's roof. They played the near-frozen water across the eaves while the men on the street below kept the pump drawing up the reluctant Black River. When fire leapt, notwithstanding their efforts, across the gap and into Helmer's attic, Utley and Elmer Yeomans kicked their way into the attic and carried the hose through to squelch the flames there.

At John Helmer's house, and one or two other skirmishes like it, the Forestport men finally dampened the fire's spread. The bucket brigades and some quick thinking had brought, at last, the fire's worst under control. Were it not for the wind's dying at about 6:30 A.M., though, all the efforts might have failed. The wind, which had whipped the flames along house to house, had abruptly subsided with an arbitrariness that one might confuse for pity.

. . .

Dawn revealed bedlam.

Ashes and blackened skeletons were all that remained of fourteen buildings. The old Getman House was gone, and Charley O'Connor's, and Michael Doyle's New American Hotel. Forestport had no more hotels, and it had, more remarkably still, no more saloons. Walt Bynon's was destroyed, as was the drinking place owned by George Helfert. Whiter's undertaking place was gone, and Whiter's barn, and Herb Helmer's store. William Morrell, the liveryman who ran the stage from Alder Creek to Forestport, had torn down his barn to stop the fire's spread. The commercial heart of Forestport was reduced to cinders. Besides the outright destroyed, another twenty-eight Forestport buildings were fire-damaged. Bureaus, chairs, stoves, sideboards, tools, and rugs so jammed the winter muck that River and Woodhull streets were barely navigable.

Michael and Jenny Doyle had saved their children but little else. His saloon fixtures, the barrels of beer and bottles of whiskey, the glasses and framed mirror, the spittoons and dusting rags: gone. The kitchen where Jenny cooked up meals for their boarders, the wood-burning stove and the squat wooden icebox, the frying pans and stew pots, the forks and knives and simple plates: gone. Blankets, photographs, beds, curtains: gone. The fire had taken nearly everything Michael and Jenny had accumulated in their eleven years of marriage. Michael estimated his total material loss at $1,500. He had but $500 worth of insurance coverage. Dick Manahan had $5,000 worth of coverage on his hotel, where he estimated his losses to total about $7,000.

Nine days after the fire, Michael Doyle became a man of property. George W. Smith, the prominent Herkimer County man who had owned the New American, sold the charred 9,000-square-foot lot to Michael for a pittance. Michael Doyle would now rebuild a hotel and saloon in his own name. It would not be grand. But using their own hands and those of the local carpenters, Michael Doyle and Dick Manahan and the others began remaking their material lives from ashy scratch. One good thing: Forestport was rich with lumber, and the February fire proved good business for the Forestport lumbermen. Everyone could pitch a hand to raise the skeleton of a new village. The *Boonville Herald* in March and May recorded the progress of rebuilding: the frame for Charley O'Connor's new hotel was up by 16 March, and Herb Helmer's new store and the undertaker H. A. Whiter's somber place revived as well.

By mid-May O'Connor had opened his new two-story hotel. It had acetylene gas lights in each of the twelve rooms, a ground-floor bar, and a dining room for which his wife, Blanche, and his two stepdaughters would do the cooking. Dick Manahan, too, had rebuilt his three-story, gas-lit hotel along solid lines. For $1.50 a night, guests had their choice of rooms and the board provided by Ida. Ever the host, the instigator of social events for which admission might be charged, Dick added a thirty-foot-by-fifty-foot hall in which dances could be held, and he began ordering again his whiskey and ale and cheap wine from Utica dealers.

In the world beyond Forestport, too, fresh starts were being made. Governor Roosevelt established on 8 March 1899 a new seven-man commission to advise him on future Erie Canal policy. John Partridge had been inspecting his new domain and committing himself to a clean and efficient canal administration. Division superintendents were cast out, and the old patronage system was put to the test. Attorney General John Davies advised a would-be canal bank watchman named Thomas Jones on 10 February that "Superintendent Partridge is going to make all the appointments himself; or, at least, they will be made after he has inspected the men personally or ascertained their merits personally" (Davies Papers). Edgar Hughes, the Black River Canal superintendent who had helped oversee repairs from the 1898 Forestport Feeder break, resigned shortly after Partridge took office. Partridge replaced him with Forestport resident Harvey Boyce, who began hiring other Forestporters, including his brother Charles to run the state's repair scow.

"It looks very much as if this locality would fare hard in the distribution of patronage," the *Boonville Herald* complained on 4 May.

In early April 1899, Partridge ambitiously declared the canal would open for business on 15 April, a demonstration that the canal was coming back. But some ditches proved not quite ready, and the weather soured, and in the end the canal opened just about when it always did, on 24 April. Nor was the canal free of problems once it opened. On the evening of 9 May, traffic stopped when a canal bank broke open in Spenceport, about ten miles west of Rochester. Muddy water inundated the village center, drowning hens, pigs, and farm dogs and floating off fresh lumber stacked for drying. It took a week to restore the burst levee, while an estimated one thousand boats lay idle.

The same month as the troubled canal opened, attorneys Austen Fox and Wallace MacFarlane finished their review of the 1895 canal improvements. The two lawyers, selected by Governor Roosevelt, sorely disappointed those who had hoped for aggressive pursuit of malefactors. Though they said they found the "suggestions of wrongdoing" in the handling of some of the canal improvements, they emphasized that the "expenditure of considerable sums" would be required to pursue any cases further (Report of Counsel 1899, 6). Moreover, Fox and MacFarlane reported, the two-year statute of limitations had run out on the most likely areas for prosecution. For instance, they found a conspicuously unbalanced bid for the T. J. Dwyer Company's work in Utica. But because this Utica contract had been let in the fall of 1896, the last chance to prosecute had passed in the fall of 1898.

Fox and MacFarlane, in any event, said they found no evidence of conspiracy between the state engineer, the public works superintendent, and the contractors. But, the lawyers added, their "decision to institute no criminal prosecutions on this evidence does not mean that in our opinion the officials charged with carrying out the great work of improving the canals have done their duty." They cited Adams for having "greatly underestimated" the true cost of the canal improvements. Fox and MacFarlane allowed that they were "not blind to the probability that the contractors may have been favored by the engineers or by the officers of the Department of Public Works" (Report of Counsel 1899, 16), but they asserted that state law left considerable discretion in the hands of those state officers. They admitted they found "extraordinary" the system by which Dwyer and other contractors were paid more for hauling dug-out canal material longer distances. They noted: "If the officials in whom the [public] confidence is reposed are without fidelity to their duties, they can be guilty of much misconduct which does not amount to a violation of criminal law" (Report of Counsel 1899, 24).

The report closed the canal cases, so far as Roosevelt was concerned.

"They had everything to gain from getting a conviction, if a conviction could be gotten," Roosevelt upbraided one upstate questioner in Steuben County following release of the Fox and MacFarlane report, as the *Rochester Post-Express* of 31 August 1899 noted. "They had no party tie

. . . 'I want you,' I said, 'to follow up on any guilty man even though that man be found closest to me in the executive chamber.' They had the time, they had the money, and they had aid of the best counsel in the state."

The skeptical questioning profoundly irritated Roosevelt. "The public mind," he complained to one friend, "has gone so clearly crooked" on the canal matter. People did not understand. "The trouble," he wrote his friend C. Grant LaFarge on 18 September, "is that the public will not see the difference between political mismanagement; or rather, mismanagement due to political pressure, and original misconduct" (Roosevelt Papers). Roosevelt, clear-eyed as ever, appreciated the difference. Neither Aldridge nor Adams, he thought, had personally profited from their canal work. They were not criminals. The real offense, Roosevelt believed, lay in having Aldridge and Adams manage the canals primarily for political purpose. Indeed, Roosevelt thought Aldridge had done a better job of administering the canal than some of his predecessors.

For his part, John Partridge was doing what he could to set things straight along the canal. He had cut some of Aldridge's men for inefficiency, and he set an entirely new standard when he declared that canal workers should not participate in partisan politics. After he had been on the job for a time, Partridge declared it unwise for canal employees to become overly active in politics, as politics had a tendency to divert their attention from official duties.

Some men ignored Partridge's declarations. Partridge's own Middle Division canal boss, Thomas Wheeler, scarcely slowed down his politicking, notwithstanding Partridge's admonitions. In mid-September, still the powerbroker, Wheeler attended the annual Republican County Convention in Utica. He placed in nomination the successful candidate for county chairman and pushed the renomination of an incumbent county treasurer whose financial dalliances had come under question.

"I would not do what he has done," Partridge said stiffly in the *New York Tribune* of 5 October when he learned of Wheeler's ongoing political activism.

Partridge, however, never removed Wheeler from office, and the public works superintendent who talked of removing politics from the canal business was forced to confess in the face of Wheeler's actions that he had no legal authority to remove the politically active unless they neglected state work. In the canal business, Tom Wheeler outlasted John Partridge. In this way and others, the canal was far more vexing than the Brooklyn fire and police departments Partridge had inherited fifteen years earlier. He was finding the section superintendents more efficient at politicking than at rebuilding. He was confronted still by the no-show inspectors, the crumbling locks, and the leaky levees of the canal itself. Already the loose threads from some of the canal improvements were starting to fray. When the 1899 season was already well underway, a Syracuse lock tender discovered a leak beneath the partition dividing two adjacent channels. The partition had been rebuilt as part of the $9 million improvement, but too shabbily, evidently, to last more than a year. The Syracuse lock leak stalled about two hundred boats for a matter of days while Partridge's repair crews bustled through a quick fix.

Then some new information slithered Colonel Partridge's way, and in the hot, drought-ridden summer of 1899 he turned his eyes from leaking locks and obstinate political operators to rough-and-tumble Forestport.

In May 1899 a Forestport resident wrote Partridge to complain about the wasteful overmanning of the North Lake reservoirs. Until George Aldridge's reign, the Forestport man wrote, one state employee had cared for the North Lake reservoirs. But since that time, the man advised Partridge, "there has been a large number of state officials, known in the woods as 'water commissioners,' whose principal duty has been to fill out vouchers for state pay, absolutely doing no work beyond the work which one man could perform acceptably and faithfully, at the expense of several thousand dollars to the state annually." The *Utica Daily Press* of 19 May 1899 reported that the fortunate water commissioners, according to the Forestport informant, included a Utica saloonkeeper, some former deputy sheriffs, and some others well placed in the Oneida County political constellation.

There was something else worth Partridge's investigating, the Forestport informant suggested, something to do with the bank watchmen hired to protect the Forestport Feeder towpath.

"There are, if rumors are true, some interesting revelations which the public and the officials in the Canal department are deeply interested in knowing their truthfulness or untruthfulness," the Forestport man wrote.

The Forestport informer limited himself to this cryptic reference. But there was, at the time, a dominating canal question around which Forestport rumors were circulating. Precisely how did it happen, men were asking, that the Forestport Feeder would break open twice in as many years? Several explanations offered themselves: canal contractors seeking work, malefactors seeking mischief, anarchists seeking disorder, townspeople seeking business.

There were any number of suspects and motives in the summer of 1899, as the Forestport mills churned through the North Country logs that had come down the Black River. Men crowded the newly rebuilt saloons run by Dick Manahan, Walt Bynon, and Michael Doyle. Michael, the old laborer who had done a touch of everything around Forestport, could take pride in his establishment. It really was the Hotel Doyle now. He could stand behind his new bar, wiping it down, polishing the rails and mirrors, counting out the ale and whiskey stock shipped up from Utica, sounding out the men who crowded about with their yarns and their schemings. But even as the new Hotel Doyle rose from the ashes, its proprietor was slipping, undermined by the same vague illness that had been plaguing him for years. As the hot summer came on and Forestport entered July, Michael grew weaker.

He had been suffering from a lingering and unspecified illness for a considerable time, a state of ill health that could only have been aggravated by the February fire and the arduous rebuilding. Day by day he slipped a little more, until, at about three in the morning of 3 July, with the town asleep, Michael Doyle died in his bed. He was forty-three years old. He left behind his thirty-year-old wife, his nine-year-old daughter, Grace, and his son, Jimmy Curtis Doyle, who was six.

It was in about this month, with Michael Doyle newly buried and the forests still burning, that Colonel John Partridge turned his serious attention to Forestport. As he had traveled the canal counties since January, Partridge had been struck by the coincidence of the two Forestport breaks, and he wanted to know more about them. Brooklyn man that he was, unknown in the more remote reaches of canal country, the old soldier and police chief traveled about doing his own reconnaissance. By September, Partridge had ventured into Oneida County.

"By personal observation and quiet inquiry, he learned that a pretty tough gang was holding sway," Partridge's hometown *Brooklyn Eagle* subsequently reported on 21 January 1900. "Whenever he mentioned the coincidence of the breaks, however, an awkward silence ensued. Gradually he learned that 'Hank's cattle died kinder sudden after he told what he heard about the '98 break,' and 'it ain't healthy to talk about that matter' and 'when Hiram was talking about that last break, he disappeared and turned up dead.' "

"I discovered that citizens of the vicinity were actually afraid to breathe of what they really knew about robberies, barn burnings, house burnings, cattle poisonings and even murder that followed so closely upon the imparting of information that a state of terror was created," Partridge recounted in the *Brooklyn Eagle* of 18 January 1900.

Forestport, admittedly, was a tough town, with its sawyers, lumberjacks, and canallers strutting the streets. The vulnerable were sometimes exploited; not every possession was safe. The week of Michael Doyle's death, the Boonville baseball team refused to travel to Forestport, claiming they could not be assured of being protected from the unruly Forestport crowd. For a season, the *Boonville Herald* of 27 October 1897 had reported, Forestport families began discovering that their best chickens were missing in the morning. Invariably the heads and feathers were found nearby. There were other scattered insults: hams taken from the Lockwood & Son's smokehouse, canned goods stolen from Henry Coscomb's house, forty cans of preserves taken from George Boyce's cellar. Even the widower Mrs. W. R. Stanburgh, whose late husband had built several Forestport mills, had ten cans of preserves stolen. Daylight was no deterrent. About five o'clock one Saturday afternoon in early December, a thief stole a whole tub of butter from the back of a wagon hitched outside Bill King's blacksmith shop.

"Forestport and vicinity," the aggrieved *Boonville Herald* had already declared on 27 October 1897, "is getting to be a favorite field for vandals of this class, who poison cows, burn barns and pillage houses, and it is high time some decisive step was taken to put a stop to their operations."

The fires were a particular problem. From 22 August to 7 September 1899, four Forestport fires blazed up from unknown causes. Forestport was not alone in confronting fire that summer—in all of drought-stricken 1899, 316 fires burned up 79,653 Adirondack acres—but the traumas were adding up. Partridge pieced together the various stories about Forestport affairs, and he picked up another rumor, that of a Buffalo man who could tell him more about the Forestport breaks. Partridge made further inquiries. This was a man, Partridge learned, who had had occasion to insinuate himself into Forestport saloon society. He was a promoter of sorts, a schemer, some would say. Usually nothing came of his big plans. He was a salesman, peddling low-grade ore, but in September 1899 his product was information about Forestport. The man's name was Howard Fordham.

Colonel Partridge pocketed the tip. He had been hired to clean up the canal, and clearly Forestport needed attending to. As he was contemplating his next step, a loud report shook awake Forestport residents. It was about 6:15 A.M. on the morning of 18 September, and once again men were running through town. Children dressed and went galloping out, liverymen hitched up wagons and drove across the Black River bridges, up Dutch Hill, and down the towpath until they could go no further. They were upon it then: the familiar tearing wound, the unloosened water ripping down the hillside. In the final year of the nineteenth century, the Forestport Feeder had broken open once again.

Chapter 10

GORDON WILLIAMS HAD NOT SEEN A THING.

The Forestport Feeder watchman passed his 5 A.M. round without incident. With his lantern and his boots, his jacket bundled against the predawn air already crisp as a fall apple, he had walked the feeder levee without incident. An hour later, Forestport sawyers trudging to their Monday morning mill shifts detected something Williams had not. The feeder water seemed low and running fast. Herbert Charboneau saw that the Black River was muddy and turbulent, as if disturbed from a foreign source. Charboneau walked to Harvey Boyce's house, where the merchant who doubled as local canal superintendent was just starting his day. Boyce could decipher the clues, and he rushed to close the locks before any more damage was done. Boyce then struck out along the towpath for about a mile until he was within shouting distance of where the feeder had broken out the year before. There, a mere two hundred feet from the repaired levee, with its triple-lap piling meant to last a lifetime, Boyce found the new break.

Even as Boyce watched, the outrushing water was gouging a broader chasm and seeking its level in the Black River about seventy-five feet below. The canyon was already fifty feet deep and one hundred feet across to the resumption of solid towpath. Uprooted and disheveled trees, which had somehow survived the previous years' breaks, littered the downslope to the Black River. The water's rush had blasted out much of the triple-sheet piling placed the year before by Dwyer's crews and had scattered the remains along the ripped hillside. The feeder's prism had been sucked out at least twenty feet deep.

The *Rome Daily Sentinel* and *Boonville Herald,* ever attentive to Forestport turmoil, recounted what happened next. Boyce hurried back to the lock tender's house and mobilized his men. Some he put to work filling sandbags and hauling timber, which they piled into the feeder to dam up the remaining water and prevent further loss. He sent out the message on the wire, and soon the world beyond Forestport knew, too, that the feeder had broken once again.

Division Engineer William H. H. Gere, who only a few months earlier had published suspicions about the causes of the previous year's Forestport break, hooked up that Monday morning with Tom Wheeler and an inspector from Syracuse. Shortly after 1 P.M., the three men boarded a northbound train for Forestport's Buffalo Head station. They rode by carriage to Forestport, and then up Dutch Hill and down the towpath through the crowd of spectators. The scene duly impressed them all: the hillside rubbled with unearthed boulders and uprooted trees, the gorge driven nearly all the way to the Black River, the crater gaping as if blown by dynamite. The growing break spanned 125 feet across by the time Wheeler and his crew arrived. Gere quickly estimated, according to the *Rome Daily Sentinel* of 19 September 1899, that he would need about sixty thousand cubic feet of earth to refill the chasm. He would need men, lots of them, just as in years past, but with some relief the canal officials gradually realized the break's severity was less than the break in either 1897 or 1898. Perhaps twenty days, no more, would be needed to finish the repairs.

By telephone the local officials notified Colonel Partridge of the break. Only recently returned from his own secret Oneida County reconnaissance, Partridge again boarded a train from Albany and arrived in Utica about ten o'clock Monday night. Emergency preparations were taking place all over. In Rome, the water and sewer commissioners prepared to hire three fire engines from the American Fire Engine Company in Seneca Falls for use in pumping water into the city's water mains. Residents were prohibited from using lawn sprinklers.

By the time Partridge arrived in Forestport on Tuesday morning, contractor James Dwyer and the engineers had settled on a repair plan. As in 1898, they would erect quick bridges over the emptied feeder so teamsters could haul wagonloads of fill dirt to the break. They would, once again, stiffen the fill with piling and puddled concrete. They would, once again, give hiring priority to the canallers whose boats were now stranded on the Forestport state pond. By Wednesday, the first crews were under the charge of Assistant Inspector Charles Tuttle. Tuttle hired a clerk and prepared a telephone so he could stay in daily touch with Partridge in Albany. The *Rome Daily Sentinel* of 20 September 1899 reported that some five hundred men were going to be needed, plus another seventy-five to one hundred wagons and teams of horses to haul the levee filling.

More insistently than ever before, the canal men also wanted to know how the break occurred. For Partridge in particular, the question of causation was paramount. His old police commissioner's instincts stood at attention.

Heavy rains had preceded the last two Forestport breaks. But in 1899, that was no answer. Forestport and the rest of upstate had been parched all summer. Nor was there any sign that water had been leaking through the base of the levee. The grass growing from the top of the berm bank to the water's edge showed that the feeder had been running low for weeks. Most disturbing was the coincidence itself: three breaks in as many years defied the odds, even along the eminently breakable Erie.

Forestport men dismissed the implications. Look at all the work it would take, they said, to cut the bank down from the top. It would take hours before the levee was sufficiently ripped, on a towpath patrolled by watchman Gordon Williams. Forestport men said the break most likely was caused by a leak, undermining the towpath through the sandy soil beneath the piling until the leak became a torrent.

"There is no suspicion of anyone in Forestport," a *Rome Daily Sentinel* report asserted on September 20, two days after the break, adding charitably: "The people of Forestport are quiet and orderly, and the lumber mills which are the principal industries of the place have been running full blast since spring. The only motive subscribed is to make work for the large gangs of men who are brought to Forestport on such occasions, and even that seems beyond belief. If the break was the result of a malicious act, it is not probable that the author will ever be discovered."

But by Thursday, state authorities had found disturbing evidence. Several of the sixteen-foot planks that Dwyer's men had pounded into the soil the previous year for piling appeared to be unnaturally cut and splintered, as if cut by an axe. Some Forestport residents, too, were already reflecting on what spirit was afoot in town. Only one week after the levee burst, the Presbyterian Church presented a Sunday evening service provocatively titled: "The Break and the Breakers." The accusatory presumption was front and center.

"There was no fullness of water to burst the banks," the *Utica Observer* noted on September 19. "There was no rainy season to break the banks. The watchmen employed were ample, in numbers at least. Now how did this break occur, and why did it get such headway before the state employees at Forestport? It might interest Superintendent Partridge, and it certainly would interest the public, to know what the watchmen up there are watching."

Some six hundred men were soon at work repairing the Forestport break. It was a rollicksome time for the town, and at the Doyle Hotel, Jenny was relying on her sickly older brother, Michael Donovan. He tended bar, filled nightly with the thirsty workers, while she sweated in the kitchen. Entertainment of all sorts filled the town. At Masonic Hall, a traveling theater troupe from New York City staged a week's worth of performances of a play entitled *The California Detective*.

It was much like old times again in Forestport, a disaster for the state and a boon for the local businessmen, but this time around, the state also caught a lucky break. Through quick work, with their emergency coffer dams and frantic efforts, Boyce and his crews had saved big portions of the towpath levee. Within only ten days, Dwyer's crews having worked nearly around the clock, the repairs were near enough completion that the state reopened the Black River Canal. The *Boonville Herald* of 28 September was able to report that nearly fifty boats, forced to tie up on the Black River Canal while the Forestport Feeder was reassembled, had started jostling their way through Boonville by 27 September. By the first week of October, the rupture had been caulked with sawed-off timber spars and

235,000 cubic feet of earthen fill. The lock tenders opened up the gates on the state pond and refilled the feeder, slowly at first, to test the integrity of the repairs, and then all the way. The Forestport Feeder was back in business.

It had cost the state $17,089.72, and seventeen days of work, to repair the latest Forestport break. That was considerably less than in 1897, when the state spend $62,781.78, and in 1898, when the state spent $50,764.47. The three-year total for extraordinary repairs of the Forestport levee had come to $130,635.97. For Colonel Partridge, the costs were unbearable. He was a law-and-order man; there were some things about the canal he could not change, but he would do his best to resolve the Forestport problem. His mind set, his backbone straightened, Colonel John Partridge by Friday called upon the good Oneida County Republican John Davies, the attorney general of the State of New York.

Davies knew canal men well. He and Tom Wheeler had been dual forces in Oneida County Republican politics for years. Poor as a youth, self-taught as an attorney, Davies had come to the tiny Oneida County town of Camden when he was twenty-one years old. Starting in 1886, he represented Camden in the county legislature, while at the same time keeping a thriving law business. He was a talented man, politically and legally, and in November 1898 he had won election as attorney general. From the start, even before the repairs were done, Davies had been voicing suspicions that the break was man-made. Not yet a year in his new job, still relatively unknown to the state at large, Davies shared Partridge's intense desire to resolve the mystery of the Forestport breaks. The only real question was, how?

Partridge's lieutenants couldn't help much. Tom Wheeler was out of the question, despite his law enforcement background. The Oneida County sheriff's office—the one formally run by Wheeler—was far too bound up in local politics to be trusted. New York State, for all intents and purposes, lacked any investigative agency of its own. The attorney general's own office was more accustomed to handling cases involving tainted milk and meat. Partridge and Davies needed outsiders, professionals. They needed the Pinkerton National Detective Agency.

Theoretically, the state might have chosen any number of outside operatives for the Forestport investigation. The turn-of-the-century Trow Business Directory for New York City listed several dozen possibilities. Just two blocks away from the Pinkerton's Broadway offices was Benjamin Franklin's Detective Agency. For the easily awed, there were the suggestively named Citizen's Secret Service and The Secret Service Bureau. For certain cases only, there was the gun-shy Wilkon's Detective Agency—"divorce cases not undertaken." But, in the public's mind, the paramount agency was the Pinkerton. It was the largest such agency in the world, with some one thousand employees in 1899, and it was still growing; fifty-eight new detectives were hired that year (Morn 1982, 164). Far and away it had the greatest reputation—and attracted the greatest controversy.

Allan Pinkerton had died in 1884, but the agency remained a family affair. William, his eldest son, was in charge of the Chicago headquarters, while his son Robert had charge of New York City and the agency's eastern operations. In 1899, at the age of fifty-one, Robert A. Pinkerton was a fleshy, diabetic, racehorse-loving man who had periodically struggled against his father's tyrannical rule. Nonetheless, Robert had secured his own reputation both as a detective and as an administrator. He had helped form the Jewelers' Protective Union and worked closely with the American Bankers Association. He also had a hand in some of the events that forever tarred the Pinkerton's reputation in the eyes of Oneida County labor activists. In June 1892 Robert personally negotiated the contract to provide three hundred uniformed watchmen to secure the Carnegie Company's sprawling Homestead steel plant near Pittsburgh (Horan 1967, 337–49).

Robert Pinkerton had collected his $5-a-day men from Chicago, New York, and Philadelphia, and on the night of 5 July 1892 the guards set out up the Monangahela River toward Homestead on two barges and a tugboat. About one-third of the men had never worked for the Pinkertons before. On Thursday, 7 July, Michael Doyle and the other men of Forestport had learned what had happened the day before.

"Bloodshed!" The *Boonville Herald* alerted its readers with a screaming headline that 7 July. "A Startling Conflict. Three Hundred Pinkerton Men Endeavor to Take Possession of the Carnegie Steel Works Where a Lockout and Strike is in Progress, and the Workmen Resist the Attempt."

The Oneida County headlines cast the Pinkertons as a virtual army deployed against the common workingmen. In towns like Forestport, Boonville, and Utica, that action secured the detective agency's reputation as a force opposed to the common man.

Slowly the picture of what had happened up the Monangahela River revealed itself. The Pinkerton barges had forfeited surprise as they were towed toward Homestead through the night, so that the men were met by perhaps one thousand men, women, and children when they tried to land. Gunfire broke out, sporadically at first, then in volleys. The two sides fell back, the workers behind their pig iron and iron plate breastworks and the Pinkerton guards behind the splintered protections of their barges. All afternoon the stranded Pinkertons traded fire with the workmen on shore. Finally, at about five o'clock, the leader of the Pinkertons raised a white flag to negotiate a surrender. Their arsenal—250 Winchester rifles and 300 pistols—was unloaded, and the exhausted, sweaty, blood-streaked men were marched out of the barges and onto the riverbank. There, a howling crowd that had grown to several thousand set upon them: spitting, punching, swinging bats and muskets, the striking workers and their womenfolk brutalized the $5-a-day temporary Pinkertons all the way to the center of town (House Committee on Judiciary, 1892, xix).

The final Homestead toll: ten workers were killed and several wounded during the day's gunfight. Five Pinkertons were killed and many more wounded. And yet, for all that, the other workingmen of Forestport received their information about Homestead screened through the anti-Pinkerton bias of the times. The Pinkertons were depicted as invaders seeking to crush the common workingman. As Michael Doyle and Dick Manahan read it in the *Boonville Herald* of 7 July: "As the Pinkertons landed, they opened fire and two workmen dropped in their tracks. This enraged the crowd, and they bore upon the Pinkertons with relentless force, driving them back to the boats."

In Homestead's wake, the Pinkerton agency stopped supplying guards to intervene in strikes (Hogg, 1944, 181). Strikes were worse than divorce cases. The work was not worth the trouble, and the agency had no shortage of other clients: the 1897 Nashville Centennial, Buffalo Bill's Wild West Show, the Ringling Brothers' circus. Nonetheless, popular distrust propelled the wildest of stories. In March 1898, as the Forestport Feeder remained locked in ice and the men of Utica's National Guard company prepared for possible war, William Pinkerton was impelled to publicly denounce an amazing rumor. The brooding, fifty-three-year-old son of the agency's founder called grossly malicious the rumors that his agency was ferreting out the secret defenses of the U.S. government and furnishing the information to the Spanish. That the story had ever gained any elevation at all showed just how tangled the Pinkerton reputation had become.

How they were perceived locally depended, in part, on the nature of their assignments. Thus, on 4 November 1895, the *Utica Observer* warned readers: "The Pinkertons are watching you!" The newspaper reported that detectives were seen "passing in and among knots of people as they gather on street corners and public places, gathering bits of conversation and other material by which they hope to silence the voice of the voters and turn certain Republican defeat into so-called victory." The *Observer* asserted that "a genuine Pinkerton, with a Bowery swagger and a bad eye" had been identified on Utica's streets, while "four or five other strangers of similar makeup and actions" had likewise been spotted. Pinkertons, the *Observer* reminded its readers, "are as repulsive as snakes" to the workingman, to whom "the name of Pinkerton is as distasteful . . . as a red rag to a mad bull."

"Look out for the Pinkertons!" warned the *Utica Daily Press* on 4 November 1895. "Nobody wants to make their acquaintance. Their appearance here will be a novelty. But there have been other novelties in this campaign. We might as well have them all."

In other cases, however, Oneida County had welcomed the Pinkertons. In the summer of 1898, not long after the second Forestport Feeder breach had been repaired, a team of Pinkertons made their way to Remsen. They were said to be trailing two suspected murderers believed to have killed a Connecticut farmer and to have stolen $9,000. One suspect reportedly had relatives in the Remsen and Alder Creek areas, including a brother up the Black River at the logging town of McKeever, a "tough nut," according to those who knew him. The men had vanished by the time the Pinkertons arrived, the *Boonville Herald* reported on 7 August 1898.

Pinkerton detective Herbert W. Bearce. Photographer and date unknown. *Courtesy of Pinkerton National Detective Agency.*

So the upstate region was not entirely foreign territory for the Pinkerton agency. Agency operatives had been in and out of Syracuse and Utica and even tiny Remsen. Even so, there were sensitive choices to be made: about who was to lead the Forestport investigation and how it was to be conducted. Would the agency attempt to insinuate a solo operative into the town, in hopes of drawing covertly close to the perpetrators? The Pinkertons had considerable experience in such infiltrations, most famously with James McParland's thirty-month-long penetration starting in 1873 into the Molly Maguires of Pennsylvania's coal country. McParland was still with the agency in 1899, as superintendent of the Denver office. A heavyset, bespectacled man who favored a walking stick, he was, of course, in no way suitable for the Forestport investigation.

But another would do; there were always nervy young men willing to infiltrate dangerous fraternities. One problem was time. It had taken the resourceful McParland more than six months just to get sworn in to the first circle of the Molly Maguire organization. Time was something

Colonel Partridge had too little of. He was a political appointee, answering to an ambitious governor.

Beyond choosing their investigative strategy, the Pinkertons had to select the man who would lead the operation. He would have to enjoy the special confidence of agency executives. With the intertwining of patronage politics and canal administration so extensive, the chief investigator would have to combine talent and discretion.

Herbert W. Bearce was their man.

A Maine native, Bearce found his way to the Pinkerton agency as a young man, and he never left it. The handsome, bearded operative never married; the agency was his family and second home until the day he retired with a trove of untold stories and a rare Pinkerton pension. When Partridge and Davies called upon his office in the fall of 1899, census records show that Bearce was sharing a Staten Island house with a German-born actor and the actor's wife. As assistant superintendent of the agency's New York City office, earning roughly $28 a month, Bearce ably juggled several responsibilities. He personally oversaw a number of operatives, whose daily reports he would read and analyze. He compiled weekly summaries of their work, and he undertook, when necessary, investigations himself. Bearce was on track, at the age of forty-five, toward becoming superintendent himself of one of the agency's East Coast offices.

But before being promoted, Herbert W. Bearce had one more field operation to run. He was going back into the field, the place where he had first made his reputation. One way or another, Bearce and the Pinkertons would break the Forestport mystery.

Chapter 11

IN THE NEW CENTURY, once Bearce and his operatives were done with Forestport, their client would hint at the methods they employed.

Colonel Partridge told an awed reporter from his hometown paper, the *Brooklyn Eagle,* how the case was broken. The Pinkerton executives had sent undercover men to live in Forestport as laborers. There, the detectives had covertly observed the townspeople through the fall of 1899. It was, Partridge intimated, on a par with the Pinkerton's best work, breaking the Molly Maguires or the New Orleans Mafia.

"It is said," the *Eagle* reported on 21 January 1900, "that the detectives became members of the desperate gang and learned how they had actually raised money for their work, buying dynamite and conducting their outlawry in a business-like manner. An organization like the Mafia was established, men being selected by lot to punish betrayers."

There are no available Pinkerton records to show how much of this was true and how much was a tabloid exaggeration. Instead, the burrowings of Herbert W. Bearce and his team of operatives can only be tracked imperfectly, by their aboveground tracks imperfectly recorded in the Utica and Boonville papers. The detectives arrived in the final fall of the nineteenth century, when upstate was aflame with change. At Trenton Falls, construction crews were pouring concrete for Oneida County's hydroelectric dam. In Utica, residents were excitedly recounting the appearance of an automobile being driven across country, while inside the

Willoughby, Owen & Company's four-story factory, workmen accustomed to making horse-drawn hansoms were crafting 135 new electric car carriages for the Columbia Automobile Company of New York. Young soldiers freshly returned from the Philippines told of America's growing empire (Clarke 1952, 76).

About three hundred businessmen, promoters, and lawyers gathered in Utica for a state commerce convention in mid-October. Meeting some evenings until after midnight, the men heard Herkimer County's George W. Smith—the same Smith who had sold the burned Forestport hotel to Michael Doyle—expound on the fatal flaw in waterborne transportation. "The canals," Smith predicted, "could not again be made profitable by further enlargement . . . and a stop should be put to further expenditure." John Kernan, the Utica lawyer who had inspired establishment of the Forestport Literary and Social Union, defended the canal as a tool to dampen railroad rates. Ultimately, the Utica convention delegates approved a resolution supporting continued investments in the Erie Canal.

Beneath this surface, the Pinkerton men were digging. Accompanying Bearce was John J. Pender, another of the agency's highly regarded detectives. Pender was thirty-five, a dark-complexioned and trimly built man of five feet five inches. A native of Manchester, England, he had been fitfully working in the United States as a hotel clerk and insurance man until finding the agency in 1891 (Pinkerton Archives).

In their union investigations, the Pinkertons had perfected the system of getting undercover operatives to file daily reports itemizing conversations, the state of local sentiment, the attitudes of local officials, and the overall conditions in the town under investigation. The early stages of the Forestport investigation would have been standard operating procedure. Dress up an operative with a fake name and an attitude, let him take a hotel room, buy the boys drinks, and troll for stories (Pinkerton National Police Agency, 1867, 7).

Bearce and his men in time also became overtly apparent through town, staying at several hotels and talking with everyone they could find. Some Forestport men appeared quite chatty. William Clark the liveryman, for one, was noted by one acquaintance to be getting on famously with a Pinkerton man. The Pinkertons could be persuasive, and they would pay

Pinkerton detective John J. Pender. Photographer and date unknown. *Courtesy of Pinkerton National Detective Agency.*

for the time spent with them. Pender, characteristically, bought some drinks and two cigars for a former Forestport bartender named Sam Bateman one afternoon, just so the two could spend two hours in a saloon going over what Bateman knew. But some men would have nothing to do with the detectives. A Boonville restaurant owner named McGuire clammed up when a pair of Pinkertons visited, and others also abided by a code of silence. The cardsharp Hugh McDonald once asked hotelkeeper Charley O'Connor what the detectives were learning.

"He told me that the detectives were not finding out a thing," McDonald said later, according to the *Utica Daily Press* of 24 May 1900. "Everybody was as mum as an oyster."

Sometimes the Pinkertons bared their teeth. A one-time bartender and wallpaper-hanger from Alder Creek named William Gorman, for one, was thought by the Pinkertons to have dissembled in his initial statements. Meeting again behind closed doors, Pender confronted Gorman and told him he should get down on his knees and beg investigators for forgiveness. Submit, Pender demanded, and then straighten up and tell the truth.

One who did cooperate was George Farley, Forestport's fifty-year-old gristmill owner. He had been doing business in Forestport since 1884. His two water-powered mills custom-ground flour and feed, and his store sold baled hay, cement, brick, and other necessities. Farley learned things, gabbing with customers across the counter of his crowded store. What he heard, he evidently shared with investigators. Farley "rendered valuable services for the State" in the investigation of the Forestport breaks, Attorney General John Davies would remind Partridge in 1901. Farley's information later inspired Partridge to speak "very highly" of him, and in a January 1901 letter to Partridge, Davies noted that Farley himself thought the state could repay him by building a water pipe to serve one of his grist mills (Davies Papers).

By early December 1899, shortly after the canal closed for the season on 1 December, the fact of the Forestport investigation was becoming apparent. Half-a-dozen strangers from out of town were spotted near the Oneida County district attorney's office in Rome at the corner of James and Dominick streets. Though still closemouthed, their purpose and their identity started to leak out. The strangers, the *Utica Daily Press* reported on 12 December 1899, "were no more or less than Pinkerton detectives . . . here looking up evidence as to the cause of the Forestport break." County District Attorney Timothy Curtin, though, had little to do with the Forestport investigation. Governor Roosevelt himself, it was said, was the prime mover.

Wild stories gained currency, once word began circulating about the Pinkertons. The *Utica Observer*'s man suggested that extradition papers were being prepared for "two Utica politicians" who had slipped away because they "know more about the break at Forestport than they care to tell voluntarily." Stretching, the *Observer* reported on 11 December that "it is said" seven different men were involved in the break under investigation, and that "the seven received a divvy of $50,000."

Shortly before 9 P.M. on Friday night, 10 December, the New York Central train eased into the Rome station at 218 S. James Street. Amid the steam and the shudder, several men stepped from the wood-paneled passenger car and onto the platform. One of the men was recognizable as Oneida County Sheriff Reese. The other, to whom Reese stayed close, was a tall, rough-hewn, sandy-complexioned fellow in his mid-forties. It was

Edward Marshall, the dodgy old log driver who had performed with such reckless courage in the Forestport fire of February last. Marshall, who had lived in Forestport the past sixteen years, had suddenly picked up several months back and decamped to a small town in northernmost Michigan, gone, his old drinking pals might have thought, for good.

The *Utica Daily Press* reported on 12 December that Reese and Marshall walked quickly to the Stanwix Hall hotel on East Whiteboro Street. Inside, they went straight to the second floor and Room 29. Two men were waiting for them. Behind the closed doors, Ed Marshall and Sheriff Reese and the two men talked for hours, until Reese and the Pinkertons got what they wanted.

The next morning, about noon, the congregation reconvened and moved to District Attorney Curtin's office. A justice of the peace named Gubbins joined them there with his law books. The men talked a while and then adjourned. Later that evening, Marshall met once more with Justice Gubbins. There, the police formally placed Marshall under arrest on charges of causing the three canal breaks in 1897, 1898, and 1899.

At noon the next day, 11 December, the detectives bustled Marshall back before Justice Gubbins for arraignment. Standing before the judge, Marshall listened calmly while the extraordinary charges were read to him. No one had ever before been convicted, nor apparently even accused, of the crime of disrupting the canals of the state of New York, but Marshall seemed indifferent to his place in history.

Not guilty, he said.

Lacking the $5,000 required for bail, Marshall returned to the Rome jail for two hours. At 2 P.M. his jailers brought him to court. By then, word had spread and at least one reporter had arrived to follow the proceedings. Marshall, however, had no lawyer with him. The snake charmer of the northern woods, who had spun so many incredible yarns in his time, was now speaking for himself in a court of law.

District Attorney Curtin summoned to the stand the middle-aged salesman Howard M. Fordham. Though only an occasional visitor to Forestport, Fordham had struck up relations with many: with Dick Manahan, at whose hotel he stayed, and with William Clark, the liveryman with whom he had journeyed out, eighteen months before, to see the wreckage from the May 1898 break. For all his schemes and stories, he always seemed a bit unmoored. Born in upstate New York, Fordham had never really settled anywhere. He had tried carpentry for a time in the Midwest, and then failed at farming in Kansas before he struck upon the idea of selling Midwestern land to New York men. He had claimed, in the past decade, at least five separate Buffalo work addresses and four home addresses. Most recently, married eleven years and childless, according to census records, he had claimed a home address with his wife and in-laws. But now, in the Oneida County courtroom, he was raising his hand and swearing to tell the truth, and it suddenly appeared there was more to Howard Fordham than had met the eye.

In May 1898, Fordham said, he had been boarding in Room 4 of Manahan's hotel. The second-floor room was directly above the hotel office, connected to the room below by a stovepipe. One night, before retiring, Fordham overheard voices floating up from the office below. Marshall and other men, Fordham said, were talking about making a break in the Forestport Feeder. Shortly after, on the early morning of 23 May, Fordham awoke to the shouts that there had been a break. He partially dressed and went downstairs, where he encountered Marshall in the hotel cloakroom. Marshall, it seemed, had already been working that morning; he was wearing rubber boots and a rubber coat covered with mud and sand. He did not seem surprised when Fordham informed him the feeder had broken.

"That's good," Marshall replied, according to the *Utica Daily Press* account on 12 December. "I hope the water will run long enough to wash out the other break, and then we will have work all summer."

Or so Fordham testified. He told Curtin that he encountered Marshall again in October 1898, shortly before election day. "I've been working on the job," Fordham testified he told Marshall; "I know everything about the break, and you'd better own up to what really happened." Marshall swore at the boys who had given up the game. What he knew about them, he said, could send one to the gallows and another to Auburn State Prison for life. Still raging, but resigned, evidently, to the truth coming out in time, Marshall then made his confession to a curious Fordham.

Marshall said, or so Fordham testified, that he and the other boys were promised $25 each and all the whiskey they needed to break open the feeder levee. On the night in question, Marshall and the unidentified others sneaked out to the towpath. They set one watchman on the Boonville and one on the Forestport ends of the towpath, and then commenced to drinking and digging. The others became too drunk to finish the job, however, and Marshall told Fordham he ended up doing most of the work himself. He sweated at it, swinging the axe as he had done for years up in the northern woods, until finally the supports came apart, the levee crumbled, and the water came bursting out so quickly that Marshall nearly got carried away.

When his turn came, Marshall denied everything Fordham had just testified to. It was Fordham, he said, who had offered him $1,000 and safe passage out of New York if he would confess to taking part in the 1898 break and reveal the names of his fellow conspirators.

"No," Fordham spoke up. "I told you that if you would tell everything that you knew about the break, it might be worth $1,000 to the parties interested."

Who those parties might be, and why they would be willing to spend such a ransom to free the information about the Forestport break remained questions unasked by Ed Marshall. He could track a deer, fight a fire, chop a tree, and ride a thirteen-foot log down a roiling Adirondack river, but in an Oneida County courtroom, he was lost. Two detectives accompanied him back to his jail cell.

Sheriff Reese told the newspaper boys he did not know a thing about the case and would not say it if he did. The reporters kept pressing. They finally learned that a hat and some tools had been found at the scene of the 1899 Forestport break: some shovels, a sharp-pointed pole, and an eight-foot-long auger with an iron grip welded on. The investigation prompted in part by that discovery had led to even stronger suspicions about the 1898 break. The reporters picked up, as well, hints of some terrible doings. From District Attorney Curtin's office, they heard that a three-year-old Forestport murder might have been committed by Marshall's associates. Five arrest warrants, maybe more, had been prepared. Knowing what they did about the Erie Canal and local politicians, the reporters asked Curtin if any well-known politician was implicated in the breaks.

After all, as the *Boonville Herald* put it on 14 December, "it has been the inclination of the public since learning that the break was caused by design to lay the crime at the door of some politician or political party, who could direct the expenditure of the thousands required to repair the break in a way to aid his or their cause."

The public's cynical inclination was the spawn of all that had come before. The $9 million canal improvement scandal, Tom Wheeler's larding of the Oneida County Canal payrolls, the sweetheart contracts stuffing the pockets of Utica's Dwyer Company: all of it had settled the canal's reputation as the plaything of the politically connected. Everyone knew how the politicians and their contractor friends took advantage of public necessity. The Rochester men with whom George Aldridge's father had done business, George and Jarvis Lord, had immensely profited from their canal repairs in the 1870s. The Utica men with whom Tom Wheeler had been in business had profited from their Utica and Forestport repairs of the 1890s. With such a history, it was easily conceivable that someone might have decided to simply make their own breaks. Doing so would be in character with everything that had come before.

But no, Curtin insisted. Whatever the public assumptions, no prominent county politicians were known to be implicated in the Forestport breaks.

"In fact, they are doing all in their power to help find the guilty ones, and no one is working harder along this line than Thomas Wheeler," Curtin said, according to the *Boonville Herald* of 14 December.

The forty-two-year-old district attorney was himself a political striver and Republican partisan. He was a teammate, after a fashion, of Tom Wheeler. He had spent his life trying to join the political establishment, not fighting it. Hungry for advancement ever since he had gone to work in the Rome brickyards at the age of thirteen, he learned law strictly on the job. He lost two of his first three political races, for county recorder and for surrogate. But by 1898, by then a past president of the Republican League Club and a man with connections throughout Oneida County, Curtin had won election as district attorney. His reassurances could not entirely squelch the rumor, as one put it, that "prominent people in the northern section were deeply implicated and under constant surveillance by the detectives." Indeed, Curtin hinted in the December 14 *Boonville Herald* that "a sort of combination" may have been formed among some of Forestport's leading citizens, the breaks having been caused "in order that the large amounts of money necessary to repair them might come to Forestport and vicinity."

Until the Pinkertons and Sheriff Reese's men finished sweeping up the other immediate suspects, any theory would remain unprovable. Ed Marshall's information only went so far, and Curtin admitted that the Pinkertons had hoped to continue the undercover part of their investigation longer. The district attorney said that he was forced to arrest Marshall, and thereby make public the Forestport investigation, only after detectives learned Marshall was about to flee the country. As to the identity of those detectives working the Forestport case, the *Daily Press* reporter scared up the names of six men who were described as "a frisky lot and dumb as oysters": Captain H. W. Bearce, J. J. Pender, W. M. Hawkins, D. D. Keyer, Charles Strong, and Howard M. Fordham.

This last was the shocker. Fordham, a Pinkerton detective? Forestport men reading the 12 December newspaper were flabbergasted at the intelligence. Not just at the deception, at Fordham's ability to pass himself off for months as a low-rent salesman, but the timing, too, was beyond belief. He had been coming to Forestport for years before the May 1898 break. Which could only mean that if Fordham were a detective, the Pinkertons had had Forestport under surveillance long before anyone had previously thought.

The supposed revelation proved a false alarm in the end, one of many that clattered throughout the Forestport affair. The reporters got it wrong, just as they got wrong their initial attempts to spell the names of Bearce—"Bearse"—and the other bona fide detectives. Fordham was not a detective but an informant, scooping dirt to the Pinkertons and hoping for some payment in return. By 14 December, Fordham's proper identity as a real estate dealer was disclosed. In an interview published that day, District Attorney Curtin said Fordham had chanced upon information concerning the breaks and, though fearing personal harm from the plotters, had presented his findings to several Forestport men "of more or less political prominence." Fordham assumed, by this account, that these unnamed worthies would deliver the news to the proper authorities.

They did not. They kept their mouths shut about what had happened in their hometown. Filled, evidently, with a zeal for justice, Fordham himself then conveyed the information to Partridge, evidently through a Buffalo intermediary.

Forestport men considered Howard Fordham a shaky character more likely to run out on a bill than to seek after justice. His testimony incited Forestport resident Byron Cool to dash off letters to the local newspapers, enumerating Fordham's debts. Fordham owed, according to Cool: $100 to Dick Manahan for room and board, as well as money to the liveryman Charles Denslow, the hotelkeeper Charley O'Connor, town supervisor Ed Curran, and others.

"There are doctor's bills and bills for borrowed money, as well as a balance due on a timber deal," Cool reported in the *Utica Daily Press* on 17 December. "On these accounts, Forestport people would be glad to have Mr. Fordham visit them in his present prosperity."

As to Ed Marshall, Forestport men knew him too. Authorities would do well, Cool suggested, to treat skeptically anything that old storyteller might relate.

"He is noted for spinning yarns for the entertainment of the crowd, which if taken seriously implicate him in many hairbreadth escapes and lead people to believe that he had led a very adventurous life," Cool observed.

Publicly, Forestport could dismiss Fordham as a scofflaw and Marshall as a teller of tales. Privately, Forestport could not be so sure. The town became a troubled, suspicious place in the final weeks of the nineteenth century. One old-timer was in jail already, the district attorney was hinting at more arrests to come, and the *Boonville Herald* was asserting on 14 December that "it is thought likely that Marshall and his allies are only tools controlled by some master hand." The men gathered in their saloons and around the radiating warmth of the stove in Utley's harness shop. They swapped their stories, trading for information and advantage, while the air grew charged as from a coming storm.

Near midnight on 3 January 1900, the Rome railroad station uncharacteristically bustled. Acting police chief D. D. Driscoll was there in his civilian clothes, as was detective Bearce of the Pinkertons. Their breaths steamed the winter air, but they kept mostly to themselves. Bearce had been absent from Rome after Ed Marshall's arrest, but in the last day he had been spotted again at the city's Arlington House hotel. Bearce, standing by the ticket window, and Driscoll spoke little on the station platform.

The 11:58 P.M. eastbound New York Central was late, and Driscoll and Bearce kept their watch until the train arrived shortly after 12:30 A.M. Bearce scanned the weary disembarking passengers until he found a familiar face. The short man flashed a signal, and Bearce turned his attention toward a slender, dark-mustachioed man in a blue flannel shirt and black hat. The stranger seemed lost at first, uncertain as to his next step, until he started down the platform toward the train engine. Bearce nodded, and signaled Assistant Chief Driscoll. Driscoll hustled to catch up with the stranger, who seemed ready to pounce.

"What do you want with me, you big stiff?" the black-hatted stranger snarled.

"You are under arrest," Driscoll told him, as the *Rome Daily Sentinel* reported on 4 January.

The stranger flared, but Driscoll was ready with a Smith & Wesson pistol pointed straight at the stranger's nose. The stranger relented, but remained tightly coiled. Together the two men began walking the several blocks toward the city police station, until they reached the James Street bridge. The stranger slowed on the bridge and gestured toward the dank water below. "What's that ditch down there?" The stranger seemed clueless about the Erie Canal. Informed about the water below, the stranger showed sudden signs of flight. Again Driscoll subdued him, this time aided by the fortuitously arriving Officer Keating. After a brief struggle, and a smack to the stranger's face, Keating clinched a pair of handcuffs on the stranger.

The threesome finally arrived at the gray granite Rome jail. There the stranger impudently identified himself as John Doe. He was a hard case, clearly, and looking harder by the minute, as his right eye blackened from the blow he had received in his struggles with Driscoll. The police took from him two .32-caliber revolvers, one fully loaded, along with six skeleton keys, two picklocks, and a pair of pliers used to crack open hotel rooms. Burglar's tools. In his small satchel, police found a notebook with numbers—3–30–26—that they interpreted as the combination to a safe. Driscoll's men shoved John Doe into a cold cell, but a few hours of scratchy sleep did not erase his sneer. When the jailer brought him his morning meal, he asked for matches.

"When I stop at the Astoria, I always have a smoke after breakfast," the man said.

John Doe was brought at 10:30 A.M. before the court recorder for arraignment. Acting police chief Driscoll swore the facts, that the stranger had been nabbed carrying burglar's tools, and the stranger was asked, once more, to give his name.

"John Doe," he repeated.

"Rather strange name," the recorder mused.

"It is a fictitious name," Doe said, according to the *Utica Daily Press* of 5 January; pressed, he explained that "I don't want my folks to know where I am."

Reporters soon gathered that John Doe was a burglar known to work hotels between Buffalo and Rome. His capture was most fortunate. The Pinkertons, reporters were reminded, "are always on the watch for suspicious characters," and so they naturally pitched in to cast a dangerous character like John Doe into the Rome jail. The suspected hotel thief seemed at first to keep his distance from most of the other prisoners. He had his own time to do and was not out to make friends, but he was willing to listen to other inmates like the garrulous Ed Marshall. In time, they would have much to talk about.

The papers were reporting that weekend on Governor Roosevelt's recent message to the state legislature, in which the governor had thumped his chest about the thorough and impartial investigation of the canal improvement scandal and "the impracticality of a successful prosecution" of Aldridge and Adams. The scandal was all water under the bridge; it was now time, the governor urged, to admire the crisp and efficient administration of Colonel Partridge.

The skeptical editors of the *Rome Daily Sentinel* reminded readers like Ed Marshall and John Doe on 3 January that "the investigation of the [canal] matter was strung over a long period until the statute of limitations stepped in and outlawed crimes which could have been punished had it not been for the delay . . . the criminals could have been convicted if proceeded against promptly." Ed Marshall and John Doe could have talked, as well, about other canal topics. The newspapers were reporting that Roosevelt's advisory panel had finished its work of evaluating the future of the Erie Canal. The commission envisioned a one thousand-ton barge canal connecting the Great Lakes with the Atlantic Ocean. Inland water transport remained commercially viable if conducted on a proper scale and managed on a professional, nonpartisan basis, the governor's commission believed.

They might have talked about this or that, Ed Marshall and John Doe, in their first weekend together in the Rome jail. Soon enough they would have new companions to talk with, old pals of Ed's. The Pinkertons were moving faster.

Early one morning on the week of John Doe's arrest, four Pinkerton detectives quietly left Rome's Arlington House hotel and boarded an eastbound New York Central. Joining them was Constable M. A. Plantz. By Sunday night, 7 January, the four detectives returned to Rome with two Forestport men in tow: the card-playing bricklayer Frank Murray and the laborer John Root. About ten hours later, Plantz returned with former pool hall owner James Rudolph. On Monday afternoon, before Justice of the Peace Gubbins, Rudolph, Murray, and Root were arraigned on charges of causing the 1898 Forestport Feeder break. The three Forestport men pleaded not guilty and then were ushered back to jail to rejoin Marshall and John Doe.

The Pinkertons seemed to be peeling away layers, drawing closer to the heart of things. Marshall was an Adirondack oddity, but his new jail companions claimed deeper roots in town. The new arrests fractured Forestport, leaving fearful neighbors on one side or another of cracks that kept subdividing further. The town, the *Rome Daily Sentinel* observed on 15 January, divided into factions: "the law-abiding citizens who wished to see the law take its course, and those who profited by the break and sympathized with the men who caused it. The latter faction has caused the detectives at work on the case a great deal of trouble, and more than once have the detectives been in ticklish positions." But the boundary dividing the upright from the dissolute was also becoming ambiguous. Jimmy Rudolph, however rough, was a man of business, and Frank Murray had upright acquaintances throughout town. Though Rudolph had recently departed Forestport for a new home in Johnstown, east of Utica, he was well remembered for his years of running a restaurant and River Street pool hall. Murray had laid bricks or loaded boats for many in town, and played cards with many others. John Root was a laborer with, it might be said, a mixed reputation. He had once been charged with stealing another man's turkeys, but with the help of character witnesses like Walt Bynon and John Conley, Root had been cleared of those charges. The charges had not prevented him from being appointed a Forestport election overseer. John Root could be trusted to do his political duty.

The lights kept burning at strange hours in District Attorney Curtin's office, and closemouthed men came and went from the four-story Arlington House hotel. The ground was shifting; dangerous new identities were being revealed.

John Doe, for instance. It seemed, on reflection, a queer matter to the *Utica Daily Press* reporter that Pinkertons investigating an Erie Canal break would so abruptly interest themselves in an alleged hotel thief. The reporter checked police station sources. Those burglar's tools and keys found in Doe's pockets, the reporter learned, were entirely new, as was one of Doe's revolvers. They seemed more like props than tools. The reporter put the pieces together and published, amazingly, his conclusion: It was apparent, the *Daily Press* stated, that John Doe was in reality a Pinkerton operative insinuated into the jail in hopes of luring Marshall and others into incriminating talk.

"Could it be," the *Daily Press* speculated on 5 January, "that the 'burglar' wired the district attorney or anyone else and gave a complete description of himself and the things he possessed so that he might be arrested upon landing here . . . if the whole thing was not a fake, how would the district attorney or any one else ever know that 'Doe' had burglar's tools in his possession?"

The paper might as well have painted a bulls-eye right on the back of

John Doe's jail clothes. Someone could wake up with a knife in the back, in that kind of business. But John Doe, as it developed, was not the only man in Rome whose life hung in the balance. Soon some men would be coming for the peddler-turned-informant Howard Fordham. They would be coming at midnight, with Forestport justice in mind.

Chapter 12

NO ONE EXPECTED DICK MANAHAN AND TOM NIGHTINGALE.

They arrived in Rome, unannounced, on the chilly night of Thursday, 11 January. They had not been summoned, and their arrival at the train station went unremarked upon. They had come armed with a warrant for Howard Fordham's arrest signed by Forestport justice of the peace John Potter. The charge: failing to pay back a debt of about $120 owed Manahan. Manahan and Nightingale crossed the corner of West Dominick and North Washington streets and entered the quiet Arlington House hotel lobby, where a night clerk escorted them upstairs to Howard Fordham's room (*People v. Manahan* 1900, 205).

When the clerk had left, and while Manahan held back, Nightingale rapped on the door.

"Who is there?" Fordham asked, after a moment's hesitation.

Nightingale identified himself, and a reluctant Fordham slowly opened the door. The constable announced he had a warrant for Fordham's arrest. He must return to Forestport. Fordham refused; that would be folly. The constable insisted, and pressed Fordham to move along. The warrant was in order, properly signed by an officer of the law. Fordham would have to face the music, in the town he had betrayed. Fordham still resisted. He would not consider boarding a midnight train for Forestport, no matter what kind of signed paper Nightingale might hold. The standoff in Fordham's hotel room lasted until an agent from District Attorney Curtin's office showed up. The agent demanded the arrest papers, and

Nightingale surrendered them. He was but a properly sanctioned man of the law, performing his duty. Fordham owed Manahan on an unpaid board bill, and justice demanded repayment.

While Curtin's agent wrangled with Fordham, Manahan slipped away to the train station, where he made the 11:58 P.M. train to Utica. He was back in Forestport before dawn.

"I wanted to get the evening train back to Utica, that was my only reason [for leaving]," Manahan later explained to a lawyer insinuatingly curious about his sudden flight from Rome (*People v. Manahan* 1900, 207).

Nightingale followed later, after being advised by Curtin's office that the witness Fordham could not be spirited off to Forestport on the basis of an allegedly unpaid board bill. The next day, Friday, a shaken Fordham told Justice of the Peace Gubbins that he feared for his life. The plot was clear, he said. Manahan and Nightingale hoped to get him into the country north of Remsen, where there was no law. Curtin and the Pinkerton agents believed likewise and asked that Fordham be retained in Rome.

"They got scared at Forestport and put their heads together to concoct some scheme to shut up Fordham, and they thought of this old board bill," Curtin speculated later in the *Utica Daily Press* of 17 April 1900. "Did [they] want to get Fordham way in the north woods for awhile, or get him under [their] control?"

Curtin or his associates tipped off reporters to the complete picture. Near Remsen, the *Utica Daily Press* of 13 January 1900 reported, there is "a very high trestle, and the train which Fordham and the constable would have taken had the former went passes over this trestle about 2 A.M. . . . while on this train . . . Fordham was to have been passed into the custody of another, and that in going from one car to another someone would slip and fall from the train into the abyss below." And then: "There would not be any Fordham to appear against Edward Marshall or any of the others implicated in the Forestport breaks."

These were astonishing allegations. Tom Nightingale was Forestport's keeper-of-the-peace; Potter the town's dispenser of justice, Manahan the leading hotelier and saloonkeeper. And now they were being accused of attempted kidnapping, of conspiring to murder.

The newspaper boys were getting other tips too. Someone close to the investigators slipped them a clue about the mysterious John Doe. He was not a common burglar, after all, and certainly he was no Pinkerton operative, as the *Utica Daily Press* had so boldly estimated. The anonymous tipster let on that John Doe had in fact been hired by "a certain class" of Forestport men concerned about Ed Marshall's arrest. These men wanted the talkative Marshall spirited out of Oneida County and far beyond the reach of the Pinkertons, and so they contracted with a Buffalo man to break Marshall from jail. A Pinkerton operative posing as a workingman in Forestport had caught wind of the plot and followed "John Doe" to the train station bound for Rome, and thereupon alerted Bearce.

"The *Press* reporter is informed from a reliable source that [Doe] is not a Pinkerton detective, and that he has no connection with that famous agency," the newspaper assured its confused readers on 27 January.

Forestport's reputation was getting dirtier every day. This latest story—that a cadre of townsmen conspired to kidnap a witness against them—broadly indicted the entire town. It apparently confirmed the criminal motives exposed in the midnight raid on Fordham's hotel, and certainly confirmed that undercover Pinkerton operatives had infiltrated the town. It surely complicated John Doe's standing within the Rome city jail. He was first identified as a hotel burglar, then revealed as a probable Pinkerton, and now exposed as notorious jailbreaker. All the waters were getting muddied.

On Saturday, 14 January, Pinkerton detectives seized John Fardette, a twenty-six-year-old laborer and occasional liveryman. Fardette lived most of the year with his mother, Maggie, in Forestport. He was said to be respectably connected in town, the oldest of eight children, but he could also be unruly. He drank and gambled, and he had been charged once for stealing oats (*People v. Manahan* 1900, 126). He was working in the woods near the Fulton chain of lakes when the Pinkertons found him. The detectives, having tracked him on snowshoes to the logging camp, escorted him back to Forestport, where he changed his clothes, and then they transported him to the Rome city jail by early Sunday morning.

Howard Fordham shortly went before two Rome judges to swear he did not owe Manahan a cent. Consider the facts, Fordham said: he had left Forestport and returned several times, and Manahan had never before said anything about an unpaid bill. He had stayed at Manahan's place, certainly. In the fire of February 1899, some of Fordham's own clothing and baggage had been destroyed. But Fordham had paid his share, in part through the transfer of the rights to cut some timber off a wooded lot not far from town. Most important, he pleaded not to be sent back to face Forestport justice.

"Only recently, since [I] gave information against several persons in Forestport, charging them with being implicated in the breaking of the Black River feeder at Forestport in May 1898 . . . [was] this alleged offense trumped up," Fordham swore, the *Utica Daily Press* reported on 13 January.

Fordham further swore that he was afraid of "personal violence and great bodily injury" if he should be returned to Forestport. The violence, he said, "would come unexpectedly from those accused or suspected of the crimes now charged, or from the friends of those who are guilty and liable to be implicated." Convinced of Fordham's sincerity, the judge agreed the unpaid board case could be removed from Forestport and considered later in Rome. Constable Nightingale returned to Rome Sunday afternoon and once again attempted to serve Fordham with an arrest warrant. Fordham and the detectives were ready for him, with an order stating that the matter of the allegedly unpaid board bill had been transferred to the Oneida County grand jury.

The arrested Forestport men were starting to consider the hands they had been dealt. It looked bad for them. Curtin and the Pinkertons held all the good cards but one and were ready to make a trade: Freedom for confession. By the time Fardette had joined his compatriots behind bars, each had submitted to the logic of their situation. Those who had not confessed already were prepared to, and Fardette would soon reach the same conclusion.

"It is said that when the details are made public, it will create as big a sensation as the county ever experienced," the *Daily Press* reported on 13 January, adding once more, to reassure those persistently cynical about the canal, that "it is said that no politicians were interested in the Forestport break."

On Monday morning, liveryman William Clark and saloonkeeper Walter Bynon heard that the Pinkertons were coming, armed with more warrants. Walt, only twenty-nine years old but aged by the rheumatism that sometimes kept him housebound for weeks at a time, revived in his fear. He could say little to his wife, Rose, or to his three young children before he hefted himself aboard one of Clark's wagons. Clark whipped the team onward, and the two men rode south toward Utica.

Dick Manahan merely waited. Bearce found him in town. John Conley, too, was taken that same day right in Forestport. The forty-year-old Conley, a trimly put together saloonkeeper, had two children and his wife, Elnora, to cry and ask what it was all about when the Pinkertons came and carted their prisoners to the Buffalo Head railroad station. By suppertime Monday, Manahan and Conley had been deposited in the Rome city jail.

Upon learning that Bynon and Clark had fled Forestport, Bearce alerted District Attorney Curtin. Curtin passed the word to the police in nearby cities, and by 2:15 in the afternoon Bynon and Clark had been seized without a fight in Utica. Informed of the capture, Curtin and Deputy Sheriff Owens bustled to catch the 2:48 train to Utica. They brought with them someone Bynon and Clark knew well: John T. Root, prudently buckled to Owens so that he might not even consider escape. But though Root was desperate, he was not about to flee. He had succumbed and had been the first to offer up an oral confession. In Utica, the confession was going to be reduced to writing.

Curtin soon had to leave Root in Utica and tend to the newly arrived prisoners, Clark and Bynon. Their flight from Forestport seemed, to Curtin, clear evidence of their guilt.

"They came to Utica by wagon, in my estimation, to avoid running into officers' hands and being arrested," Curtin told Judge Andrews that Monday afternoon, the *Boonville Herald* reported on 18 January.

More likely, Clark and Bynon had skipped out to Utica in hopes of securing a lawyer before the detectives caught up with them. By the Monday afternoon court hearing, they had representing them one of Utica's best-known attorneys, Josiah Perry. Well acquainted with Forestport's ways and a familiar face around Utica's political circles, Perry pressed for bail lower than the $5,000 sought by District Attorney Curtin.

"I personally think that these men are innocent," Perry assured Judge

Andrews, according to the *Herald*. "The men charged came to Utica this morning and could very easily have escaped, but apparently, knowing they are innocent, they were willing to surrender."

Perry's word could usually be relied upon. The forty-nine-year-old Remsen native and one-time schoolteacher had been practicing law in Utica since 1877. An active Republican partisan who had come tantalizingly close to winning election as county district attorney in 1886, he moved in all the expected fraternal circles: the Imperial Council of the International Order of the Odd Fellows, the Skenandoah Lodge of the Freemasons, and Utica's own Arcanum Club. Perry already knew Forestport well from several forays into the village to investigate those selling liquor without a license. Back in September 1892, he had barely lost the Republican nomination for county judge to Watson Dunmore (Wager 1896b, 61). Soon Dunmore and Perry would be meeting again.

Judge Andrews initially resisted lowering the bail. Finally, after adjourning and reconvening that night at the well-established Butterfield House hotel, Andrews agreed to a bail amount that Clark and Bynon could afford. Forestport mill owner George Farley—the very man later praised by state officials for his help in solving the Forestport breaks—joined with Forestport store owner Charles Bingham in putting up bonds for Clark. Bynon had three acquaintances put up bonds, and he and Clark were released shortly after midnight.

Ed Marshall was no longer with them. The old river driver and storyteller had been quietly moved to the Utica jail, and Curtin passed on that Marshall would face no charges. This announcement was altogether strange. Marshall, after all, was the man whom Pinkertons had retrieved all the way from Michigan, the man Howard Fordham had pegged as one of the muddy-booted conspirators. But now Curtin and the Pinkertons had concluded that Forestport men were right all along about wild Ed Marshall.

"It would appear from the evidence," Curtin or his representatives advised the *Rome Daily Sentinel* of 15 January, "that Marshall is one whose ambition it is to be thought a bad man. He was in possession of many of the facts of the three crimes, and when they were mentioned in Forestport he would smile in a knowing way or make some remark intended to give the impression that he was one of the persons who committed the deeds."

By Tuesday, 16 January, Marshall was let go. John Doe, the black-eyed man from Buffalo, was charged with attempted burglary. And, in what were described as sealed indictments, seven men were charged with the Forestport breaks.

Sealed indictments were used when investigators had not yet captured the accused. The Pinkertons, then, still had more gathering to do beyond the men they already had in hand. Not simply the breaks were being exposed as the Pinkertons began lifting rocks around the village. The detectives learned of two cases of suspicious death. One case involved a man who had, some time back, come howling out of the north woods flush with logging money. He started on the Forestport tour, one saloon followed by another, until he was falling-down drunk and helpless. Then, detectives understood, some of the same men accused of causing the breaks poured more alcohol down his throat and lifted $90 from his pockets. The last wash of alcohol did the man in; he died, the coroner concluded, from acute "alcoholism." The allegation floated up like a corpse, untethered to courtroom-worthy evidence. It was simply, as the reporters put it, "said that" or "understood." The small town continued fracturing, fault lines of doubt and suspicion dividing neighbor against neighbor. The allegations vexed the good people of Forestport, who were being tarred, as one put it, with the image that "one-half of our citizens are dangerous criminals and the other half [are] engaged in shielding them."

"It seems to us up here," Forestport's deputy postmaster Frank Connors complained in the *Boonville Herald* of 25 January, "that someone is trying to make a reputation and using this case to do so, with Forestport-at-large as the scapegoat."

The authorities denied any suggestion that they had it in for the town. They declared themselves to be simply in the business of dividing the innocent from the guilty.

"The proof against the men under arrest is positive," Bearce declared in the *Boonville Herald* on 17 January. "The state will have little trouble making the strongest kind of case against each one of the conspirators. We have gone to the bottom of the case and have all the information necessary to clear up the matter."

One day after the grand jury handed up the sealed indictments, Ida

Manahan steeled herself and traveled to the Rome city jail. She brought with her an estimable Utica lawyer named Thomas S. Jones, the man who would join in trying to save her husband.

The fifty-nine-year-old Jones knew Forestport firsthand, having begun his legal practice in the village in 1862 shortly after graduating from the Albany Law School. After a few months, he had returned to his native Boonville, where he spent the Civil War years practicing law and politics. Jones served on the Democratic State Committee during the 1880s, and after moving his practice to Utica he had twice won election as Oneida County district attorney. He had worked closely, at times, with Tom Wheeler during Wheeler's turn as county sheriff. Since leaving office, Jones had specialized in fire insurance law. With his tidy posture, mustache, and thinning white hair, he looked like a reliable man (Wager 1896b, 44). He was, in all, a prosperous, solid member of the county bar and perhaps just the man to save Dick Manahan.

Jones was, moreover, not the only upstanding citizen interested in the Forestport gang. On the same day he and Ida Manahan visited the Rome jail, what the *Rome Daily Sentinel* characterized as "four of the moneyed men of Forestport" scouted about town in hopes of arranging bail for at least some of the prisoners. They needed to cover bail that had been set at $40,000, and by the time they had gathered the money District Attorney Curtin had left Rome for consultations in Albany.

John Partridge, with whom Curtin presumably met, was a satisfied man. On Thursday evening, 18 January, he held forth for reporters more expansively than ever before. He recounted how he had learned about the 1897 and 1898 Forestport breaks shortly after taking office, and how he had picked up clues "from the western part of the state, partly by accident" that the breaks were deliberately caused. This was apparently a shaded reference to the tips provided by Buffalo salesman Howard Fordham. Partridge detailed his own reconnaissance, his consultations with Attorney General Davies, their decision to hire the Pinkertons, and the detectives' "step-by-step" investigation. Partridge felt free to speculate on the breakers' motives.

"There was doubtless a mercenary motive back of all this," Partridge said in the *Boonville Herald* on 19 January. "The money which the state has had to pay for the repairs on the feeder has gone into the pockets of the laborers, teamsters and others, and much of it eventually found its way into the saloons and pool rooms."

An official theory of the breaks was becoming clear. Those men arrested were of two classes: laborers and shovel-toters like John Fradette, Frank Murray, and John Root, and business owners like Manahan, Conley, and Bynon. The owners of Forestport's saloons, hotels, and pool halls had the motive to incite the breaks, and men like Root, Murray, and Fradette had the muscle to make the breaks happen. But if the state's prosecutorial theory was becoming more apparent, many particulars remained under seal. On Friday morning, 19 January, attorneys Thomas Jones and William Townsend asked for a copy of the indictment against Manahan. Townsend was a Yale man who had worked with Jones since their time together in the district attorney's office. The partners told Justice Andrews that though the indictment had been filed a week before, the man charged had never been given a chance to read it.

Curtin, back from his Albany consultations, urged Justice Andrews not to break the seal on the indictment. If opened, it would tip off men not yet arrested.

"One of the defendant's attorneys tried to get the indictment from the clerk," Curtin said, "and I understand they have gone to the jail to see other prisoners regarding this matter. They are all seeking to secure information."

"If you state that, you state something that is not true," Jones declared. "You are not a gentleman!"

"Other attorneys have been to the jail to find out about these matters," Curtin replied. "I understand you have been there."

"You," Jones said, according to the *Boonville Herald* of 19 January, "are neither a man nor a gentleman."

Curtin was not easily rattled by such courtroom wrangling. In the two years since winning election, Curtin had only lost two minor cases. He had prosecuted murderers and every lesser manner of bedchamber sneak, blackleg, boodle-passer, cracksman, and ruffian. Though Jones floridly pled his case, Justice Andrews rejected the request. Nor did Andrews agree to order an immediate arraignment of Manahan; a "reasonable time" was all he set. By Friday afternoon Manahan and Conley were asking through their lawyers for release on bail and for an elaboration on the charges. Curtin offered a few more details. Both Conley and Manahan, he revealed, stood accused of involvement in the 1898 and the 1899 Forestport breaks. This was a new twist, for the town and for the accused alike. Section 479 of the New York State Penal Code, the section Conley and Manahan were accused of twice violating, made it a felony to willfully injure the state's canals. Curtin believed no one had ever before been convicted under the law. Conviction on the two separate counts could send the men to Auburn State Prison for fourteen years of hard labor and cost them $2,000 in fines.

By late Friday afternoon, Manahan had arranged for his release on a $10,000 bond. Conley remained in jail. There, he was about to be joined by others. Even as Manahan returned to Forestport under bail, the Pinkertons were scouring the local woods and camps for his alleged co-conspirators. Shortly after 7 P.M. on a gray Saturday, Boonville Deputy Sheriff Wetmore found the man he was looking for near Forestport.

Frank Bassett was thirty-six years old, a canal bank watchman and occasional sawmill laborer with five children and a wife named May. He was of modest height and weighed about 175 pounds. A black-mustachioed, tobacco-using, eighteen-year resident of Forestport, he was regarded by his neighbors as honest and straightforward. He was trusted enough, after all, to have been named canal bank watchman. The Saturday evening arrest of Frank Bassett near his home on the Alder Creek road proved especially "heart-rending," in the words of one reporter. His children were young and his wife, May, was vulnerable to trauma. Though not everyone knew it, her death records would show she was epileptic and could have a seizure in trying times. The distraught family watched helplessly in a driving rainstorm as Wetmore and a Pinkerton man put Bassett aboard a double sleigh led by two white ponies and took him away to jail. Everyone was miserably soaked by the time they arrived in Rome three hours later. Jailers placed Bassett in his jail cell and told him he was charged with causing the 1899 Forestport break.

On Monday, Utica attorney William Townsend sought a $5,000 bail for Bassett. Curtin agreed to it. Bassett was brought from Rome to Utica in anticipation of his release, and several propertied Forestport men indicated they would go his bail.

But then Bassett informed them Monday that he had already confessed to the Pinkertons. With that intelligence, Bassett's ostensible friends, the lumbermen George Ainsworth and James Gallagher, turned around and returned to Forestport without him. If Bassett were spilling the beans, he could take care of his own affairs. Ainsworth and Gallagher, the *Rome Daily Sentinel* stated on 22 January, concluded that in light of his confession, "they had better keep their unencumbered property for the bonds of any others who might be arrested and from whom a confession could not be pumped."

Forestport was closing ranks against outsiders. That night, a forlorn Bassett lamented to one of the Pinkerton detectives about the perversions of the bail system. Why was it that someone manly enough to confess his sins was not able to secure bail?

Bearce understood. The Pinkerton detective had seen injustice in his day, and not all of it committed by criminals. The night Bassett returned to the Rome jail, Bearce mused aloud to a visiting reporter. Some attorneys were enough to make a grown man cry. Take old Ed Marshall, for instance, the big talker who was the first to get locked up on the Forestport deal. He happened to have $60 in his pockets when he was arrested, and a Rome attorney with a pipeline to the jail rushed quickly down to see him.

"He made Marshall think that he was surely going to be hung or electrocuted," Bearce said in the *Daily Sentinel* on 24 January. "Marshall would not listen to any [other] advice, and he gave the attorney an order for $50 . . . and he never so much as lifted a finger on Marshall's behalf."

The Pinkertons kept gathering. On Saturday evening, 27 January, a deputy sheriff named Waite from the town of Camden arrived in Port Leyden up the Black River. He found his way to the livery stable of William Morrell, who had formerly run the stage connecting Forestport and the Buffalo Head railroad station. Waite was a stranger to him, just another customer, it seemed. Waite said he would pay to be taken by Morrell's wagon to West Leyden. The men set off, Morrell unsuspecting and Waite biding his time. Once they had arrived in West Leyden, Waite revealed his identity, announced Morrell's arrest on a bench warrant, and ordered

Morrell to drive them both down to Rome through the Lansing Kill gorge. Shortly before dawn on Sunday, the deputy delivered a dispirited Morrell into the hands of the Rome jailers.

For the next three weeks, the Forestport men—save Manahan, who had secured his bail—waited behind bars while the Oneida County grand jury heard evidence. Directed by Bearce, two Erie Canal engineers began surveying the Forestport Feeder from the village to Boonville. Prosecutors wanted not just confessions, but levels and elevations, the incontrovertible facts about the flow of water. The Forestport men's lawyers prepared in their own way, talking with the imprisoned or the bailed-out as was necessary. The jailed men could hear the news, as well, from the faraway world, like Governor Roosevelt's firm proclamation of 12 February that "definitely that under no circumstance could I or would I accept the nomination for vice presidency." Behind the scenes, Roosevelt had advised Platt in a 1 February letter that he "should like to be Governor for another term, especially if we are able to take hold of the Canals in serious shape" (*Barnes v. Roosevelt* 1915, 2471). From visitors, the jailed men could learn of more local affairs, of the factions dividing Forestport.

But still, despite repeated attempts, they could not learn of the particulars upon which they had been indicted. It would be, District Attorney Curtin assured Judge Dunmore, improper to disclose the names of all the other men who had been charged in the indictment. Judge Dunmore agreed. The charged men would remain in the dark, though some light was starting to expose other aspects of the Forestport investigation.

John Doe, the enigmatic burglar who had been sprung from jail earlier, was now being spotted keeping company with the Pinkerton detectives. His black eye had healed and his clothes were spiffed up. Any remaining doubt about his affiliation vanished the March day when John Doe carried into the grand jury room a box of tools being presented as evidence in the Forestport breaks investigation. The Utica newspaper reporter had been precisely right months before with his first intuition: John Doe was himself a Pinkerton, planted to spy upon the incarcerated Forestport men. The subsequent report that John Doe was part of the Forestport plot, dispatched to spring Ed Marshall out of jail, was simply part of the Pinkertons' practiced deception.

"John Doe," the *Utica Daily Press* marveled on 9 March, "is one of Pinkerton's brightest detectives . . . He got all kinds of evidence in connection with the Forestport breaks, for he worked his bluffs to the queen's taste, so to speak, and the prisoners on the job 'coughed up' everything to him, and through him it was that several of the confessions were obtained."

The man called John Doe left Rome on the evening train of 9 March, bound for New York City and what reporters predicted would be "another important case." Having served his part, he apparently never returned to Oneida County, nor was his identity ever revealed.

For the next several weeks, Curtin kept secret several of the indictments he had already obtained. But it was becoming evident, the *Rome Daily Sentinel* noted on 8 March, "that more people were implicated in the plot than was at first supposed." The investigation's focus, moreover, had expanded beyond the 1898 break.

On Monday morning, 19 March, detectives returned to Forestport and reached into the Hotel Doyle. Their target was Michael Donovan, the brother-in-law of the late Michael Doyle. An unmarried man, suffering from rheumatism, he had moved into the hotel to help his sister Jenny after Michael's death the year before. Michael Donovan had company for his late afternoon train trip down to Rome. District Attorney Curtin, having secured the additional indictments he had sought, had ordered as well the re-arrest of William Clark, Walt Bynon, John Conley, and Dick Manahan. The four men, already out on bail and charged with complicity in the 1898 break, now faced additional charges of involvement in the 1899 break. Bynon was laid up when the officers came for him, stricken by his chronic rheumatism. After some consultations, the two Rome constables accepted an attestation by Forestport's Dr. George Kilborn that Bynon was too ill to move. He was placed on bed arrest, the *Utica Daily News* reported on 20 March. The remaining Forestport men were bundled by wagon to the Buffalo Head station, and then south to Rome, arriving shortly after 5 P.M. Within half an hour they were gathered in a courtroom thick with vested lawyers. Thomas Jones reappeared to enter pleas of not guilty on behalf of Dick Manahan, Perry pleaded not guilty on behalf of

William Clark, and Rome-based attorney Joseph Sayles pleaded not guilty for John Conley.

For the politically attuned, the appearance of Sayles on Conley's behalf marked one more intriguing twist in the politically tangled Forestport case. It could have been read almost as a grudge match, with Sayles's real target being canal boss Tom Wheeler. Sayles and Wheeler despised each other. More than a decade before, Sayles had bitterly contested Wheeler's bid for Oneida County sheriff. Sayles, the *Utica Daily Observer* had recorded back on 5 November 1888, had been thought to be the anonymous author of a scurrilous 1888 circular that broadcast Wheeler's past misdeeds and youthful indiscretions, and linked him with the "worst elements" in county politics. Sayles attracted the eye of courtroom watchers for another reason. The forty-six-year-old Albany Law School graduate had a reputation for defending men in life-threatening trouble, including more than thirty charged with capital offenses (Wager 1896b, 39). Conley had hired a serious man to defend himself against serious charges.

Dunmore set $4,000 bail for most of the Forestport men and $5,000 bail for Michael Donovan. Later that evening, Michael's younger brother William and brother-in-law James Gallagher posted the necessary bond.

The next day, lawyers entered formal pleas of not guilty on behalf of the newly arrested men. Conley, looking wan, was in court to support his lawyer's argument against the imposition of additional bail. Conley was but a poor man, Sayles assured Judge William Scripture, and his health was in a bad way. If more bail were required, he would have to stay in jail and that could only weaken him further. Curtin was unsympathetic. Conley's drinking habit, he said, was the real problem. Judge Scripture peered more closely at Conley. Scripture was a fifty-six-year-old Republican stalwart, a former Rome postmaster and the father of eight children; he had been on the bench long enough to know the look of decline (Wager 1896a; Wager 1896b, 39). He could tell that, whatever the cause, Conley was clearly fading. Scripture allowed that no further bail would be required if the defendant could present a statement signed by a reputable physician.

The common Forestport defense was crumbling. The district attorney already held several confessions in his pocket and more on the way. Frank

Bassett, whose confession was already common knowledge, was prepared to plead guilty. There was but one man left, apparently, for the Pinkertons to scoop up. This was William Evans, a hard case from Forestport who some said was the leader of the gang of breakers. Evans was widely known as a dangerous man, a barn-burner and likely suspect for any criminal plot around Forestport. He had decamped for Pennsylvania and had not yet been gathered in. Curtin was not worried. He would collect Evans soon enough, and convict all the breakers regardless of who confessed. Curtin's confidence seemed upheld on Wednesday, 21 March, when the lawmen made two additional Forestport arrests.

At the Buffalo Head hotel, immediately upon leaving the train, the constables found Cornelius Breen, a sociable man who ran the hotel once owned by Dick Manahan. The officers took him and stage driver William James. By Wednesday evening, the two men were appearing before Rome's Judge Scripture and having their $5,000 bonds posted.

Whether through arrests, allegations, or blood ties, hardly a Forestport family was left untouched by the investigation. The liveryman and stage driver James had his bond posted by the eminent George Ainsworth of the Forestport Lumber Company. Going Breen's bond was the storied Sol Carnahan, one of the North Country's hard-driving, hard-living lumberjacks. Carnahan was the kind of man who would jolly a horse into a saloon for laughs, or throw down a roll of $500 cash so he and his jacks could rent a bar for an hour (Thomas 1958, 25). When he was flush, he would share, and so it was that he pitched in to get Conny Breen out of jail.

Jail prospects weighed heavily on the captured men, especially hotelkeeper John Conley. Not having posted bail since his re-arrest on 19 March, he had been withering in the dank, closed space until finally the jailhouse physician swore an affidavit that Conley was suffering from nervous prostration. The doctor warned continued imprisonment might cause serious deterioration. The judge had already seen how poorly Conley was doing, and he accepted the affidavit. A pale Conley returned to Forestport on Friday evening, 23 March.

Jail was somewhat less onerous for other Forestport men. Indeed, the treatment of Rudolph and Murray had become the talk of Forestport. They had only stayed in the common jail cells for about a week following their January arrest. Then, their fellow prisoners reported, the two men had been taken upstairs, along with John Root, and their lives had taken a material turn for the better. They had their own rooms and the use of a hallway, and they were served edible food. To while away the time, the *Boonville Herald* of 19 April would later report, Murray said he and his friends "also had a pack of cards for our amusement." Periodically Bearce showed up for a chat, until the Pinkertons were satisfied. Late one night, when the other inmates were sleeping restlessly, Jailer Owens escorted Rudolph and Murray outside and told them they were no longer needed. They carried their few possessions out into the dark street, where a horse and carriage and the Pinkerton detective named Strong were waiting.

"I was surprised when I got outside," Murray said later, "and I was surprised that I should be let out at the time I was" (*People v. Manahan* 1900, 103).

The former prisoners and their new companion, Strong, bundled up against the cold and rode the two-plus hours from Rome to Utica, where they stayed overnight at the Dudley House hotel. Early the next morning, Rudolph and Murray boarded a train for their new home. They were going to Johnstown, in Fulton County, to start a new life. They were no longer Forestport men.

But they had not precisely left Forestport for good. Rudolph and Murray would each be returning, if not to the town, then to the scene of the crime. Their minds focused by three weeks in jail, Frank Murray and James Rudolph now had a story to tell. It was the story that cost them Forestport forever but that bought them their freedom, the story of what happened the night of 23 May 1898.

Chapter 13

AND THIS WAS THE STORY THEY TOLD.

Spring revived Forestport, even in the dullest of years. The river drivers hit town, paid-up and strutting, by the third week of May 1898. The sawmills were running again, whittling through the logs piled up on the state pond, and boats once more were easing down the feeder. Men had money in their pockets, and places to spend it. In his small, smoky card room, where in months past Frank Murray fleeced the chumps, Jimmy Rudolph convened one weeknight with Murray, John Root, and John Fardette. It was about nine o'clock at night.

"I've got an old pick down in the cellar," Rudolph said. "We can take that."

"I've got an axe," Root said.

"Shovels," Fardette offered. "I'll bring the shovels."

"We'll need a signal," Murray said, in case one of the watchmen comes by. "I've got a whistle, and I'll bring that."

The men next talked timing. Timing was crucial, and Jimmy Rudolph took the lead.

"We'll go this week," Rudolph said. "We'll do it Saturday night. Nine o'clock, we'll leave from my place" (*People v. Manahan* 1900, 103).

The men agreed. Saturday was perfect. The town was flushed and the saloons preoccupied with enough comings, goings, and bottle-breakings that four men slipping away would not be noticed.

The plotters scattered from Rudolph's card room with the agreement to meet on Saturday night. They passed the next few days holding close their secret plan. It was one more thing the women in their lives would not be told, not John Root's mother, nor Jimmy Rudolph's wife, Emma. It was a man's business they were about, though they spoke of one another casually as "the boys." They went about their unremarkable lives until Saturday night, when Rudolph was walking down River Street and looked inside Manahan's hotel.

"I did not see any of the boys," Rudolph said later (*People v. Manahan* 1900, 104).

Still he stopped in. Dick and Ida had been grooming their place, and on some nights Manahan's became the town clubhouse. Rudolph began ordering foaming glasses of beer from Billy Gorman the bartender and, soon enough, the gang began arriving. First Charles O'Connor, and then Frank Murray, and Walt Bynon, and William Clark the liveryman. With every new arrival, there would be another new reason to drink, another new person to order the rounds. Michael Doyle strolled in and greeted the boys. Conny Breen arrived in the company of Howard Fordham, the Buffalo salesman who had been talking up various ventures.

"Drinks for everyone," Breen called.

The boys stood about the bar, saluted Conny, and finished the round, and then Manahan bought another for the house. Things were revolving around Manahan's bar; the room was spinning, for some.

"There was an old German in there, and a number of people having lots of fun; the old German was singing and dancing," Root recalled (*People v. Manahan* 1900, 132).

The clubhouse talk loosened, as if it did not matter who heard them. They talked carelessly of this and that, until finally someone said straight out that it was time for a canal break. That's right, another said, a break right through the feeder, make it run.

"Why in hell don't you go make it, then, and not be belly-aching around here?" Manahan said (*People v. Manahan* 1900, 132).

Michael Doyle, too, had had enough of all the blather.

"You all are a bunch of damn fools to be talking about a break so loud," he said, and stalked out, back to his own saloon.

The rest of the men stayed and drank some more. After a time,

Rudolph, Murray, Root, and Fardette walked with the spurious buoyancy of drunken men out into the night. Down by Doyle's hotel, in an alleyway next to Sandy Denslow's livery stable, the plotters wove together their intentions. Rudolph had reached a conclusion.

"It's a helluva job to get those pilings out," Rudolph said. "It's too late to be starting a big job like that now."

The boys agreed; they would try the next night. Rudolph ordered the men to stay home and out of sight the next day. After dark, at nine o'clock, they would meet at the Dutch Hill bridge. The men scattered. The next day, Forestport was at its serene Sunday best. Washed by the recent rains, the lush spring air enlivened the good folk on their way to morning services at St. Patrick's and the Presbyterian church. Rudolph, Murray, Root, and Fardette stayed home and apart that day, men cloaked in domestic camouflage.

About 9 P.M. that night, Rudolph sauntered across River Street. Root and Fardette were already in the alleyway by Sandy Denslow's livery, armed with shovels and ready to go. Rudolph remembered his own pick. He went back home, retrieved the pick, and returned to the alley only to find that Root had taken off to get a bottle from Manahan's. It was shaping up as a long night, and Root had the right idea. In a moment he returned with a half-pint of whiskey. With their booze and their tools, the men were set. One at a time, Root and Fardette and finally Rudolph discreetly set off for the feeder towpath. Rudolph walked down River Street as casually as if returning from digging a neighbor's cellar. Forestport was a workingman's town, and there was nothing unusual about a man lugging about his work tools. Still, Rudolph kept his guard up, especially when he noticed the canal bank watchman coming down the street.

"I didn't want him to see me, so I crossed over the street," Rudolph said (*People v. Manahan* 1900, 105).

Cautiously Rudolph picked his way through the shadows until he and the oblivious watchman had passed one another. In a few minutes more, Rudolph had made his way across the Black River bridges to Dutch Hill, where the boys awaited him. Rudolph told them of passing the watchman, a cautionary note, and the four men struck off down the dark towpath. For a half-mile or so they walked, their voices subdued. The men knew where they would set about their business. It was a carefully chosen spot, close to where the feeder had broken the year before, and high enough above the Black River that a break might cause maximum damage.

The men dropped their tools on the towpath and fixed their assignments. Murray walked back a hundred yards or so, around a bend toward Dutch Hill, and Fardette proceeded ahead several hundred yards. They would keep the first watch, while Rudolph and Root commenced. The breakers took a pull from Root's whiskey bottle, then set their minds to it.

"And Root and I," Rudolph said, "went to digging."

The two laboring men knew what they were about. Positioning themselves beyond the arc of the other man's swing, they bit into the towpath with the picks until the tamped-down soil was loose and crumbly, then they shoveled it off to the side. They did not worry about making an incriminating pile of dirt. Once the feeder burst open, the water would wash away all evidence. They entered the wordless rhythm soon enough, stopping only briefly to backhand the sweat off their foreheads, or to pull another swallow from the whiskey bottle. They dug a trench about two feet wide and about three feet deep, working from the outside of the towpath in, leaving intact two feet or so of the embankment adjacent to the water's edge. That kept the feeder water safely contained while they excavated into the depths of the towpath. Through the night, while Forestport darkened and settled in for rest, the four men labored. Root and Rudolph worked with a vengeance, digging straight across the towpath until they reached the wooden piling that James J. Dwyer's men had pile-driven down the previous summer. This was the hard stuff, the bony skeleton that would have to be splintered apart before the feeder ruptured.

Rudolph was the first to need a break. He climbed out of the hole he had dug, laid down his pick, and went around the bend to where Fardette sat watch. He directed Fardette to go help Root dig. Obediently Fardette went back down the towpath, but Root, too, had other plans for him. Root told Fardette to continue down the towpath and fetch Murray. Fardette kept walking, another hundred yards or so. Murray handed Fardette the whistle he had brought and set off.

Murray and Root then continued digging, working out a new, deeper ditch on the far side of the piling. They grunted harshly, involuntarily, when their picks bit the packed earth. They rammed the shovel blade into the picked-over crumble and clods, teased it back and forth for a rounded load, and tossed it with a quick twist of the hip off to the side. The palms of their hands reddened and warmed around the handles of the shovel, the pick, the axe. They sweated and swore, and worked as hard and as whiskey driven as the men who two generations before had built the feeder into the Forestport hillside.

When Rudolph felt rested, he returned to where Root and Murray were still digging. Rudolph told them he did not think it was necessary to keep watch on the other side of the towpath. If anyone were to be coming along, it would be from Forestport, Fardette's side. The boys agreed; it was fine with them, one more man to be digging. Rudolph continued down the towpath to where he figured Fardette would be.

There was no one there.

Rudolph kept walking, one hundred yards, two hundred yards. The towpath was empty.

"When I thought I had gone farther than he was, I turned and went back," Rudolph said (*People v. Manahan* 1900, 106).

The two men saw each other then, shades in the unilluminated distance. Eerily, Fardette seemed to have materialized so that he was between Rudolph and the other breakers. It was hard to fathom, but somehow Rudolph had passed by him the first time without seeing. Maybe Fardette had been down off of the towpath, hiding or reclining on the hillside or relieving himself.

Hey, Fardette. A whisper.

Fardette saw the shade walking toward him, fumbled in his pocket, and found Murray's whistle. He did not recognize Rudolph; all he saw was an approaching man. A watchman maybe. Fardette nervously bleated on the whistle, and then he turned and skedaddled down the hillside. He did not stop running until he was back at his mother's home in Forestport, where he shed his incriminating work clothes and fell asleep. Temporarily safe under his covers, he was done with his part of the break.

Murray and Root heard the whistle, dropped their tools, and scrambled from the ditch, seeking safety.

"It scared Root and me," Murray said later. "We went over behind the towpath a little ways from the ditch and laid there" (*People v. Manahan* 1900, 116).

Lying on the steep hillside that sloped to the Black River, Murray peeked over the top of the towpath. He could see the shade of a man coming along. For several minutes, Murray and Root slithered down the hill and waited for the shade to pass. After a time, they worked their way along the hillside a distance and climbed back onto the towpath. Muddy from their hillside scramble, tired from their exertions, and possibly a bit befogged by the whiskey they had been drinking, Murray and Root neared the ditch. Rudolph was down there, already working. They could hear him at his hard labor.

Whatever his vices, Rudolph was a man who took care of business. Not knowing how far his pals might have run, or if they would be returning at all, Rudolph had simply rolled up his sleeves and solitarily resumed the work. He had dug the ditch deep enough and close enough to the feeder's edge that water was filtering out. A trickle, at first, that merely muddied the bottom of the ditch in which Rudolph worked, but the trickle grew, soon sloshing up against the remaining timber piles.

"By the time the boys had come back, I had the water running pretty good," Rudolph said (*People v. Manahan* 1900, 107).

Rudolph told them what had happened, how he had somehow passed Fardette in the dark and been mistaken for a watchman. Trading places, they commenced on a new three-foot-deep hole next to the piling. The dank, buried piles of timber were the last stubborn barrier to a good break. When they had got their new hole ready, just big enough for a man to swing an axe, they began attacking the posts. It was cramped, ragged work, as the men resorted to one tool and then another.

"We chopped and split and pried," Murray said.

"We slivered it up, and pried it out the best we could," Root said (*People v. Manahan* 1900, 117).

The three men kept at it, knowing the feeder itself would become their strongest tool. The men just had to chop and dig enough to give the water its head, to tilt the balance. Their time, however, was about done. Faintly, in the east, the barest tease of light warned the night sky. Spurred on, the men chopped out more of the timber piling. They were spent, but finally the water was rippling out of the feeder, lapping around or over what remained of the timber posts. The break had been set on its inevitable course.

Though some timber posts still impeded the feeder water, the men knew their work was done. It was time to seek cover.

"We dared not stay any longer," Rudolph said (*People v. Manahan* 1900, 107).

Murray, Root, and Rudolph retreated down the towpath toward Boonville. They walked, more or less, west, several hundred yards to the spot where the feeder and the Black River below nearly converged. Then they struck out down the hillside to old Phil McGuire's dam. The river was not high enough to be going over the spillway, but the men still had to take care in crossing. The ten-foot-wide spillway was slick enough to steal their balance and plunge them headfirst to the river below.

One at a time, the men cautiously crossed McGuire's dam on their hands and knees, awkwardly clutching the tools that, fallen into the wrong hands, would be considered evidence. Spied from afar, they might have seemed a pack of animals returning from a night's predations. Once they had reached the Forestport side of the Black River, the shadowed creatures rose to their hind legs and dispersed.

Rudolph, now alone, walked through McGuire's lot and a neighboring barnyard. He squeezed through a fence and in a few minutes more he was at the back of his own house, where his wife, Emma, and the children were still sleeping. He lit a kerosene lamp so he could clean his muddy clothes and brush off his soaked and clodded-up shoes. He scrubbed away until he heard a knock.

"It was Murray," Rudolph said. "Murray said he wanted to come in and tell me where he left the shovels so nobody could see them" (*People v. Manahan* 1900, 107).

Murray, after the men crossed McGuire's dam, had gone straight to Rudolph's house and deposited inside the front hallway the two shovels he had been hauling. After striking off for home, Murray realized he needed to ensure that Rudolph knew where the incriminating tools were, so they might be properly secured. Murray then went around to the rear of Rudolph's house, where he saw the kerosene light by which Rudolph was cleaning. Murray rapped on the back door, and the two men had their final brief conversation of the night. Shortly after, Murray proceeded home and Rudolph slipped into his own bed. Rudolph was drifting there, or asleep, when the dawn fog started lifting and Al Schoonmaker began running down River Street, thinking he was saving the day.

. . .

It happened, the four confessed breakers assured Bearce and the detectives, just like that. The drunken Saturday night gathering in Manahan's place, the postponement of the job until Sunday, Fardette's panicked bleating of the whistle, and the long stretch toward dawn when Murray, Root, and Rudolph hacked away at the old towpath and its underpinnings. The stories told by all four men wove a coherent yarn suitable for hanging.

Their story, though, begged other questions. Accept that Murray, Root, Rudolph, and the skedaddling Fardette were the breakers. Why did they do it? If these four men were only the tools, whose then was the master hand that guided them? These were the questions Oneida County District Attorney Timothy Curtin intended to answer publicly in April 1900.

Chapter 14

THE HONORABLE WATSON T. DUNMORE ruled a reasonable courtroom.

A former school superintendent, he could discipline the unruly. A graduate of Wesleyan University and the Hamilton College law program, he comprehended complicated legal and financial dealings. He could be quick, or he could be patient: one of his cases in private practice had dragged on twenty years before his client won. A Knight Templar and Odd Fellow with fourteen years as a county judge, he knew both the fraternal and the legal codes in which the truth sometimes hid. He was a man of property; he had served, while still on the bench, as an executive of the New York State League of Building and Loan Associations (Wager 1896b, 23). He was also a man of some political assertiveness. Shortly after the Pinkertons hauled Ed Marshall back to Oneida County, Dunmore had asked to meet with Governor Roosevelt. The reasons were not made public.

The morning of Monday, 9 April, was crisp and windblown. The curious drawn to the start of the Forestport trials kept themselves bundled until they were safely inside the forty-nine-year-old Rome courthouse. The back benches of Judge Dunmore's courtroom filled quickly. It had been a long time since such consequential crimes had been brought to justice in Oneida County. At the front of the courtroom, arrayed beneath Dunmore, were defense attorneys Thomas Jones and Josiah Perry. Manahan sat near his nervous wife, Ida, flanked by the attorneys. Ready for the biggest case of his career, District Attorney Curtin sat with Deputy Attorney General John E. Mason. State officials wanted this trial to turn out right.

At 11:30 A.M. Judge Dunmore gaveled his court into session. The trial of Richard J. Manahan had begun.

. . .

First, the lawyers sought Manahan's peers.

The opposing lawyers each held five peremptory challenges. Each could also attempt for-cause challenges, and toward this end Jones and Curtin put their questions through the remainder of Monday afternoon and the start of Tuesday. Had the jurors formed an opinion in the case? Would they convict based on circumstantial evidence? The lawyers asked potential jurors whether they would place confidence in the testimony of an admitted criminal—a key question for a case that rested on the admissions of admitted breakers Rudolph, Murray, Root, and Fardette. Jones wanted to know whether the jurors were prejudiced against men in the liquor trade. That, too, was crucial. Temperance sentiments could indict saloonkeeper Dick Manahan.

The defense and prosecution eventually settled on a jury that included two salesmen from Rome, a machinist from Utica, a quarryman from Prospect, a laborer from Oriskany Falls. They were not a particularly worldly group. One man needed an explanation of the term "accomplice." They were, mostly, farmers: from Camden, Deerfield, Verona, and Vernon Center.

Tuesday afternoon, Timothy Curtin arose for his opening oration. He told the jury how important and unusual the case was. It was important because of the utter disregard for public property shown by the defendants, their scorn for the rights of the state and the people. The canal, he said, belongs to the people of the state of New York, and not to those who choose to disrupt it for their private gain.

For forty-five minutes Curtin sketched his prosecutor's road map. The Forestport levee, after the 1897 break, had been repaired with extra precautions, making it stronger than those of the Erie or Black River canals. It was strong enough to withstand all but the foul human plotting concocted in Manahan's hotel. The state would show how the breakers were overhead conspiring, how they were too intoxicated to complete the work on Saturday night and so put it off to the following Sunday, how the four men skulked off to the towpath and set to digging through the night, interrupted only by Fardette's false alarm. For their work, the men had been promised $25 each.

Here, for the first time, Curtin disclosed the thrust of the state's case. The Forestport breaks were designed, he said, by the town's saloon owners to bring more working men to town. It was a business proposition.

This is a case prosecuted for the clearest of reasons, Curtin summed up: We have, he said, a superintendent of public works who is interested in the *honest* discharge of his duties. It was a new era along the canal, enforced with soldierly rigor by Colonel John Partridge, and the prosecution of the Forestport conspirators would set the example of it. The implied contrast with the old ways of George Aldridge and his ilk was clear to all hearing Curtin's words.

Curtin first marshaled the hydraulic facts. A civil engineer named Albert A. Evans presented a map of the Forestport Feeder, showing how the site of the 1897 levee break was 6,100 feet from the Forestport canal lock. The site of the 1898 break was 6,700 feet. Evans spoke only of what could be measured. The feeder was seven and one-half feet deep and forty-five feet wide. The towpath was thirty-two feet wide on the south side, where it had been broken in 1897, and forty-two feet wide on the north side. Farther along, the towpath was thirty-eight feet wide where broken in 1898. The elevation drop from the towpath's top to the Black River below was sixty-two feet.

About the time the sun was setting, Judge Dunmore adjourned court for the day. Two officers led the jurors out of the courtroom, down the street, and to their rooms in the Arlington House hotel, now doing bang-up business off the trials.

The next morning, Bearce sat watching along with Colonel Partridge, but it took an hour or so before the courtroom's back benches filled with spectators. The engineer's numerical droning of the afternoon before had been dry stuff. Even Manahan appeared disinterested. Engineers and foremen appeared through the morning and early afternoon, describing the disruption at the scene of the 1898 break and the nature of the repairs. The Erie Canal's general inspector, J. Nelson Tubbs, explained that the triple-lap piling installed in the Forestport levee following the 1897 break could not be easily undermined unless water somehow found its way underneath.

"From my examination," Tubbs said, as the *Utica Daily Press* reported on 12 April, "I am unable to say that the break was impossible from natural causes. Very few things are impossible. I should think it improbable, however."

Boonville foreman Eli McClusky described the scene when he arrived about 9 A.M. on the morning of the break. The water was still rushing out of the feeder, and the banks were still crumbling away. When he was able to wade through the upheaved muck to examine the remains of the towpath pilings, he found distinctive marks.

"They were made," McClusky said, according to the *Rome Daily Sentinel* of 12 April, "with a pointed square instrument, like a pick or a timber bar."

Having shaped the clay, Curtin then began breathing life into his case. He summoned Hugh McDonald, the card-playing sharpy familiar with all the gaming men of Forestport. McDonald said he had been living in Forestport in both 1897 and 1898, and had worked in Jimmy Rudolph's pool hall. Jones, knowing what was about to come, periodically tried to trip up the flow of McDonald's story with objections. The objections were, for the most part, routinely dismissed, though the *Utica Daily Press* account of 12 April showed how they allowed the attorneys to snipe away at one another.

"I assume," Curtin sniffed following one objection, "that I know how to examine a witness."

"I don't think," Jones replied, "it is worthwhile to quarrel over the truth of that assumption."

McDonald testified he had been staying in a small room above Rudolph's card room a few nights before the break. Downstairs, Murray, Root, Fardette, and Rudolph were talking. Upstairs, listening through a stovepipe connecting the two floors, happened to be Hugh McDonald.

"An axe and a pick," one of the downstairs men said, "that's what we'll take." McDonald, a curious fellow, began listening more closely.

"There'll be more in this job than the other," Fardette said, as the *Rome Daily Sentinel* reported on 12 April.

The other men grumbled their agreement. They were owed.

"We won't get beat out of our money this time," Rudolph vowed.

The men talked tools and signals: Rudolph said he had a pick in his cellar, and Root pledged an axe he had at home. Two men could keep watch while the other two dug. They would get to the work soon.

"O'Connor and Manahan want this job done right away," Fardette said.

Or so Hugh McDonald testified. He had, however, his own tangled connections to confess. On cross-examination, McDonald identified himself as Jimmy Rudolph's son-in-law. He had entered into the marriage following the 1898 break, when Lulu Rudolph was blossoming at eighteen. And what was it, Jones wanted to know, that you were doing in Forestport?

"I was sporting it," McDonald said, in the *Rome Daily Sentinel* account of 12 April.

"Well, what do you mean by 'sporting it'?"

"I was spending what money I had," McDonald said.

"Was it that, or were you spending other people's money?"

"Any way you please," McDonald said.

"Did you play cards for money?"

"Some of the time, when I felt like it."

"And you felt like it," Jones suggested, "most of the time when you were awake?"

A card cheat was Hugh McDonald, and partner for a time with this Jimmy Rudolph who would soon take the stand as the state's central witness.

"And would you say," Jones asked, "that you are a good fellow now?"

"No," McDonald said, "I would not say that I am a good fellow now."

Jones let the admission settle into the jury's consideration. This, then, was the kind of untrustworthy character summoned by the state: a card cheat, who would be followed by a sordid gaggle of bill-skipping salesmen, ruffians, and admitted lawbreakers.

Howard Fordham, for one. From his early mistaken identification as a Pinkerton detective, to the aborted effort to spirit him away for Forestport justice, Fordham had attracted attention. Now, under oath, he told his full story publicly for the first time.

For the past fourteen years, Fordham said, he had lived in Buffalo and worked as a real estate salesman. For about the same length of time, he had been coming to Forestport, where he had come to know and do business with a number of the town's men. He had organized the Forestport Water Company, with Charley O'Connor as president and Dick Manahan as one of the directors. This commercial venture proved a dry hole, but it showed Fordham's standing in town. Other men were willing to partner with him to make money. He chanced to be staying at Manahan's hotel the night before the 1898 break. He was in town to check on land owned by his sister, from which he had heard reports that timber had been stolen.

Fordham said he retired upstairs about 10 P.M. that Saturday night. Remarkably, his room shared one characteristic with the room used by Hugh McDonald in Jimmy Rudolph's place—both were connected to first-floor rooms by stovepipes that could carry sounds as well as smoke. So it was, Fordham testified, that he could still hear Charley O'Connor, Murray, Root, Fardette, Manahan, and the others. They were talking of the good another break might do the town.

"Dick, a break in the canal would be worth $2,000 to me," O'Connor said, by Fordham's recollection.

"I cleared $750 by teaming and hauling officers down to the last break," Clark said. "If the break happens near the old break, so as to take it out, I can make more than last year."

"If you want to make a break," Manahan said, "why don't you do it? There's $25 in it for you and all the whiskey you want. What are you bellyaching around here for?"

This was it: the Forestport conspiracy, laid bare. Manahan would pay $25 to each for the breakers, and reap in return the business from all the thirsty workingmen brought to town as a result. There had always been men to profit from canal breaks: the Lords of Rochester, the contractors from Utica, the patronage controllers from Albany. The Forestport Feeder break would be cut from this same cloth.

Fordham recounted how the Forestport men were seriously upset Monday with Al Schoonmaker, whose premature alert had stopped the break from cracking wider.

"If that Schoonmaker had kept his mouth shut, the old break would have been washed out," Clark told Fordham.

Manahan agreed. The son of a bitch, he said, ought to be kicked, or worse, for telling of it too soon. That was not quite all. Fordham said that, some months after the 1898 break, he had told Manahan that Charley O'Connor was intimating he might tell someone, possibly Tom Wheeler, who made the break. Manahan, Fordham recalled, jumped from the chair in which he was sitting and swore.

"I knew that he would tell of it to save his own neck," Manahan said, and then he went behind the bar for a consoling drink.

Curtin let the jury consider that final incriminating image, of fleshy, red-eyed Dick Manahan chasing his guilty fears with a whiskey shot. The district attorney was done, for the moment. He sat down, and Thomas Jones arose to confront the dangerous witness. Jones would follow the first rule of cross-examination: if the story displeases, undermine the storyteller.

"Tell me," Jones said, "about this water company that you formed in Forestport."

Fordham then described how Manahan and O'Connor and the other investors had pledged $50 each to capitalize the Forestport Water Company. The venture came to no good. No pipe was ever laid, no water ever transported. Relations turned sour; there was, Fordham acknowledged, a subsequent disagreement with Manahan over a board bill. He denied in sequence a series of accusatory questions. No, he was not intoxicated while in Forestport. Yes, he did drink some. No, he had never offered Ed Marshall $1,000 in gold to tell who made the breaks.

Jones failed to shake the fundamentals of Fordham's story. That Fordham was rather a huckster, the jury could plainly see. But his core story, about overhearing the plotting and the incriminatory statements afterward, remained intact as court adjourned for the day.

The next morning, Al Schoonmaker described the cloudy, wet dawn when he had discovered the break, and George Klinck described his efforts to shut off feeder gates. Then the toughest Forestport man yet to enter the courtroom took the stand, swore to tell the truth, and brought the damnable conspiracy home.

Chapter 15

THE SUMMER OF THE 1897 BREAK, James Rudolph recalled, had been hot for everyone in town. The Forestport hotels and boarding houses were full, and everyone had money to spend. It was a festival remembered, one spring night in 1898, by Rudolph, John Root, and Michael Doyle. The three men were about the bar.

"I would give $25 if there was another break," Michael Doyle said, by Rudolph's remembering.

Manahan's attorneys objected. Michael Doyle was a dead man, in the ground nearly a year. How was it that he could be verbally indicted by the prosecution's witnesses? Dunmore dismissed the objections, and Rudolph continued with his story about the conception of the Forestport plot. With his offer, Michael Doyle became the first Forestport businessman to suggest paying for the break of 1898. Rudolph and Root had no moral compunctions about the proposal, but $25 seemed insufficient for the work.

All right, Michael Doyle said, maybe more money could be got.

The next day, Rudolph testified, Root came to the pool room flush with possibility. He had been busy. He had taken Doyle's proposition and seen Conley, and Bynon, and Clark, and Manahan, and O'Connor; all the Forestport liquor men, and others besides. Several of the men, Root told Rudolph, were willing to join in putting up $25 each for the break. All that was needed was to recruit two others, so there might be two diggers and two watchers. The deal was struck, and the levee, in time, was broken.

River Street, Forestport, ca. 1911. Photographer unknown. *Courtesy of Dorothy Mooney.*

But once the work itself was done, Rudolph testified, the breakers could not collect their due. The morning of the break, Charles O'Connor told Rudolph he had no money with which to pay his $25 share. Rudolph then encountered John Conley, who also begged off.

"I can't pay just now," Conley told Rudolph, "I've been on a big drunk, and have no money."

One after another, the Forestport co-conspirators ducked their obligations. Walt Bynon said he would forgive Frank Murray the $8 saloon debt that Murray owed, but beyond that, Bynon could afford to give no more. Clark the liveryman, too, said he would forgive a debt owed by Rudolph, but would have no cash to give. Manahan paid some amount to John Root, and when Rudolph came calling looking for his share, he was told to get it from Root. Michael Doyle paid Rudolph $5 and Murray another $2.50. As soon as he made more, Michael promised, he would pay the rest, but apparently he never did.

The vaunted Forestport conspiracy sounded, in Rudolph's telling, more slapdash than terrifying. The dime-novel dramas hinted at by Colonel Partridge in his pretrial newspaper interviews—the suggestions of secret passwords, and Mafia-like gangs, and even murder—were nowhere substantiated in Rudolph's testimony of unpaid debts, broken promises, and drunken men loudly singing their plans.

But however threadbare, the Forestport plotting as retold by Rudolph was still enough to send men to Auburn. When Curtin had finished with his questioning, Jones immediately began undermining the witness's character. Rudolph had much to admit to. Yes, he had once served six months in jail for assault; but, no, he had not helped Ed Scoville escape from that same jail. He had simply kept his mouth shut while Ed broke out. Yes, he had been in business with the cardsharp Hugh McDonald; but no, he had not been aware that McDonald was marking the cards he played with. Yes, he once had a saloon in the town of Wilmurt; but no, he did not have a license for it.

Jones then began probing the circumstances that led Rudolph into the state's hands. Rudolph said he had talked several times with the Pinkerton men, the first time being in Johnstown when detective John J. Pender had visited. Once arrested, Rudolph had been kept in the main Rome jail for a time before being brought to the more spacious upstairs.

"How were you fed upstairs?" Jones asked.

Curtin objected. Of what possible interest could Mr. Rudolph's dining habits be?

"I propose," Jones replied, according to the *Rome Daily Sentinel* of 12 April, "to show that this man's evidence is a product of one of the foulest plots ever concocted."

The rhetorical match was now even. The Forestport breaks were either, as the prosecutors claimed, a result of one of the most damnable conspiracies in the history of the state; or, as Jones put it, the prosecution was a foul concoction of historic proportions. Substantively, Jones meant to suggest that Rudolph and the other witnesses were bought off by favored treatment: clean sheets and a good steak. Judge Dunmore, however, would have none of it, and after a few more questions Rudolph stepped down without ever divulging his Rome diet.

Curtin next introduced Joseph Casbacker of Port Leyden. Casbacker had worked on both the 1897 and 1898 Forestport levee repairs, and for two months had kept bar at Manahan's saloon. The breaks, by Casbacker's account recorded in the *Boonville Herald* of 19 April, were a subject of near-constant discussion. So, Casbacker queried Manahan, the breaks are a good thing for Forestport?

"If it wasn't for the breaks," Manahan said, "we would starve."

Another time, a man greeted Manahan cheerfully and asked, "Dick, when are you going to have another break?"

"Oh, pretty soon, I guess," Manahan said.

Curtin continued with his parade of confessed criminals. Frank Murray related his version of the breaks and recalled how he had contemplated the possibility of using dynamite to blow out the levee. Bynon and Clark, pragmatists both, had replied that they did not care how the break was done just so long as it got done. The men's voices were rising in Manahan's saloon, dangerously so.

"You are a lot of fools for talking so loud," Michael Doyle told the men that Saturday night, and then, Murray recalled, Michael stood up and went home.

Murray allowed under cross-examination that jail conditions had improved once he, Rudolph, and Root were moved upstairs. Each of the men, after they had begun talking to the investigators, had been given the luxury of a separate room, the wandering space of a hallway, and a pack of cards for their amusement.

It had already been a full day, but Curtin pressed on once Murray stepped down. Tom Wheeler took the stand to describe the feeder repairs, but he was also a reminder of how canal business was done. He had to submit to some impertinent questions on cross-examination concerning his business dealings with the contractor James Dwyer. Some men had been suggesting Wheeler was Dwyer's silent partner in the deal to repair the 1898 Forestport break. Wheeler angrily denied it. His last partnership with Dwyer, he said, had been to fill in the old Chenango Canal back in 1888, when Wheeler was Oneida County sheriff.

John Fardette took the stand. Like Rudolph and Murray before him, he described how the little gang had come together and then how, once the work was done, there proved precious little loot to be divided.

Fardette, though he had fled early on the night of the break, still expected payment from the Forestport saloon owners. A deal was a deal. So he asked, several days after the break, what Manahan was going to give him. Manahan, Fardette testified, replied that he had already given Root $10.

"I said," the skeptical Fardette testified, according to the *Utica Daily Press* of 13 April, "that it was strange that Root had not spoken of it."

Still, dutifully, Fardette asked his co-conspirator about the money.

"What Manahan says is a damn lie," Root told Fardette, "and I'll be damned if I'm going to go see him."

In the end, Fardette said, he received $2 from the liveryman Bill Morrell and $10 from the hotelkeeper John Conley. This was less than half of what he believed to be his fair share: $25, for one night's work.

"So," Jones pressed on cross-examination, "you would consider $25 fair compensation for committing a felony?"

"I did not know," Fardette blandly replied, "that it was a crime. If I had, I would not have assisted in the work."

Jones turned then to Fardette's criminal history. Yes, Fardette acknowledged, he had once stolen oats. And yes, he said, he had once paid money for some stolen turkeys—but, Fardette distinguished, he had not done the actual stealing itself.

John Root was the last of the breakers to take the stand. The longtime Forestport resident described his conversations with the town's saloonkeepers and their debate over the best location for making the break. Manahan and Bynon argued for a point somewhere beyond the waste weir, but the liveryman Clark had another idea. The farther from town the break occurred, he said, the more rigs he would be able to rent out to the state.

It was close to dinnertime, and the sun was nearly expired outside. Curtin, though, had one more point to draw out before sending the jurors back to the Arlington House hotel for the night.

"What happened," Curtin wondered, "when you learned Pinkerton men were prowling through Forestport?" Each of the four breakers pledged their silence to one another; but one day, Root said, they heard that Charley O'Connor had squealed.

"I went down to see O'Connor and asked him if he had told on us," Root recalled. "He said that it was a damn lie."

The next morning, Root described on cross-examination how he had been walking by Manahan's hotel several weeks after the break. Manahan was standing in the front door and called him over. "Here's $10," Manahan said. "It's all I can afford, because I haven't made that much from the breaks." Root kept the money himself; he had no recollection of denying to Fardette that he had been paid. For Jones, seeking every vulnerability he could find in the prosecution's case, this was a small but telling point. The jurors had now heard two of the prosecution's star witnesses contradict each other over the $10 paid by Manahan. Fardette recalled asking Root about the money; Root recalled no such discussion. One of them had to be lying. Where, then, did the lies stop?

Curtin rested his case at about 10:30 in the morning. A ten-minute break gave lawyers a chance to compose themselves and jurors a chance to briefly reflect on what they had heard for the past four days. It looked bad for Dick Manahan. The state's four primary witnesses had named him as a chief instigator of the breaks conspiracy in which they confessed their own involvement. The confessed breakers might be unsavory, but their testimony had stood up.

But now it was the defense's turn, and the jurors would hear lapel-grabbing, table-thumping courtroom rhetoric at its most florid. Though it had been Thomas Jones who had been most active in objecting and cross-examining so far, the defense's opening statement would be delivered by his partner, Josiah Perry.

"These men who confessed are drunkards and not reliable in any way," Perry declared from the outset. "Would it not be foolish for Manahan, Bynon, and Clark to trust such men?"

As if the Forestport Social and Literary Union ladies were better suited for breaking open the feeder. But no matter. Perry lavished special attention on the man most central to the state's investigation. Howard Fordham, Perry said, is the worst kind of freebooter. He was drunk all the time in Forestport, when he supposedly overhead conversations about a coming break. He had a grudge against Manahan, besides, because he owed the hotelkeeper for an unpaid board bill. As to the break itself, Perry noted that it had been raining in the days prior to the levee's collapse. The sandy soil along the bank had caved in in several places. The break could easily have resulted from natural causes. But it certainly was not a break sought and paid for by Dick Manahan, a family man of good character.

"His wife and children are in court," Perry said. "Not for sympathy, but because this is their place, beside the husband and father who is foully accused."

Perry followed his stirring statement with a handful of banal witnesses: bank watchmen and others supporting the defense claim that slipping sand had dammed up the canal and forced water over the towpath.

With the one-time bartender Billy Gorman, Perry entered the core of his case. Gorman in 1898 had been working for Manahan. He had been in the saloon all night on the Saturday prior to the break and said neither Manahan nor anyone else, within Gorman's hearing, had talked about causing trouble. In an unexplained coincidence, Gorman related that he had quit work in Manahan's saloon following an unspecified "unpleasant incident" occurring the very day the 1898 break was discovered.

Ed Marshall—the tale-telling wild man of the woods—followed Gorman to the stand. Ed had been out of the public's eye since the Pinkertons released him from jail, and his appearance was an odd turn. First he had been accused by Fordham of being one of the Forestport breakers, based on his own exaggerated yarns, and now he was speaking for Manahan's defense. He was a roll of the dice for the defense.

Marshall said he had been driving logs for the Forestport Lumber Company in the days before the break. By mid-May, the Adirondack logs had been corralled and the river drive was done, and Marshall was rooming on the third floor of Manahan's hotel. On the Saturday before the break, Marshall said, he had gone the rounds of Forestport. He had stopped off for a drink at Doyle's saloon and eventually ended up back at Manahan's, where he shared a drink with Howard Fordham. Never, Marshall said, had he heard any talk about causing a break.

Marshall stepped down momentarily so that Alonzo Denton, the upright Forestport lumberman, could testify. Denton was the backbone of Forestport society. He had been in business for thirty years and had employed in that time many men. Rudolph, he said, had worked for him seven or eight years earlier. Rudolph did not have a very good reputation in town, he said, and he would not believe him even if he spoke under oath. Fardette, too, was said by Denton to have a bad reputation in town and should not be believed. The same went for Root and Murray.

But the state, too, had some questions, and Denton, a truthful man, would answer them. People in Forestport, he said, had certainly been discussing the four confessed breakers a great deal. They were considered bad men, Denton reported, but the reason had nothing to do with their turkey-stealing, card-playing, hard-drinking pasts.

"People in Forestport," Denton testified, according to the *Boonville Herald* of 19 April, "thought they were bad fellows for telling."

Upstanding Alonzo Denton had just revealed Forestport's hidden bond. Everyone in town benefited from the breaks, no matter their cause. Denton himself had sold a good deal of lumber to the state for use in repairs. Curtin drew the lumberman into acknowledging that he had begun hearing bad things about the four confessed breakers only after word of their confessions had gotten around.

John Potter, insurance salesman and part-time justice of the peace, followed Denton to the stand. He knew each of the confessed breakers; with the exception of Murray, he said, they were not to be trusted.

Curtin pounced on cross-examination, reminding Potter that he had done business with Manahan. He had signed, at Manahan's request, the papers ordering the questionable arrest of Howard Fordham. He had been to Manahan's saloon both before and after the arrest, and to Doyle's place, and Conley's too.

"But Mr. Curtin," Potter protested stiffly, "I am not a drinking man."

With every defense witness, another Forestport layer was peeled back. Perry summoned his witnesses to repeat a simple refrain: Rudolph and the breakers were known to be bad men, and their testimony was not to be trusted. Only on cross-examination were the other truths revealed.

Manahan's lawyers summoned the hotelkeeper Charley O'Connor. He was on the spot. He wanted to help Manahan, but he was also facing his own liability. Measuring his words carefully, he related how he had managed the Getman House hotel from about 1891 to 1897. Since his marriage to the former Mrs. Getman, he had started a new hotel. He had spent considerable time at Manahan's hotel, but he had never heard men talking about causing the break. He did not hear Manahan urge others to cause the break. None of the incriminating conversations related by the prosecution's witnesses had occurred within O'Connor's earshot.

Curtin, when it was his turn, wanted to know more. Had not O'Connor stated once that he had made several thousand dollars off of the increased bar business from the break? O'Connor denied the sum, while admitting he had made some money. Most had, in Forestport.

"The break," O'Connor said, according to the 14 April *Rome Daily Sentinel*, "was a good thing for the town."

When O'Connor stepped down, the most delicate moment of the trial arrived. Dick Manahan had decided to speak in his own behalf. He would need to tell a good story if he were to avoid Auburn State Prison.

His own attorney gently introduced the jurors to the innocent side of Dick Manahan. He was married, with three children, the youngest of whom was barely ten months old. He had started off in the working world when he was but twelve and living in Utica. When his family moved to Forestport two years later, Dick had worked on the canals during the summer and in the woods during the winter until he was twenty-one years old. He was a responsible man, running in succession the hotel at Buffalo Head, a livery in Lowville, and a hotel in Boonville before moving back to Forestport and buying the old Getman House.

With his character burnished, Manahan then began erecting his denials one on top of another. He had heard nothing in advance of the 1898 break's occurring. Certainly he had not offered to chip in his own money to help make a break. Though he knew Root, he had never had anything to do with him, or Rudolph, or Fardette. He knew Murray from when he had hired him to build a solid stone wall at the old Buffalo Head hotel, but that was the sum of their business dealings.

Curtin had been anticipating Manahan's cross-examination for a long time. The district attorney was confident of his own ability to dismantle a defendant, and with the Pinkertons' help he had identified several likely avenues of attack. He stood and appraised the accused, letting Manahan sweat a little.

Curtin then demanded to know what had happened the previous January, when Manahan had obtained a warrant for Howard Fordham's arrest. Suspicious timing, the district attorney suggested, to seek Fordham's arrest just when the Buffalo man was preparing to testify before the grand jury. Manahan insisted it was a coincidence. He had not known Fordham was going to be presenting evidence against him. He had obtained the warrant lawfully, and for legitimate reasons had accompanied Constable Nightingale to Rome. He stood by at night, then, in the Arlington House hotel's corridor while Nightingale tried to serve the warrant.

Didn't you fear, Curtin asked with barbed humor, that Mr. Fordham might have been lost if brought back to Forestport so late at night?

It was a matter of justice, Manahan repeated. Fordham owed him money, and he had to pay. Nothing dark should be read into his decision to quickly depart the Arlington House hotel once he spied the Pinkerton man known as Brooks. Manahan said he simply wanted to go home.

The jurors, because of prior newspaper accounts, had reason to think otherwise—and Curtin knew it. It was hard for anyone to forget the stories from several months back, alleging without evidence that Forestport men had planned to throw Fordham from the midnight train.

Through Saturday afternoon, Manahan spoke more of his business. Usually, he said, he would sell two to four barrels of ale a week. Curtin reminded Manahan he had bought nineteen barrels of ale shortly before the 1898 break. Curtin rustled the bills, further reminding Manahan of the seven hundred pounds of foodstuffs hauled in from Buffalo Head station shortly before the break. Manahan admitted he had never before bought so much ale or so many canned goods.

Manahan finished shortly before 3 P.M. on Saturday afternoon, and the court soon after recessed to return Monday. He had acquitted himself reasonably well. He had told his story and exposed the better aspects of his character, and had not collapsed during the cross-examination. But, in truth, the state had presented a strong case. The confessions of the four breakers and the testimony of Howard Fordham fairly pinned Manahan and the other saloonkeepers. Manahan's own actions, moreover, seemed suspicious at the least. The late-night visit to Fordham's hotel and the sudden departure smelled of dark plotting. The fortuitous purchase of ale and canned goods shortly before the breaks suggested advance planning. If Manahan were to remain a free man, his lawyers would have to spin some wondrous last words.

At 9:30 on Monday morning, Manahan's attorneys returned briefly to the witness Ed Marshall. He recounted, again, how Fordham had offered him $1,000 to tell of who had made the breaks.

"I can't tell you if you gave me $10,000," Marshall replied, by his recollection.

"You name anyone," Fordham assured him, "and we will furnish the proof against them."

It was an incredible statement, recorded in the *Boonville Herald* of 19 April. It sounded, indeed, fitting for a tale told around campfires or wood-stoves, and Curtin, in his brief cross-examination, brought out Marshall's tradition of tale-telling. No, Marshall said, it was not true that he had bit the tails off of snakes in the Adirondack woods; but yes, it was the case that people said he had. Yes, he himself told stories at times.

One other thing, Curtin wanted to know. Where are you staying in Forestport, since your return from Michigan?

At Manahan's, Ed Marshall replied.

. . .

Thomas S. Jones was ready for the final act. The jury was an audience to be won over, with facts if the facts were on his side, and with words and bombast if the facts were unhelpful. At ten o'clock he faced the twelve Oneida County men who had heard all the facts and the reporters from Boonville, Utica, and Rome who had been taking it all down.

"We are here," Jones said, "to consider whether this man, who has shown himself honest and industrious, who has shown himself a man among man, is guilty of a crime against the state, which has been hounded by this army of Pinkertons."

Simply mentioning the name Pinkertons evoked the workingman's memory of Homestead, the railroad strikes, the infiltration of the unions. They were ruthless tools, not to be trusted any more than the pack of scoundrels who, by their own admission, had caused the break by their own hands.

Jones allowed that he was "amused at the little slender thread of evidence" presented by the prosecution. This notion that Manahan's guilt was proven by his prescient ordering of beer and canned goods made no sense. Did it not stand to reason the saloonkeeper would have waited till the day of the break before ordering the goods? With two trains running to Forestport every day, it would have been a snap to bring up whatever was needed. Only an innocent man would do something that looked as guilty as stocking up before a break.

"Manahan," Jones assured the jurors, "has never been accused of being an idiot or an insane man. If he had been looking for a break and placed these orders as he did, he should be in an asylum."

The four confessed breakers came in for special attention. They were blackhearts and scoundrels, every last one: Rudolph, who spent time in jail for assault; Fardette, charged with stealing oats and accepting stolen turkeys; Root, who stole the turkeys; Hugh McDonald, the card cheat.

"These four fellows," Jones said bitingly, "recited their concocted stories like a class which they had rehearsed while in jail living on the fat of the land. While the other prisoners downstairs lived on mush and bread and water for committing some petit larceny, these felons dressed nicely and conspired with the state to send an honest man to prison."

And Fordham. He began, this Fordham, as a promoter of Kansas lands, selling worthless property to trusting men. His shady business then in Buffalo must not have been doing well, though, because he had the time to hover about in Forestport, time, supposedly, to overhear Forestport men of a Saturday night discussing the break to come. But that made no sense whatsoever. Would men plotting such a deed shout out their criminal intentions in a crowded saloon? And Fordham, if he were an honest man hearing such intentions, why would he not have warned the canal authorities?

As the morning ended, Jones turned to Manahan himself. Here was a man who had forthrightly taken the stand, who had never taken a penny from his brother man dishonestly. An honest, industrious man, whom the state was now trying to convict on this trumped-up evidence.

"It has been said," Jones summed up at the end of two hours, "that it is far better that 99 guilty men should go unpunished than one innocent man should suffer. I leave this case to you, in the belief that before God this man is absolutely innocent."

It was high noon when Thomas Jones settled back down at the defense table. He had raised as much dust as was lawyerly possible. Even so, the logic of his case appeared flimsy. He seemed to be offering two mutually exclusive theories for what had happened on the Forestport towpath: either water had worked its natural way across the sandy levee and undermined it, or Rudolph and the other breakers had caused the damage themselves and then sought to divert blame elsewhere. But if the levee had broken naturally, as Jones had repeatedly suggested, then why would Rudolph and his little gang take credit for it?

Shortly after 2 P.M., Curtin rose for the most closely watched closing argument of his legal career. Throughout the week, a representative of Attorney General Davies had monitored the progress. For those not in the courtroom, the *Rome Daily Sentinel* of 18 April carried all the details.

"There is no case," Curtin began, "paralleling this in viciousness and wantonness. There is no case on record which shows such a total disregard for the rights of the state and the people."

The stakes thus clarified, Curtin spoke of the solidity of the Forestport levee. It was a bank that had stood for years until 1897; a break, he added, that the state would generously assume came about naturally. When the state had completed its 1897 repairs, the Forestport levee was even more indomitable than before: strengthened by piling and the piling backed by another twenty feet of packed earth. It was built to last. Curtin then moved to defend the integrity of his own case. The defense, with its insinuations, had attacked the state's witnesses and had charged there was a buying of testimony.

"Could I pay $1,000 to any man?" Curtin asked. "I have to give an account for every dollar I spend, and it is the same with Colonel Partridge."

Character was central to Curtin's case, as it had been for the defense. And though the defense had assailed Rudolph and the others, the prosecutor said he would gladly contrast them with the dissipated Manahan.

"I would be willing," Curtin said, "to put Root, Murray, and Fardette side by side with Manahan, and I am willing to say that any stranger would pick one before Manahan."

Curtin revisited Manahan's night trip to the Arlington House hotel. The district attorney suggested it was damningly simple. The defendant Manahan perjured himself before the Forestport justice of the peace in order to obtain the warrant for Fordham's arrest. Curtin conjured the image of Manahan and the constable Nightingale, skulking through Rome to spirit away a threat.

"They were afraid of Fordham," he said. "They thought that if they could silence Fordham they would be safe."

Consider the nineteen barrels of ale and seven hundred pounds of groceries, Curtin urged the jury, all bought conveniently just before the breaks occurred. The invoices proved the purchases, and no one could deny them: the seventy-pound case of tomatoes, the ninety pounds of corn, the forty-pound case of salmon, the one hundred-pound case of pickles. Manahan bought all that because he knew he would be needing it.

"If these breaks continue," Curtin concluded, "the Canal might as well be abandoned. Take this case, gentlemen, and do with it as you feel is your duty."

The district attorney sat down, after having spoken for barely an hour. He had summed up his case in roughly half the time taken by the defense, and without the same rhetorical glossing. It was a sign of confidence. The weight of evidence was clearly on the state's side.

The jury attended to Judge Dunmore's instructions for the next twenty minutes before retiring. It was four o'clock in the afternoon, and the shadows were gathering. The spectators slowly scattered, considering the fine points of what they had heard. Dick and Ida Manahan huddled with the defense lawyers and accepted whatever reassurances could be offered. For the next six and one-half hours, everyone waited while the salesman, the quarryman, the laborer, and the farmers decided Dick Manahan's fate.

Some jurors declared from the start that Manahan was guilty, and over the course of the next few hours other jurors became persuaded of the same thing, but unanimity was elusive. Foreman Fred Clark of Rome tried guiding them through the vexing questions, but by 10:30 that night the jurors advised Dunmore they remained divided.

The jury continued working. At 1 A.M. the vote was still stuck at nine to three for conviction. It was a tense night for everyone, and the jurors got little if any sleep. All day Tuesday, in a room grown stale, they continued picking through the conflicts, while a few holdouts seemed unheeding of the evidence.

"You could not touch them with any argument," one juror recounted in the *Utica Daily Press* of 18 April.

Finally, at 4:50 on Tuesday afternoon, after nearly twenty-four hours of exhausting deliberations, Fred Clark the foreman gave up. No amount of extra time would avail. He sent word back to Judge Dunmore, and led his men back into court. When they had settled, Clark reported that the jury was deadlocked. Dunmore asked if there were any prospect of agreement. Clark said no, and apologized.

"I am not blaming you," Dunmore assured him. "It is one of those things that cannot be helped."

Curtin did not mask his frustration. He had much riding on the case. If he failed with Manahan, the core conspirator, the other dozen Forestport defendants might slip away as well. There was no question about his next move: he would retry Manahan, as soon as possible.

Manahan departed Rome Tuesday evening, not entirely free. Though the Forestport boys shook his hand on his arrival, welcoming good old Dick back from the clutches of the Pinkertons, he still felt the imminence of his retrial.

Back in Judge Dunmore's courtroom, after Manahan's jury was sent home, the lawyers kept haggling. Josiah Perry, representing William Clark and Walt Bynon, urged the judge to postpone any further trials.

Curtin, fuming over seeing Manahan walk unshackled from the courtroom, shook his head. There were too many delays being sought. Clark was not ready, nor Bynon, and saloonkeeper John Conley, another future defendant, was starting to plead infirmity.

"He's suffering from the same disease as Bynon," Curtin said unsympathetically, "and that is too much liquor."

Dunmore said the matters would rest until 30 April, when the district attorney might move to proceed with Manahan's retrial. Once the state had disposed of Manahan, Bynon and then Clark would be addressed. The lawyers agreed, and it was done. For the next two weeks, Judge Dunmore's courtroom would lie dormant, before men would try once more to settle Dick Manahan's fate.

Chapter 16

ON MONDAY, 30 APRIL, Judge Dunmore welcomed the lawyers back to his courtroom. It had been a busy two weeks since the first trial ended. Beyond Rome, the Republican maneuvering for the upcoming presidential convention consumed Platt, Roosevelt, and others. George Aldridge, already recovering his political footing after his canal humiliations, had been running delegates at the Republicans' state convention. Roosevelt had been steadfastly resisting the push by Platt and the state's corporations to slide him out of Albany and into the vice presidency. The canal was near opening.

In Rome, both sides had been preparing for the rematch. Curtin and his investigators riffled again through the dog-eared evidence, culling additional witnesses. Jones consulted with Manahan, who had tried despite his distractions to keep his Forestport saloon running as the Forestport Feeder readied for the 15 May opening.

That Monday morning, Manahan summoned himself upright for the jury's consideration. The lawyers straightened their papers and nodded their readiness. Thirty-eight men summoned for the jury pool waited their turn for questioning. Spectators filled out the room. They knew the script, but they could not know the improvisations to come. Almost immediately, though, the character of the new trial made itself apparent.

"Assume that this defendant kept a hotel and sold liquor," Jones said to the first potential juror called. "Would that create a prejudice in your mind against him, and would you have a prejudice against a man engaged in that business" (*People v. Manahan* 1900, 15)?

"A slight prejudice," admitted Mr. D.S.V. Gardiner, a farmer from Vienna.

But to the dismay of Jones, Gardiner's acknowledged prejudice did not matter in Judge Dunmore's courtroom. The judge, who had frankly expressed his frustration at the first mistrial, seemed eager to move justice along. Repeatedly the judge denied Jones's efforts to reject jurors on the basis of prejudice. Gardiner, over Jones's protests, took the first seat in the jury box.

J. D. Pierce of Bridgewater said he had read the accounts of the first trial. He had subsequently formed certain convictions about Dick Manahan.

"The fact that a man is indicted and charged with having committed a crime would create some prejudice in my mind against him," Pierce acknowledged, adding, "I don't like the liquor business" (*People v. Manahan* 1900, 17, 19).

It did not matter.

Doubly prejudiced, his head filled with the newspaper accounts of Manahan's last trial and his sober mind soured against saloonkeepers, Pierce was nonetheless retained. It quickly became obvious that the jury pool was widely infected with information. The saturation coverage of Manahan's first trial made it virtually impossible to find jurors who were innocent of the case. Tom McCarthy of Rome said he, too, held an opinion based on the accounts in the *Rome Daily Sentinel.* Like Pierce, he admitted to being prejudiced against those charged with a crime.

Jones sought to exclude McCarthy, but Dunmore let him stay. Another potential juror bluntly stated that, given the prejudices he had coming into the case, he would find Manahan guilty even if left with some doubt at trial's end. It did not matter. Another likewise conceded he had formed an opinion from his newspaper readings. It would take additional evidence, he said, for that opinion to be reversed. It did not matter. Dunmore rejected the defense's challenge on grounds of bias, and Jones was forced to use up one of his peremptory challenges.

After fifteen potential jurors had been questioned, and five accepted,

Dunmore adjourned. The next day, 1 May, questioning dragged on. Jones exhausted all his peremptory challenges. George Parkhurst of Oriskany was dismissed after admitting he had previously said what others thought—that the Forestport break was rooted in the larger Erie Canal scandals.

"They began at the wrong end to try the cases," Parkhurst said; the real beginning, he was quoted as saying in the *Rome Daily Sentinel* of 1 May, was in Albany.

Parkhurst was dismissed. Finally, at the end of the second full day, the twelfth juror was seated. Jones's efforts notwithstanding, it was a panel engineered for conviction. There were eight farmers, a shoemaker, a laborer, an inspector, and a clerk. Many had followed the day-to-day coverage of the first trial; some held liquor sellers in disfavor, some would require additional evidence to grant Manahan's innocence. The burden of proof had perversely shifted. It would now be up to Manahan to disprove the state's case and dislodge the assumptions planted in the jury's mind. When Timothy Curtin stood at 5:10 in the afternoon of Wednesday, 2 May, for his opening statement, every juror already knew too much about Dick Manahan from Forestport.

Curtin had also honed his arguments. He laid out for the new jury a clear road map toward conviction. It went like this: The Forestport conspirators, having learned in 1897 how lucrative a break could be, concocted their plans for another one in 1898. Dick Manahan, the liquor seller, had prepared himself with his incriminating pre-break purchases of booze and food.

Curtin again drew first upon the engineering witnesses to explain the workings of the Forestport Feeder. Manahan's attorneys, through periodic objections, insinuated that the engineers were part of a Pinkerton plot to railroad an innocent man. Judge Dunmore usually sustained Curtin. Dunmore had had enough of Thomas Jones's bombastic courtroom flourishes.

With Colonel Partridge watching Wednesday afternoon, Curtin retrieved cardsharp Hugh McDonald. McDonald again spun out his story of overhearing his father-in-law James Rudolph and three others discuss making the break. He explained that he had not alerted anyone about the pending break because he did not want to interfere with what he thought was an all-but-accepted practice. But under a cross-examination captured in the 3 May edition of the *Rome Daily Sentinel,* he was compelled to describe his own card-cheating schemes.

"You played there with your friends using marked cards, did you?" Jones asked.

"I don't know that I had any friends there," McDonald said.

"Well," Jones said, "I guess that is so."

On Thursday morning Curtin ushered in new witnesses, including a Forestport-area postmaster named Enos Crandall. He had heard talk on the Saturday night before the 1898 break, among Manahan and the other accused men, about how commercially beneficial canal breaks could be. But as he conceded on cross-examination, Crandall shared Manahan's sentiment.

"I said a good many times myself that a break made lively times," Crandall said (*People v. Manahan* 1900, 81).

Howard Fordham followed Crandall, and for nearly two hours repeated his testimony of the first trial: he was staying at Manahan's the Saturday night before the break, in the second-floor room directly above the hotel office. A stovepipe carried Manahan's words upstairs.

"He said, 'if you boys want to go and make a break, why in hell don't you go ahead and make it and not be belly-aching around here. There is $25 apiece in it for you, and what whiskey you want,' " Fordham recalled (*People v. Manahan* 1900, 89).

Defense attorney Jones pounced in a lengthy cross-examination, forcing Fordham to concede he had had five or six beers on the Saturday before the break. He acknowledged his vaporous pipe dreams—the real estate, the water company, the electric rail service to North Lake. The Forestport Water Company, in particular, was dissected, to suggest the tensions that had arisen between Fordham and his former Forestport partners.

Though the courtroom had thinned out during the dry engineering presentations of the day before, it filled back up when court reconvened on Thursday afternoon following Fordham's tour on the stand. The witness Jimmy Rudolph was bound to entertain.

"Michael Doyle was the first one that spoke to me about it in his place," Rudolph said. "He said, 'if there was another break tonight, I would give $25 in the morning. Why don't you go to work and make one?' I said, 'It is too late; besides, one man cannot make a break [and] $25 is not enough anyway.'

"Just then," Rudolph went on, "Root came in. [Doyle] said, 'There is Root, why don't you get him to help you?' I said, 'I don't know how Root would take it.' He said, 'I'll call him over and see what he thinks about it.' He told Root the same as he told me; he said, 'I was just telling Jim that I would give $25 for another break' " (*People v. Manahan* 1900, 101).

" 'I will tell you what I will do,' he says," Rudolph said. " 'I will go down and see the rest of the whiskey fellows and report. I will see Charles O'Connor and tell him to go and see Dick for me. He will tell him, and as soon as I hear from him I will tell you all about it.' "

There was still more to Jimmy Rudolph that Jones brought out on cross-examination. When the question was put, Rudolph finally peeled back another layer that had been cloaking the Forestport Feeder.

"I helped make the break of '97," Rudolph said. "I and John Fardette and William Evans made it" (*People v. Manahan* 1900, 109).

It was now official. Until this moment, the 1897 Forestport Feeder collapse had been cast as just one of the inevitable breakdowns along the Erie Canal system. Now, with Rudolph's testimony, the human plotting was shown to stretch further than anyone had previously alleged. Conspiracy, not chance, had caused the Forestport Feeder to break open three years running.

Rudolph, after muddying himself with the 1897 levee-busting, said he profited from "thirty-five or forty" boarders he and his wife put up at his River Street pool hall. After Rudolph concluded his testimony Thursday afternoon, Fardette added his own sullen confession about the 1897 affair. The *Rome Daily Sentinel* of 4 May captured the exchange:

"Didn't you tell me on the other trial that you never committed a felony before making the break of '98?" Jones asked Fardette on cross-examination.

"No," Fardette said.

"Why didn't you tell of making the '97 break then?"

"I wasn't asked," Fardette replied.

Fardette, as on the first trial, spelled out how he had been drawn into the 1898 conspiracy. It had not taken much convincing; things were dull, and he needed the money. Indeed, as Fardette recalled it, there seemed to be a standing offer around Forestport. He testified that William Clark the liveryman "had told me he would be willing to give $10 any time I was willing to make a break," while Conley "said he was willing to give $25 any time a break was made."

But John Root, it had become clear, had played a central role in pulling the conspirators together. Michael Doyle may have been the first to mention paying for the 1898 break, and James Rudolph may have captained the crew of breakers, but it was Root who roped in the Forestport businessmen. He took the stand Friday morning, while a freakish May snowstorm swirled outside.

Root said he had heard all the saloon boys—Manahan, Bynon, Conley—agreeing that another feeder break would do them well. Bynon had been boasting that he had cleared $700 during the 1897 break, and he and Manahan both sounded ready to pay for another. Root, advised of Michael Doyle's offer, told Rudolph he would recruit the other businessmen. He knew their inclinations.

"I asked [Rudolph] if he meant what he said about making a break, and he said yes," Root testified. "Then I went to see Bynon, and asked him if he meant what he said about making a break, and he said he did. I told him that Manahan and Doyle said they would agree to give $25 to make a break, and he said he would give the same" (*People v. Manahan* 1900, 130).

Root was rolling by the time he got to Charley O'Connor. He told him that Bynon, Manahan, and Doyle all said they would give $25 to make a break. O'Connor joined up quickly.

Liveryman William Clark told Root that he would pitch in what he could. He also offered some technical recommendations. If the break were made far from town, then Clark would be able to rent out more rigs and wagons.

Having recruited at least five contributors, Root consulted with Rudolph. They agreed Frank Murray and John Fardette would be good men for the job. But after the breakers had worked all night to dig through the canal levee, nothing had happened as it was supposed to. Manahan slipped Root $10 and said that was all he could afford to give. The other liquor boys likewise welshed on their end of the bargain. The only thing everyone agreed on was that Al Schoonmaker deserved punishment for having called the alarm too damned soon. Root, under questioning, recalled Manahan's fuming at a saloon near the Buffalo Head railroad station.

"He was talking about Schoonmaker, and what a sneak he was for hollering," Root said. "Manahan said he ought to kill him. He wished somebody would kill him."

Jones could not shake Root's testimony on cross-examination. The most the defense attorney could do was illuminate the witness's character.

"I take a drink of whiskey when I want it; I drink all I want to," Root smirked, in response to Jones's questions.

How often have you been drunk, Jones wanted to know.

"I've never kept a memoranda of how many times," Root replied (*People v. Manahan* 1900, 135).

District Attorney Curtin told judge and jury that the prosecution was resting its case. It had been a presentation of facts and allegations little different from Manahan's first trial. The mainstay witnesses had told largely consistent stories of the conspiracy's hatching and the levee-breaking itself, but their character flaws had already been amply illuminated. And from the start of Josiah Perry's opening statement Friday afternoon, it was clear the untrustworthiness of the prosecution's witnesses was still central to the defense.

Perry asked: How could anyone be convicted based on the inherently questionable testimony of accomplices? If Howard Fordham had overheard such a tale as he claimed, why had he not run to warn the state authorities? And as for the cardsharp Hugh McDonald, a slippery man known as One-Eyed Mike . . .

Mason objected to the term.

"All right," Perry relented. "I'll call him the Honorable Hugh McDonald."

With his first witnesses, Perry sought to flesh out the basic argument that Manahan had an innocent reason for stocking up on supplies prior to the break. A former salesman for the Fort Schuyler Brewing Company in Utica, F. X. Schmelsle, was called to recount conversations he had had with Manahan. Schmelsle had advised Manahan that Congress intended to raise the tax on beer by one dollar. With that looming, Manahan had ordered the big lot of ale in early May.

But prosecutors interrupted the exculpatory story. They successfully objected to his recounting of the conversation, though Dunmore had permitted comparable hearsay testimony when presented by the state. Perry was thus forced to move on, to a second tier of witnesses.

As on the first trial, lumber company leaders Alonzo Denton and George Ainsworth undercut the character of the prosecution's witnesses. But as Curtin drew out on cross-examination, even the esteemed Forestport sawmill owners were connected to the breakers. Ainsworth recalled going to Utica to bail out Frank Bassett after Bassett was arrested on charges of causing the 1899 break.

"He confessed to me that he made the 1899 break," Ainsworth said, "and I then refused to go on his bond because he confessed to it."

Ainsworth's testimony invited diverse interpretation. Was he part of the Forestport brotherhood, letting Bassett languish in jail because Bassett had broken a code of silence? Or was he an upright man unwilling to provide bail for an admitted criminal? It was a question never answered before Judge Dunmore let everyone go for the day.

Saturday morning, Manahan's lawyers continued with their parade of Forestport men who swore the breakers must not be believed, and Curtin continued undermining the witnesses' own reputations. Justice of the Peace John Potter swore that each of the confessed breakers had a bad reputation about town. This was the same Potter who had signed the questionable arrest warrant Manahan had used in the failed effort to snatch Howard Fordham back up for Forestport justice. Potter, it developed, also had past dealings with John Root as well. Curtin had a few questions for him.

"Didn't you appoint this supposedly untrustworthy John Root to be inspector of elections?"

"I will not say I did not," Potter said.

Curtin, smiling, presented a town record book and asked Potter to examine the listing from 7 March 1899. Potter conceded he recognized his own signature next to the account of Root's appointment. Curtin, whose predator's smile finally incited Perry to "object to the counsel laughing and grinning all the while," pressed Potter on the inconsistency. The *Rome Daily Sentinel* of 5 May reported what happened next.

"I found out his character was bad years ago," Potter allowed, "and yet as an officer of that town I appointed [him] to that important office, knowing it was bad."

The Pinkertons had really done a job on the town. Everyone's past had become part of a file. When constable and former Forestport highway commissioner Tom Nightingale took the stand to denounce the character of the four confessed breakers, he was also forced to deny Curtin's assertions that he had once assigned state workers to labor on his farm.

But none of the defense witnesses was confronted with his own past more than Edward Marshall.

He related, as soberly as he could, the same story he had told in the first trial: he had been staying at Manahan's, in Room 14 on the third floor, and had been with the boys downstairs in the saloon all night the Saturday before the break. He had not heard a thing about the breaks. There then followed, on cross-examination, an exchange reported in the *Rome Daily Sentinel* of 5 May that better illuminated Marshall's character:

"Did you ever put a live snake in the your mouth and bite off the [head]?" Curtin asked.

"No, sir," Marshall said.

"Did you ever do so with lizards?"

"No, sir."

"Did you ever put a live animal in your mouth?"

Here Marshall hesitated.

"Yes, sir," he finally allowed.

"What was it?" Curtin wondered.

"A frog," said the ostensible snake charmer of the North Woods.

Curtin washed his hands of the witness Marshall and the court broke for lunch. Everyone was tired, including one juror who, feeling peaked, had to lie down on a divan placed for him in the jury box. But there were more Forestport reputations to undermine. Any man taking the stand on Manahan's behalf faced diminishment. Doctor George Kilborn, eight years a Forestport physician and himself son of a town doctor, offered minor testimony concerning Walt Bynon's sickness. Doctor Kilborn was as respectable as Forestport got. More than once, afflicted Forestport families paid him in barter because they had no cash. Curtin was unimpressed.

"I do get drunk," Kilborn admitted, after describing for Curtin his habit of frequenting Bynon's and Manahan's saloons. "I don't remember that when drunk I have drawn revolvers upon people in saloons, but will not swear that I have not."

Curtin and the Pinkertons were scorching the Forestport earth. The town, by their accounting, was a nest of criminals, boozers, gamblers, accomplices, turkey thieves, blind-eye-turners, and frog eaters. By Monday morning, when Dick Manahan took the stand, he was facing a jury ready to convict the entire town.

Guided by his attorney Jones, Manahan briefly recounted his life and then described the supply purchases he had made upon buying the old Getman House hotel. But when he tried to explain the timing of his large ale purchase as a consequence of learning of a pending $1-per-barrel tax, Curtin's objections cut him off. Try as he might, Jones could not phrase the questions such that Judge Dunmore would allow them, and so Manahan was left without one of his primary defenses. He and Jones had built their case around the explanation that fear of future taxes, and not preparation for a future break, motivated the purchases of early May. Dunmore, however, blocked them at every turn.

Manahan denied, at length, the various conversations the prosecution's witnesses had testified to. He had never talked to Root about causing a break. He had never heard Walt Bynon talk about the desirability of another break. He had never offered anybody any money for causing a break, and he certainly had never talked about causing harm to Al Schoonmaker because of Schoonmaker's premature alarm. As for the business with Howard Fordham, Manahan said, that was simply a matter of getting back what was owed. Fordham had run up a bar tab of $35 and a room-

and-board bill of $140 during his extended Forestport stay, and only about $50 of it had been paid. That was why Manahan and constable Nightingale had gone to Rome about midnight back in January.

When it came time Monday afternoon for cross-examination, Manahan was forced into admitting he had twice paid fines for selling liquor without a license.

Manahan was then walked once more through his relationship with Howard Fordham. The Buffalo salesman had left his lodging in Manahan's place in the fall of 1898, and returned in time to have his clothes burned up in the fire of February 1899. The lumber Manahan used in rebuilding his hotel came from Fordam's wooded lot, but it did not satisfy Fordham's accumulated room, board, and bar bill. That was why Manahan and Nightingale made their midnight raid on Fordham's room in Rome. He had not read anything in the several Utica newspapers about arrests being made in the Forestport matter.

"I did not have any suspicion that Fordham knew anything about me," Manahan insisted (*People v. Manahan* 1900, 207).

This statement stretched credulity. The story of Ed Marshall's being hauled back from Michigan and of Fordham testifying against him had been bannered across the newspapers back in December. One Forestport resident, Byron Cool, had felt compelled to write the newspapers denouncing the character of the Buffalo scofflaw. Manahan had every reason to believe Fordham was going to prove a witness against him, and Curtin, of course, knew it.

Manahan, finally, was able to complete his explanation for the ample beer purchases when his attorney guided him through an artfully worded redirect examination. The beer agent had told him, Manahan said, that the extra beer tax was soon going to be imposed.

"He told me he wanted to sell me twenty five barrels, and I could take it along as I wanted it," Manahan said. "If any of it spoiled, they would give me another barrel without extra charge" (*People v. Manahan* 1900, 210).

Manahan's story was now fully out for the jury to consider, and at 3:40 Monday afternoon the defense rested.

With all the witnesses done, lawyers cleaned up a few loose ends. Jones sought to have struck certain bits of evidence, like Fordham's testimony about the midnight raid on his Rome hotel, on the grounds that it had never been connected with the underlying charges. He had a point. Though there was certainly a suspicious odor about Manahan's late-night effort to arrest the man who had been publicly identified as the key witness in the Forestport investigation, no evidence had been presented to support the prosecution's conspiracy innuendo. It tainted the jurors' perceptions without substantially helping them reach the truth. Nonetheless, Dunmore rejected the bid. He allowed the Fordham testimony as evidence, however sketchy, of Manahan's supposed "guilty knowledge." Then he sent everyone home, to return at 8:30 Tuesday morning for the big rhetorical climax.

Thomas Jones faced a tough audience. The jury had been double-exposed to the Forestport case because of the publicity from the first trial, and Judge Dunmore had not filtered out biased men. The state had also presented a strong case against his client. The *Rome Daily Sentinel* of 8 May recounted how he changed the subject.

Look at the prosecution's pack of thieves, Jones urged the jurors. Those four confessed criminals had enjoyed the state's largesse, while poor Manahan had been persecuted. Jones's voice was biting as he reminded jurors of who was casting stones against his client. Jimmy Rudolph and Hugh McDonald, One-Eyed Mike himself, were gamblers who made their living by stealing at cards. And look at the Pinkertons, those unsavory tools.

Jones could not entirely ignore his client's disordered qualities. It is true Manahan pleaded guilty to selling liquor without a license, he conceded, but he paid his fine like a man. And, Jones correctly though fruitlessly pointed out, that incident had nothing to do with the crimes for which he was now charged. Other problems of perception remained: not just Manahan's ongoing engagement in the saloon trade, but his somewhat unsavory appearance. He was a calloused and heavy man, thick under the eyes and ragged around the edges. Life had worn on him. Jones sought to have the sweeter Ida Manahan, who had faithfully sat by her husband during his ordeal, reflect some sunlight into Dick Manahan's undeniable shadows.

"Dick may be a rough diamond," Jones said, "but he has a good family."

Curtin had presented a strong case. But as he rose at about 11 A.M., Curtin also knew he had to lock down Manahan's motives—and he had to make sure the jurors did not hold the employment of the hated Pinkertons against the state.

"Colonel Partridge," Curtin said early on, "who is charged with the safekeeping of the public works of the state, has been criticized for calling to his aid one of the ablest detective agencies of the country, an organization that has existed for over seventy years."

In truth, Allan Pinkerton was still an eleven-year-old child living in Scotland seventy years before, in 1830. He did not establish his detective agency until 1850. Curtin, in any event, did not want to linger on the Pinkertons. The less said of them, the better, so far as the district attorney was concerned. He had some other reputations to rebuild. Rudolph and the boys needed recasting as credible men. Certainly, Curtin conceded, they had had spots of minor trouble. John Fardette may have paid a fine once, Jones said, but it was only $5, and he only paid it to avoid annoying his mother. Root may have been charged with chicken stealing, but he was acquitted. Rudolph may have been arrested for fighting, but that was twenty-one years ago, when Rudolph was but a boy. In truth, Rudolph had been in his early twenties at the time he was convicted of assault. But put all this into context, Curtin suggested.

"Doesn't that compare favorably with anything they have up in Forestport?" Curtin asked. "Doesn't their record compare favorably with Richard's?"

If Manahan really had a proper regard for those family members that Jones had invoked, then he never would have undertaken the conspiracy in the first place. This was a dangerous man. Had he succeeded in snatching Howard Fordham back up to Forestport, Curtin said, Fordham "would have never lived to tell his story."

"I believe," Curtin sternly proclaimed, "that one of the most damnable conspiracies has been hatched up by this defendant and others at Forestport . . . this man got these poor ignorant fellows to do his dirty work, and didn't even do as he agreed by them."

As if Manahan deserved condemnation for breach of contract for his failure to pay the breakers, on top of everything else. But the notion of contract was, in a way, fitting for mention. The lust for commercial advantage motivated Manahan and his co-conspirators, Curtin said. Certainly Rudolph and the boys had not broken the levee simply for sport. With breaks to repair, there would be men swarming Forestport in need of food, drink, and lodging; that, Curtin said, was Manahan's incentive.

Curtin thought he was finished. The jury was tired and hungry, and more than ready for a break; but as Curtin sat down, a juror named Charles Dawes rose. Dawes was a weathered farmer from the town of Clinton, and he was unhappy.

"Mr. Curtin," he asked, "should not every man implicated in the break be brought to the bar of justice, though he be not indicted" (*People v. Manahan* 1900, 223)?

The question was fraught. The prosecution's case was built on the testimony of admitted criminals. Manahan's jurors were faced with the prospect of convicting one man while others complicit in the same crime walked free. It was not an unusual tradeoff, to let lower-order malefactors go free in exchange for their testimony against their higher-ups in the criminal hierarchy, but it was, evidently, distasteful to Mr. Dawes. Curtin could answer only one way, if he wanted to satisfy this juror whose vote he needed.

"Certainly," he said.

Curtin settled back into his chair, declaring his job done. In the jury box, a weary Rome clerk named Horace B. Case sighed.

"Amen," Case said, the *Daily Sentinel* of 8 May reported dryly.

After lunch, Dunmore spent forty-five minutes explaining the charges and the jurors' responsibilities. He enunciated the statute making it a felony to willfully injure any of the New York state canals, and he emphasized a man might be guilty even if he was not the one to wield the shovel.

"The person who first suggested the commission of the crime, the person who encourages it . . . may be a far more dangerous criminal than the mere puppet who commits the act," Dunmore opined (*People v. Manahan* 1900, 225).

Dunmore further explained that New York required the testimony of accomplices to be accompanied by corroborative evidence. But that corroborative evidence, he wanted understood, need not be strong enough on its own to merit a conviction; anything, he said, "which fairly tends to connect this defendant with the commission of the crime" would suffice: Manahan's beer purchases, for instance. He explained how to judge the veracity of Curtin's Forestport witnesses; if their testimony was to be impeached, he said, it would have to be based on their general reputation in town, and not on what one or two people might think. If no one had questioned their character until they turned state's witness, and if the character questions were raised by friends of the accused, all that should be taken into account. Not, Dunmore added, that he was expressing any personal opinion on the matter. Nor, Dunmore said, was he suggesting what weight jurors should place on the evidence presented that Manahan had tried to snatch the witness Fordham from his Rome hotel. Just think about it, he said, for yourselves.

Dunmore then summed up what he considered the strongest pieces of corroborative evidence. He all but repeated the prosecution's case: the plotting that Hugh McDonald and Howard Fordham claimed to have overheard, the assorted Forestport conversations about how profitable another break might be, the hearsay evidence concerning Manahan's anger upon hearing that Charley O'Connor might squeal to Tom Wheeler.

Dunmore made sure jurors understood that a "reasonable doubt" had to be much stronger than a "vague conjecture" as to innocence; "strong evidence," he said, must be attended to. And he stressed that Jones's anti-Pinkerton effusions were not relevant to the jurors' deliberations.

Dunmore also wanted jurors to appreciate how reasonable it was for the Pinkertons to be hired. If authorities believed that repeated Forestport breaks were caused by bad men, he said, "do you think they deserve criticism for employing professional detectives to discover if possible who committed these crimes, or to find the persons whom they believed to be destroying the property of the state?"

"I am not," Dunmore said, "expressing any opinion about it."

In fact, Judge Dunmore had been making his own opinions abundantly evident throughout the second trial. He had sat jurors who had followed Manahan's first trial, who had formed an understanding as to Manahan's guilt, and who had confessed an anti-liquor prejudice. He had ruled against nearly every one of the defense attorney's myriad objections, he had summed up the strongest elements of the prosecution's case, and he had defended the state's hiring of controversial detectives.

At 3:05 that Tuesday afternoon, 8 May, two deputies led the jurors to a nearby room. Lawyers, investigators, and the curious drifted outside, where spring showers had been dampening the town. Manahan and his attorney Jones, not knowing how long the jury would take, left the courthouse altogether. But barely two and one-half hours later, the deputies posted outside the jury room heard a sharp rapping on the door. A verdict, so elusive in the first trial, had been expeditiously reached.

It took another fifteen minutes before Manahan and Jones could be retrieved and brought back into the second-floor courtroom. Ida Manahan, strung tight by the ordeal, remained downstairs. Dick settled into his chair and scrutinized the faces of the men who had just determined his fate. Dunmore's clerk asked for the verdict, and the foreman, R. H. Doxtater, stood up. He was a farmer from the tiny crossroads of Stacey Basin, without a fancy education but intelligent and practical.

We find, Doxtater said, the defendant guilty.

Manahan's lawyers immediately demanded the verdict be set aside on the grounds that jurors had misbehaved in asking whether other Forestport men would face trial. Once Dunmore rejected that long-shot request, Jones demanded a new trial on the grounds of jury bias and Judge Dunmore's erroneous rulings. Jones promised a quick appeal.

None of which really mattered for the moment. Dick Manahan accepted his lawyers' commiserations, their earnest pledges to keep fighting, while other Forestport men offered such sympathy as they could. It was all just talk. Nothing, now, could save Dick Manahan from hard time at Auburn. Guilty in the eyes of the state and his Oneida County peers, the convicted Forestport conspirator stood up and looked about him at the Rome courtroom, at the new world he had just been ushered into.

Chapter 17

"FROM THE FIRST," THOMAS JONES SAID the night of Manahan's conviction, "I have believed Manahan innocent, but the result of a jury trial is never a surprise to me."

Once the door shut on the jury's deliberations, the lawyers could only plan for the appeal to the appellate division of the New York Supreme Court. That would take time, though, and could not come soon enough to save Manahan from being dispatched on the Auburn train.

Ida visited her husband in the Rome jail the next day. For his family and friends, Dick remained stalwart. He seemed the cool customer, but his passions were running hot when the subject of the state's investigators arose.

"The Pinkertons worked hard in this case," Manahan said in the 9 May *Rome Daily Sentinel.* "They knew that they had to have some kind of evidence to support their charges, and so they got those men, Rudolph, Root, Fardette, and the others, to come down and swear as they did. I hope those men will get their share out of the proceeds of making the case. That's all the wish I have regarding them."

Until the Pinkertons started uprooting Forestport, Manahan said, no one had thought much about how the canal breaks happened. Manahan's despondency ripened as he spoke of his family and the difficulty they would face keeping the hotel and saloon running. His voice was thick, his face flushed, his eyes red. Curtin had drawn jurors' attention to Manahan's run-down condition during trial and suggested it illuminated his depraved saloonkeeper's life. Actually, Manahan said, he was suffering from a bad cold.

By Thursday, the day of his sentencing, Manahan had recovered his emotional footing. At two in the afternoon, when deputies ushered the prisoner into Dunmore's courtroom, a large audience of the titillated and the respectful stood by. Dunmore gazed down on Manahan and ordered him to stand. For the record, Manahan first had to swear to the bare facts about himself. The *Daily Sentinel* of 10 May recorded the facts given: Manahan was forty-one years old, a Forestport resident, and keeper of a hotel. His parents were dead. He was married and a Catholic, and, he was compelled to say, he was intemperate. He was in the hands of the state, with few secrets remaining.

"The crime of which you are convicted is not a repulsive one," Dunmore told Manahan. "It is somewhat out of the ordinary. I shall not impose upon you the extreme sentence of the law, and your good conduct in prison will shorten it."

With that, Dunmore sentenced Manahan to four years in Auburn, less than the seven years maximum authorized for the crime of damaging the New York State canal system. And if he submitted properly to the prison regime, Manahan might shave his time served to three years.

"Thank you," Manahan said.

He seemed cool enough, courtroom spectators thought. His voice held, he did not break down, and he did not futilely shout his innocence one last time. He took his punishment, that is to say, like a man. Except later that afternoon, when the spectators were gone and a *Daily Sentinel* reporter visited: Manahan's stripped nerves were again apparent.

"This is wrong," Manahan said in a cracking voice, "all wrong."

Manahan had begun to more fully appreciate the nature of his prison sentence. Auburn's reputation preceded it. The state men's prison was a hybrid of rank brutality and lockstep discipline, part of a twenty-acre, inmate-built complex in the center of the town of Auburn. It was old in almost every way; Auburn prisoners had helped cut stone for the original Erie Canal construction three generations before (Shaw 1966, 129). The very spring of Manahan's trial, a group of prison experts had declared the 1,300-cell facility to be unsanitary and unfit for the confinement of prisoners. Auburn's ninety-year-old cells, stacked six high, were criminally tiny and ill-ventilated: three and one-half feet wide by seven and one-half feet long and seven and one-half feet tall. They stank from the iron sewage buckets prisoners squatted over and then lined up to empty each morning. Even the state prison superintendent confessed in his annual report that "the air is bad and foully contaminated" throughout the prison, while the walls were "loaded with the crusts of tens of years of use" (New York State Superintendent of Prisons 1899).

Though reformers had started revising the old penal system, Manahan would be entering Auburn when the old rigidities still largely ruled. The prison keepers would take from him his wedding ring and any other possession, and uniform him in a shirt with narrow blue-and-white stripes, a rough gray suit, and a gray cap. His hair would be clipped short when he entered, and he would be keeping his eyes straight ahead during meals, eating on tin plates, submitting to the wordless orders communicated by the keepers' rapping of a staff. He would be working for eight hours a day at what the state termed "hard labor," making brooms, or beds, or furniture for schools. If inmates rebelled, as they had two years before, Manahan and the rest would be placed on a bread-and-water diet until they properly submitted. Strap whippings and cold showers kept obstinate individuals in line.

Dunmore may have thought himself lenient, but four years in such a place would be retribution enough for Dick Manahan's sins.

"I am totally innocent of this charge [and] I think my sentence severe enough," Manahan told the *Daily Sentinel* reporter. "Tell the Rome people I am very miserable."

Elsewhere, though, Manahan's misery was considered properly instructive. Colonel Partridge, having inherited a canal system apparently riddled with corruption and patronage schemes, believed Manahan's conviction and prison term would send a salutary message statewide. Those who would prey upon the canal were now on notice. In Albany, Partridge declared Manahan's conviction "the first step toward putting a stop to depredations on state property; not alone in the Forestport region, but in all parts of the state."

"Manahan's conviction and sentence alone is a wholesome warning to the lawless classes, who in the past have made free with the state's property," Partridge went on, in the 11 May *Daily Sentinel.* "When his companions in these plots have been sent to join him behind prison bars, I believe that state property and private property, also, will be safer than it has been in the past."

The opinion-shapers at upstate newspapers likewise considered Manahan's conviction a proper object lesson. "The moral influence," the *Syracuse Post-Standard* declared in an editorial cited in the *Daily Sentinel,* "is good, and it is safe to predict that breaks in the Black River Canal near Forestport will be less frequent."

On Saturday morning, 12 May, Manahan left for Auburn. Arm in arm with Ida, unchained but accompanied by Rome jailer Hugh Owens, Manahan walked from the jail to the train station to catch the 11:09 New York Central. Many of his Forestport friends gathered there, including liveryman William Clark, on the verge of his own trial. The *Daily Sentinel* of 12 May reported that the sympathetic crowd lifted Manahan's spirits; he joked with the boys until the train pulled into the station. Dick and Ida embraced affectionately.

"Be a good boy, Dick," Ida urged, "and keep up good spirits. We shall see each other again."

With that, Manahan stepped up to the train, where a Utica undersheriff was ready to accompany him to Auburn. The Forestport crowd lingered while the train pulled from the station. Everyone knew Manahan's strong back would be sorely tested by the Auburn ordeal, and that Ida would have to struggle to keep the hotel and saloon afloat. But even as she stood on the railway platform, Forestport sympathies were distracted by another in their midst. William Clark had bid Dick Manahan luck and farewell with special fervency. The liveryman knew he might soon be following Manahan down the tracks.

. . .

A little more than a week later, Clark sat in Dunmore's courtroom. The cast of players was much the same as in both of Manahan's trials. Curtin was once again presenting the state's case, while Josiah Perry and Thomas Jones shared the defense. By Wednesday, 23 May, a jury had been selected: nine farmers, a Utica mechanic, a Deansboro businessman, and a carpenter from Waterville. Clark's attorneys had tried weeding out the obviously biased, but the jurors were tainted by their inevitable exposure to the publicity surrounding Manahan's two trials. They knew too much, even before Curtin rose to present an opening statement reprinted in the 23 May *Daily Sentinel.*

"This is the first time in the history of the state," Curtin said, "that the public highways and canals have been maliciously destroyed for private gain."

Clark's private gain amounted to $700 or $800 for renting out the rigs that carried workers to and from the break. He had hoped for even more. Among the Forestport conspirators, Curtin said, it had been Clark who had urged that the 1898 break be made far from the village, so that the need for rigs and teamsters would be greatest. Unlike Manahan, whose hotel and saloon profit from the breaks came indirectly, Clark was on the state's temporary payroll. When big Tom Wheeler took the stand on Wednesday afternoon, he disclosed a memo showing the state had hired three of Clark's single-horse rigs and four of his two-horse rigs. For up to forty days each, the state had paid Clark $1.60 an hour for the single rigs and $2.80 an hour for the double rigs. It added up, Wheeler said, to $555.50.

The cardsharp Hugh McDonald, his father-in-law Jimmy Rudolph, and the card-playing mason Frank Murray all related much the same testimony as they had in Manahan's two trials. When Howard Fordham took the stand Wednesday afternoon, Clark's interest in the breaks became clearer still.

Fordham, prodded by Curtin, told jurors of a conversation in which Clark had bragged about how busy Forestport became during the 1897 break repairs. The streets had been lined with people from the center of the village to the Black River bridge, Clark had said. Inspired by the memory, he invited Fordham to tour the Forestport Feeder with him. They rode in one of Clark's rigs up Dutch Hill and then down the towpath for a while before getting out and walking, while Clark jovially revealed the canal's vulnerabilities.

"There," Clark told Fordham at one point, "would be a dandy spot for a break." They walked further, over the repaired 1897 break, and on toward Alder Creek until Clark pointed to another spot where, he said laughingly, "the next break will occur." Later, Fordham said, he had been at the Getman House bar while Clark and Charley O'Connor talked about the profit to be made from another break.

" 'Manny' ought to be in on this," O'Connor said.

"Yes, a break would be a good thing for Manny," Clark replied, according to the 24 May *Daily Sentinel.* "I cleared $750 out of the other one."

Manahan himself arrived shortly afterward and joined the three men for a drink and, by Fordham's account, a little wishful thinking. Clark toasted the prospects for another lucrative break and offered Fordham an unsolicited job recommendation.

"Dick," Clark said, "if there is a break, you'll have to get two bartenders. Fordham would make a good one after you got him broken in."

The men laughed and drank some more. Soon enough, Fordham testified, the Monday morning broke when he heard Al Schoonmaker shouting in the street that the feeder had burst. Fordham told jurors how he bustled down from his hotel room to the River Street sidewalk, where Clark swore about Schoonmaker's calling the alert too soon.

Josiah Perry pulled a concession, on cross-examination, that Fordham had originally sworn to state investigators that the loony snake charmer Ed Marshall had been the one to cause the 1898 break. Perry let the implication sink in about the shifting sands of Fordham's testimony.

"Isn't it a fact," Perry asked, "that while you were in Forestport you had the tremens?"

"No, sir," Fordham said.

"You drank a great deal there." Perry made it a statement, not a question.

"Oh, I drank some," Fordham conceded, "but not so much that I did not know what I was about."

But no question asked or implication thrown seemed to undermine the state's case. All Clark's attorneys could do was try to rattle witnesses like Adelbert Larrivey, a Boonville man who had once worked in Clark's livery. Larrivey had once asked Clark how it was possible to make a living in a town like Forestport. Clark, Larrivey said, had enthusiastically recalled how he had made $750 out of the 1897 break. Larrivey's testimony seemed banal enough, and delivered by a man who himself had recently spent time in the Rome city jail on the charges of having carnal relations with a teenage girl. Soon enough, however, Larrivey's appearance for the prosecution would have some unexpected consequences.

John Root's testimony on Thursday afternoon, 24 May, more directly implicated Clark in the criminal scheme. Root had been wrung out for all he was worth. He had been confined to the Rome jail since his January arrest, and only his betrayal of former friends would save him. As in Manahan's trials, Root related how he had solicited Clark's contribution toward an 1898 break. Doyle and Manahan were not particular about where the break should occur, but Clark insisted it be far from town. That way, he had explained to Root, he would have more opportunity to rent rigs to the state.

Then, Root said, Clark had stiffed him and the other breakers on what they were owed.

"All you fellows owe me," Clark told Root. "I will call your accounts square."

That rankled. Root and the boys had done their share, and Clark and the others had profited from the resulting business. It got so that, one night shortly after the break, inside Manahan's bar, Clark asked Root when he was going to buy a round.

"I will if you will pay me what you owe me," Root snapped back.

"Why don't you pay your own bills?" Clark replied.

"There's Rudolph," Root said, conceding his own debt and turning his attention to another. "He's a poor man, why don't you pay him?"

"Rudolph owes me, too," Clark said, according to the *Utica Daily Press* of 25 May.

For Clark and the other investors in the canal breaks, the money saved by stiffing Root and the boys was penny wise and pound foolish. Fardette, promised $25 like the others, received only $3.25. Nonpayment inclined Root and the others toward disloyalty and mutual suspicion. When the Pinkerton operatives showed up in town, Root began wondering why

Clark seemed so chummy with one of the detectives. Maybe, Root wondered aloud, Clark was helping the Pinkies out so as to save his own skin.

"No," Clark insisted, "you don't have to worry about me."

Shortly before 5 P.M. that Thursday, Curtin having rested his case following Root's testimony, Thomas Jones arose for his opening statement. The four confessed breakers were untrustworthy men and confessed criminals. The notion that a solid citizen like Clark might have told the likes of Howard Fordham where he wanted another break was completely absurd.

"I ask you, gentlemen," Jones said. "Did ever a man in his sane mind, who contemplated committing a crime, make such a statement?"

The jurors had Thursday night to think that one over. Unfortunately for Clark, it was easy for them to imagine such blatant talk about a canal break. They had already heard enough about Forestport during the trial and knew its lawless reputation. They soon enough learned more. A sawmill owner from Hawkinsville named John Wells, testifying early Friday morning, said he had known Rudolph for twenty years. Wells formerly lived on property owned by Rudolph, and things had gone sour. Rudolph, he said, was thoroughly untrustworthy. Curtin was not impressed. He wanted to know precisely why Wells thought Rudolph so untrustworthy. It's what people say about him, Wells replied. Like who? The *Utica Daily Press* of 26 May reported the roundabout answer.

"Samuel Hunt," Wells ventured.

"Who's he?" Curtin asked.

"He's dead."

"Give us the name," Curtin insisted, "of one who is not dead."

"Oh, a lot of them."

"Name one," Curtin challenged.

"James McDonald."

"How long ago did he say anything about Rudolph?"

"Ten or 12 years ago," said Wells, caught out.

How many times, Curtin bellowed, had Wells himself settled with the state for taking lumber that did not belong to him? Wells insisted it had not happened. How many times, Curtin persisted, had Wells been sued in the last two years for taking the state's timber?

"Never," Wells said, "in the last fifty years."

His denial probably did not matter. Curtin's questions left a least a residue of doubt in the jury's mind about Wells's own character. It would be much the same for most of the others who followed him. Henry Nichols, for one. The owner of Forestport's general store and brother of lock tender Garrett Nichols, Henry was a loquacious man of property. He had held assorted local offices in the forty-four years he had lived in Forestport and had entered into various partnerships; he was one of the men who had put up Manahan's bond. He distrusted all of the confessed breakers save Fardette.

"Where did you stop last night?" Curtin asked, a curious question, tinted with implications.

"Mr. Curtin," Nichols replied tartly, according to the *Daily Sentinel* of 25 May, "I don't know as it is any of your bread and butter where I stopped last night."

Pressed further, Nichols allowed he had stayed at the Arlington, where, he went on, someone had tried to knock him down and rob him the night before. The robbery effort failed, but the news of it left one more bad taste in the jurors' minds. Forestport men attracted trouble wherever they went. Charley O'Connor, who was facing his own legal problems, testified that he had been staying at Manahan's hotel the Saturday before the 1898 break. He had not heard the supposed conversations Fordham claimed to have overheard. Clark was not even at Manahan's place that night, O'Connor said. Even more than the other defense witnesses, however, O'Connor was vulnerable to Curtin's questions. Curtin pressed him: The newspapers have reported on Frank Bassett's confession; he implicated you as one of the fellows who paid for the break. Jones fervently objected; Dunmore, for one of the rare times in any of the Forestport trials, upheld him. It did not matter. Through his questions alone, Curtin painted O'Connor as he had painted most of the Forestport men.

Ida Manahan survived a brief turn on the witness stand without being overtly ridiculed by Curtin. She also told the jury something no one in either of her husband's two trials had heard: that the boarder Howard Fordham approached her before the 1898 break and complained about cigar smoke filtering up into his room through the stovepipe and register. Ida said she tacked a piece of oilcloth over the open register. That would have blocked the smoke; it would also have blocked, presumably, the conspiring voices Fordham said he had heard floating up the Saturday night before the break.

It was curious, Curtin considered, that Ida hadn't related this exculpatory information at her own husband's trials. Had the defense attorneys simply overlooked it then, or had something happened in the meantime to refresh Ida's memory? Ida explained she had been sick during her husband's trials and under a doctor's care. Dick, she said, had directed that she not be called to court. Curtin let the point pass.

On Friday afternoon William Clark started speaking on his own behalf. Nobody else presented so far had really undermined the prosecution's case, and his attorneys had to hope Clark would favorably impress the jurors. He had, in that regard, some advantage over the fleshy and weary-looking Manahan. Clark's trim, clean features prompted his lawyer to call him "handsome," and a reporter said that with his "frank, intelligent countenance, he resembles a prosperous young farmer more than anything else."

Clark told how he had briefly run a Forestport saloon before starting his livery business. He knew the four confessed breakers, certainly. John Fardette had been a regular worker in his livery, receiving $18 a month plus board. But Clark and Manahan had never been on good terms. They were competitors, because Manahan also kept horses for rent, and Clark seldom ventured into Manahan's hotel or saloon. Specifically, he was not at Manahan's on the Saturday before the 1898 break, nor, he said, had he ever driven Fordham down to the feeder to show off the site of the 1897 break and identify likely locations for a repeat performance. He had talked with Fordham, undeniably; he had even ridden with him down to the feeder on the morning of the 1898 break, but he had never spoken of causing a break or of exacting revenge on Al Schoonmaker.

Clark answered questions unhesitatingly and did not collapse under the cross-examination. Still, his simple denials of involvement sounded thin. Though he had had defense witnesses deny seeing him at the Manahan hotel the Saturday night before the 1898 break, he had presented no alibi witnesses to say where else he might have been. Moreover, Perry made the questionable tactical decision to let a handful of shaky character witnesses follow Clark to the stand. Instead of letting Clark's direct first-person claims of innocence linger as the climactic notes of the defense, the *Daily Sentinel* of 26 May reported how Perry called the snake charmer and frog-eater Ed Marshall for a further attack on the prosecution witness Howard Fordham. Marshall was a wild card and vulnerable to the kind of character-slashing questions dealt out by Curtin. Dutifully Marshall asserted his yarn that Fordham had offered $1,000 in gold for information relating to the 1898 breaks. Righteously Marshall said he could not have provided any such information even for $10,000.

Curtin did not delve into the more eccentric twists of Marshall's character. He did draw out, however, that Marshall was pals with a number of the Forestport accused. He was friendly with Charley O'Connor, had stayed at Dick Manahan's hotel, and was indeed still living at Manahan's.

"You are there now, aren't you?" Curtin asked.

"No," Marshall wisecracked, "I'm here."

By late Friday afternoon, both defense and prosecution were ready to wrap up. The trial had moved quickly: barely three days for the presentation of witnesses, and without the lawyerly squabbling that marked Manahan's trials. They were well practiced. By the time summing up began Saturday morning, none of the lawyers needed notes. Josiah Perry went first, rousing for an hour and forty-five minutes all the lush courtroom eloquence he could muster. He summoned attention to all the extraordinary measures the state had taken to solve the Forestport breaks: the hiring of Pinkerton detectives, the involvement of the state attorney general's office, the close attention being paid by the superintendent of public works, the personal engagement of Mr. District Attorney Timothy Curtin himself. It all reminded him, Perry said, of the French state's persecution of the scapegoat Captain Alfred Dreyfus, an innocent man consigned to Devil's Island based on perjured testimony and conspiring witnesses.

"There have been murder cases in this court," Perry said, "where the district attorney has not made half the effort to find the defendant guilty."

Perry reminded jurors of the skulduggery committed by Rudolph and the other confessed breakers, and dismissed Fordham as "a schemer." He recalled Ida Manahan's swearing that she had covered over the stovepipe and register, so that Clark could not possibly have overheard the pre-break conspiring. He scornfully questioned whether any man would be so foolish as to tell another of his plans for a canal break. But mostly, Perry played the heartstrings. He revealed that he had, years before, been young William Clark's schoolteacher. He knew the man's good heart, and he urged the jury to envision how the next Sunday might be in William's humble Forestport home, with the family united once more around their justly exonerated father.

"It will not be the elaborate seven-course dinners eaten by Superintendent Partridge," Perry said, "nor will it be the sumptuous dinners that the Pinkertons have eaten at the Arlington, but it will be a dainty dinner prepared by a neat wife and a loving hand. There will be two little golden-haired children there, and William Clark will sit at the head of the table."

The mirage shimmered in the dry courtroom air; for one moment, everyone felt the illusion. Clark and his wife cried openly. Even Curtin, after a short break, had to admire the oratorical skill that could sculpt such an image.

"He's a man," Curtin said of his opposite number, "who can cry at will, tell you stories, tell you about France and wind up by picturing a family scene in Forestport. If you should do as the counsel asked you, you would open the prisons and let the criminals go free."

Then Curtin returned to the grounded facts. He had, Curtin reminded jurors, the confessions of four breakers. Clark, Curtin pointed out, had freely associated with Rudolph and the boys long before the 1898 breaks; they were all part of the same Forestport mob. Naturally, Curtin said, it took a great deal of effort to crack such a mob.

"We have been trying to unearth one of the most gigantic conspiracies that was ever concocted in the state," Curtin roared.

The *Daily Sentinel* of 26 May reported that after about ninety minutes, Curtin sat down and Dunmore let everyone out for lunch. Returning in the mid-afternoon, the jurors listened carefully to the judge's instructions. Unlike in Manahan's second trial, Dunmore correctly ordered the jury to disregard some of the hearsay evidence that the cardsharp Hugh McDonald had presented. But Dunmore also noted that even criminally charged witnesses were capable of telling the truth, thus upholding the testimony of Rudolph and the other breakers. He asserted that the evidence proved man-made violence had been done to the timber piles found chopped amid the debris of the 1898 break, and he ordered jurors "not to be swayed by any sympathy for the defendant or his family if you are convinced of his guilt."

At 3:25 P.M. the jurors filed out to their courthouse room. An Oriskany Falls farmer named Burdette Minor was quickly selected as foreman, and his first-impression ballot showed that eight jurors favored conviction and four favored acquittal. The men rolled up their sleeves and got down to work, unaware of a shocking report just arriving from the Forestport Feeder.

Chapter 18

JOSEPH LARRIVEY WAS NOT A WELL MAN. But the friendly, Danish-born former tannery worker had some connections. He had once run restaurants in Alder Creek and Boonville, and he had secured a job as a night watchman along the banks of the Forestport Feeder. One Wednesday night, Larrivey was feeling especially poorly, and the *Utica Observer* of 26 May reported that he had asked his nineteen-year-old son, George, to walk the canal for him. George, an inoffensive fellow some called "Forest," had a lot on his mind during his night patrol. His brother, Adelbert, was in legal trouble, charged with carnally knowing a teenage girl, and on Thursday Adelbert was scheduled to testify for the prosecution in Clark's trial. George was thinking on these matters and more when he started on his rounds about 8 P.M.

As he later reported, George rested a while at a small grocery store adjacent to the towpath near Hawkinsville. About midnight, he heard a noise coming from the Forestport direction of the towpath. Leaving his lantern on the store's porch, he went out into the towpath's middle. Almost immediately, he heard a sharp report and felt something sting him on his right side, just above his hip.

He had been shot; someone was trying to kill him.

Young Larrivey drew his .32-caliber revolver and, seeing the shadow of a man running down the towpath, he fired three times. All three missed; when he tried firing a fourth time, his revolver jammed.

He needed help, fast.

Larrivey pounded furiously on the door of the grocery store, but no one answered. He ran to the next house along the towpath, but there were only two women and a young boy at home there. He kept running, to the Union Hotel, and woke up the proprietor, a Mr. Weigert. Weigert declined to help. Too dangerous out there for either of them. He suggested the young watchman return home to Boonville.

"This Larrivey bravely refused to do," the *Rome Daily Sentinel* subsequently reported on 1 June, "and he cautiously returned to the towpath and put out his light."

When Larrivey reported the incident the next morning, investigators knew exactly what to suspect. Surely it was no coincidence that the brother of a prosecution witness was fired upon.

"It is clearly evident that there is a desperate gang in the village of Forestport, who do not stop at anything when they are looking for revenge," the *Utica Observer* averred on 26 May, the day Clark's jurors started their deliberations.

Bearce's Pinkertons started looking into this latest outrage. Colonel Partridge was furious. The shooting, an obvious attempt to frighten off a prosecution witness, showed yet again how unruly life had become along the Forestport Feeder. It was past time, Partridge vowed grimly, that canal order be restored.

"If this assailant goes unpunished, his crime may be the first of many of like character," Partridge declared in the 29 May *Utica Observer*. "We will protect the Forestport Feeder, and break up the lawless element in that section of Oneida County if it takes thousands of dollars to do it."

Clark's jurors, meanwhile, analyzed their gathered facts and impressions all Saturday night and toward dawn Sunday morning. It was an unmerciful schedule, without recess or chance for resistance to gather strength. One by one, the four jurors who voted initially for acquittal relented to the majority. By midnight, only one juror held out. Through the night, he held his solitary ground; for hour upon hour of futile argument until, inevitably, he capitulated near dawn. He assented to a guilty verdict, so long as it was accompanied by a recommendation for leniency. That was acceptable to the rest of the jurors. A verdict was their only real responsibility, and sentencing would be left up to the judge.

Shortly after 5 A.M., after more than twelve unrelieved hours of deliberations, one juror rapped on the inside of the door and informed the sleepy deputy outside that their work was done. It took another ninety minutes to summon Dunmore, the various attorneys, and Clark to the courthouse, where they arrived amidst signs of imminent rain. When all had gathered, and the puffy-eyed jurors had filed in, the foreman stood and declared the verdict.

"We find the defendant guilty," he said, adding a special recommendation for leniency in sentencing.

Clark, his face white and his jaw set, did not visibly flinch. He let the next words roll off him as Perry rustled up the usual demand for a new trial, and Dunmore announced his intention to postpone sentencing until Monday. The $10,000 bond that had kept Clark out of jail had run its course, and deputies escorted him away. Colonel Partridge, proclaiming himself pleased with the trial's results, bustled off to catch the Sunday morning train out of town.

Clark's wife visited him in jail later that morning, while their six-year-old son and three-year-old daughter played on the lawn in front of the jail. The talk offered scant consolation. Fordham and Fardette especially galled him. They were utter losers, penniless until they started testifying for the state. The local newspapers, too, infuriated him, with their printing of Pinkerton-planted stories that spun the jurors' minds against Forestport. The detectives, he believed, had coerced or lured the witnesses to appear against him. He had already heard jail talk that Fardette was complaining about being compelled to speak against Clark, and he derided Adelbert Larrivey's new suit of courtroom clothes as being Pinkerton-bought.

"I tell you one thing, and you will see if I am not right," Clark told the 28 May *Daily Sentinel*. "That gang will convict every one of the boys. They have started out to do this, and they will do it."

On Monday afternoon Clark stood again before Dunmore and recited the facts required of a newfound felon. He was thirty-five years old, Protestant, married; his parents were dead. He had a common school education, and was intemperate. He was, he said, an innocent man. Perry repeated the claim, and recalled again how he had taught school to the young Clark. That was less meaningful, however, than Perry's next assertion: that he had talked to some of the jurors, and "some of them are still in doubt as to his guilt." If true, a miscarriage of justice had just occurred. Conviction was supposed to come only after the elimination of doubt.

But it was too late for that.

"Personally," Dunmore told Clark sternly, "I do not see why any distinction should be made between you and Manahan. The crime of which you have been convicted is an extraordinary one."

Still, Dunmore said, the jury's request for leniency carried some weight. Taking the jury's request into consideration, he sentenced Clark to three years in Auburn. Though less than the seven years Clark might have received and one year less than Manahan's, it was hardly lenient; instead, Dunmore explained, it would be "a warning to you and others."

"When these cases have been disposed of, I trust that we shall hear of no more breaks at Forestport except those resulting from natural causes," Dunmore said in the 28 May *Daily Sentinel.*

The authorities shared Dunmore's hope that the message would even spread beyond Forestport. Sorry as it was, the Forestport gang through its destruction could yet show that the rule of law had been restored to canal country. New Yorkers were watching the Forestport trials and could learn from them, just as, upstate observers knew, the Forestport men had been for years learning perverse lessons offered by others' misuse of the Erie Canal. That was the dirty little secret of the whole Forestport affair. The breaks conspiracy may have been unique in its particulars, but it was disconcertingly cut from the same pattern found along the Erie Canal down all the years.

"The Forestport gang had been taught by bad examples that men much higher in the political world than they could ever hope to be did not hesitate to filch from the State treasury by various subterfuges," the *Utica Observer* said on 28 May, the day of Clark's sentencing. "They had seen the state dams and feeders dotted over with fellows drawing good salaries for no adequate performance of duty. . . . [so] if a pet of the political machine could be sent into comfortable quarters with a half-dozen other boon companions to pout in at $100 a month, when there was no reasonable work for them to do, why could not a countryman profit by selling whiskey, beer or food to men engaged in repairing an intentionally made break in the state feeder."

This was the larger meaning of the Forestport breaks. Well-placed men had engorged themselves on the canal for decades; as the *Observer* noted, such men could commit robbery "by legislation or administration." Men had cut corners, served their allies, and abused the public trust. They had, unwittingly, set an example for canal exploitation that the Forestport men took to another, explicitly criminal, level. That the common men of Forestport were being made an example of did not go unnoticed in some Democratic circles. The *Utica Observer* again noted scornfully that Governor Roosevelt had appealed to voters two years earlier who had hoped for "a stop to the extravagance and the punishment of the Canal fund plunderers." Instead, Roosevelt had utterly failed to prosecute the Erie Canal scoundrels, and his administration, the *Observer* complained, was just as "Platt-ridden."

William Clark had all the time he needed to sourly contemplate such parallels and inequalities. Shortly after 11 A.M. Tuesday morning, he walked from the Rome jail in the company of a jailer and a deputy sheriff. He had been holding firm in public since his conviction and the jailers felt no need to handcuff him for the short walk down James Street to the train station. Few people paid attention to the trio, shadowed by a *Rome Daily Sentinel* reporter, but at the station several of Clark's friends waited to bid him farewell just before he boarded the 11:09 New York Central to Auburn. He shook hands with each and accepted the kiss of a woman distantly related to his wife.

"Good-bye, my boy," the woman called.

. . .

Other Forestport defendants folded up like kites following Clark's conviction. The conspiracy was now an accepted fact in Oneida County; there was not a potential juror around who had not followed the case. On Thursday morning, 7 June, saloonkeeper Walt Bynon dressed up in his best dark suit and resignedly advised Curtin he wanted to plead guilty.

Knowing he was Auburn-bound, Bynon had already spent the first week of June paying off some $300 in debt to various Utica businesses.

Dunmore appreciated Bynon's show of character. The judge observed that Bynon was not one of the prime instigators of the Forestport conspiracy and did not deserve as strict a sentence as Clark or Manahan. Bynon nervously heard out the judge, periodically wiping his sweat from face and neck. Still, Dunmore wanted to send a message, and over Josiah Perry's urgent pleas for leniency he sentenced Bynon to a year at Auburn.

"I trust," Dunmore said, "that this punishment will be a lesson to you, that your conduct while in prison will be exemplary, and that when you come out it will be with the determination to lead a better life."

Other Forestport men, too, had given up the fight, sparing Curtin the aggravation of further trials. But at least two Forestport men were still resisting, though only one of them legally. John Conley, one of the hotelkeepers charged with helping instigate a canal break, had watched the Manahan and Clark convictions and decided he had seen enough. On Tuesday, 12 June, Conley's attorney A. F. Sayles stood alone when his case was called. Sayles had not seen his client in days, and had already informed Curtin the previous Saturday that he had been unable to contact Conley.

"I understand," Curtin said in the 12 June *Daily Sentinel,* "that Conley has been seen in various places in an intoxicated condition."

Two days later Conley was nabbed in Forestport late at night by a deputy sheriff and one of Bearce's men. Conley claimed he had been sick, laid up in bed and incapable of making it to the Rome courthouse. Whiskey sick, the detectives thought; they bundled him into a carriage around midnight and returned him to Utica.

A second Forestport defendant awaiting trial was also resisting surrender, legally. Cornelius Breen, the forty-six-year-old proprietor of a popular hotel near the Buffalo Head railroad station that served Forestport, had hired early on M. H. Powers of Rome. The fifty-year-old graduate of the Hamilton College Law School had carefully observed the front-page coverage of the Clark and Manahan trials. He knew the Oneida County jury pool was so thoroughly tainted with pretrial publicity that a fair trial was impossible. On Saturday afternoon, 9 June, while Walt Bynon was boarding the train to Auburn, Powers filed a petition for change of venue. If Breen were to be tried, Powers said, it should be far away.

"Since [the] three trials and two convictions; and, in fact, since about the month of December 1899, the newspapers of Oneida County have teemed with sensational articles and alleged matters of mysterious deaths and murder committed at Forestport," Powers noted in the 9 June *Daily Sentinel.*

Powers asserted that Bearce and his Pinkertons had instigated the stories casting Forestport in such a malign light. He claimed Partridge, too, had soiled the waters through his various interviews and stated intention to convict the Forestport breakers at any cost. Half-a-dozen Oneida County men signed affidavits attesting to what Powers said. Andrew Delos Kneeland, the thirty-eight-year-old former Rome attorney hired by Charley O'Connor, seconded all of Powers' arguments and likewise was calling for a change of venue.

Powers also had one more, rather startling, point to make. It happened that Colonel Partridge was offering a $1,000 reward for information leading to the arrest and conviction of the person who had shot at young canal bank watchman George "Forest" Larrivey. But Powers claimed, in his declaration to the court, that the canal bank watchman had "accidentally or purposely" discharged his own revolver. The story about a desperado trying to frighten or murder the brother of a prosecution witness was a concoction. The supposed assault was a bit of theater whose motive one might only guess at, but whose consequence was the further defaming of Forestport's reputation at the very time Forestport men were on trial.

For the next five months, John Conley languished, unbailed, in the Rome jail while Conny Breen sought to get his own case transferred somewhere out of Oneida County. The county court was adjourned for the season, and Forestport men went about their usual summer business. The sawmills ripped through the logs floating on the Forestport state pond, and the patched-over canal boats brought the fresh-cut lumber down the feeder into the main channels of commerce.

On a cold Tuesday morning in November, John Conley surrendered to the inevitable. Through his attorney he had sought out the best deal remaining to him. So had Conny Breen and Charley O'Connor. Though they had tried removing their cases to another county, they had concluded they could not escape the facts at hand. They watched while Conley confessed his guilt in conspiring to cause the 1899 Forestport break. Curtin then explained what had come to pass. He had been consulting with Colonel Partridge and Attorney General Davies, and had been quietly negotiating with the attorneys for the remaining Forestport defendants. It was time to finish up: to give Conley another year, and his cohorts a fine, and call the case closed.

"Considering the large expenditure necessary for the trial of these cases," Curtin told the judge, in the *Boonville Herald*'s account, "and considering that it would be more beneficial for the taxpayers and Oneida County generally if these people would plead guilty and take a fine . . . I have concluded to recommend a fine."

Conley's attorney reminded the judge that Conley had a young family dependent upon him. He was a businessman with an otherwise good reputation about Forestport. He deserved mercy, but Conley, on the judge's asking, had nothing further to say on his own behalf, and Dunmore sentenced him to one year. With good behavior, Conley might be home in Forestport in a matter of months.

O'Connor's attorney, A. D. Kneeland, then stood. He sought leniency for his client, a man, Kneeland suggested, of otherwise solid reputation.

"Up to this time," Kneeland said, "he has never been charged with crime. The reason that he was implicated in this one was because he entered into it in a joking manner, little dreaming that any man was criminal enough to commit the act."

Dunmore told O'Connor that he was satisfied that the Forestport ringleaders were already in prison. O'Connor's role in the breaks, though perhaps not quite trivial, was certainly marginal. Dunmore ordered O'-Connor to pay a $500 fine.

"The punishment," Dunmore said, "is not for revenge, but to protect the state from such acts in the future."

Breen, too, escaped with a $300 fine. Both he and O'Connor paid the fines that day. A few days later, it was Michael Donovan's turn. Michael had been bed-bound for weeks. He was, in any event, only a bit player in the Forestport conspiracies. His late brother-in-law, Michael Doyle, may have instigated the 1898 break, but Michael Donovan was only a spare hand. He had struggled from bed and, obviously fatigued, made it into Dunmore's courtroom on Monday morning, 23 November. Curtin recommended a $200 fine, and Dunmore assented.

Frank Bassett, the bank watchman charged with helping out in the 1899 break, did not fare so well. He sought leniency, reminding the judge of his five children and promising to "attend to business hereafter." His wife, May, had already written a heartfelt letter asking that her husband be spared, and his friends had likewise urged mercy. Frank Bassett was a well-regarded man. He had already served nearly a year in the Rome jail, simply waiting trial. Though he had no money to pay a fine at present, Bassett assured Dunmore that he would "try to secure it in some way."

The judge was not impressed.

"Justice would not be done in your case by a mere fine or suspended sentence," Dunmore told Bassett. "You were employed to protect the canals, and you helped to destroy them. I think that justice would not be properly meted out unless you go to prison for the offense."

With that, he sentenced Bassett to Auburn for a year. A few minutes later, he ordered the prosecution's witnesses Root and Fardette freed from jail. They had been locked up, like Bassett, for nearly a year. They had been wrung dry, and there was nothing left to be gotten from them.

With the late November sentencings, Curtin, Colonel Partridge, and the Pinkertons had reason to believe the Forestport breaks cases were entirely resolved. The canal was sound once more, the prime conspirators were locked up in Auburn, and a message had been sent not just to Forestport but to all of canal country. Law and order had been reestablished.

"It was a big undertaking," Curtin wrote Partridge in a letter reprinted by the *Boonville Herald* on 26 November, "but I believe that all concerned may feel compensated for the effort."

Bearce, the driven bachelor detective who had led the Pinkerton operation, won the highest honor the agency could bestow. Not long after the William Clark trial ended, Bearce moved to Philadelphia to serve as superintendent of the active Pinkerton office there. Curtin and Partridge, too, had reason to believe their work in solving the Forestport breaks would be rewarded. Most broadly of all, the authorities hoped the stern message sent by the Forestport trials would reward the state with peace and discipline along the canals. With the final sentencings, state officials believed the story of the Forestport breaks was over.

But it was not over. Soon enough, lawyers would again be in the courtroom, arguing for the freedom of Forestport men.

Chapter 19

DICK MANAHAN DOURLY WELCOMED Clark, Bynon, and Bassett when they arrived at New York's oldest prison. With practice and good luck, Auburn could be survived. As "A" class nonviolent first offenders, the Forestport men were treated less harshly than the prison's murderers, rapists, and hardened recidivists. Amid the some 1,100 prisoners, the Forestport men were somewhat unique. There were, in 1900, only seven Auburn inmates who had been convicted of crimes relating to destroying property (New York State Superintendent of Prisons 1900).

Day to day, the Forestport men marched to their prison factory jobs, to their meals, to their rank and confining cells. They read the approved version of Auburn news in the sanctioned and tirelessly uplifting prison newspaper. When the untoward occurred, like the suicide by hanging of a burglar in August, they heard the grittier account over the inmates' grapevine. They could receive, on rare occasions, the brief visits of their loved ones.

And in the spring of 1901, the Forestport men learned the entirely unexpected.

As they had promised, Josiah Perry and Thomas Jones had appealed Manahan's conviction to the Rochester-based appellate division of the New York Supreme Court. In early April, the paperwork proceedings having run their course, Jones and Curtin presented their oral arguments before a five-judge panel. Lush rhetoric did little good before these seasoned professionals, and Jones sharpened his presentation to several key points: Manahan's jury was contaminated by the information spinning out from the highly publicized first trial, the prosecution was allowed to present illegitimate evidence, and the defense had been unfairly prohibited from presenting its own best evidence.

Curtin, during Manahan's trials, had buttressed the breakers' confessions with the evidence about Manahan's pre-break purchases. Manahan had responded, during trial, that his purchases were customary; he had just bought the old Getman House, after all, and the spring season was just beginning with his stocks low. The only unusual purchase, he conceded, was the fifteen barrels of ale bought from the Ft. Schuyler Brewing Company. Manahan contended he bought them because he had been advised that Congress was preparing to levy a war tax.

Judge Dunmore, however, had thrown numerous obstacles into the straightforward telling of the tale. Salesman F. X. Schmelsle was not allowed to say what he had told Manahan, nor was Schmelsle's boss allowed to testify that Schmelsle had been the agent serving Forestport, nor was Manahan initially permitted to explain how he had bought the extra ale at Schmelsle's urging. It was this inability that struck the appellate judges as unfair when they issued their opinion at the end of April.

"His explanatory evidence was not improbable," Judge Frank C. Laughlin wrote on behalf of a unified panel (*People v. Manahan* 1901, 108).

Laughlin was a Roosevelt man, new to the appellate bench. The forty-two-year-old former Buffalo city attorney had only been named by Roosevelt to the New York Supreme Court's appellate division the year before, after four years as a trial-level judge. But he did not lack in confidence, and he could dissect arguments. He laid out the timeline. Congress had declared war on Spain on 25 April 1898. On 13 June, President McKinley signed into effect a war revenue tax that included a $1-per-barrel increase on the beer and ale tax. Laughlin said it was "quite likely" that word of the tax increase was spreading across saloons in the period between late April and mid-June. Moreover, Laughlin noted that Manahan's first jury had been permitted to hear the full explanation of the ale tax. That jury, deadlocked, had not convicted Manahan, while the jury that had been blocked from hearing the ale-tax explanation had convicted him. It was only reasonable to consider that the excluded testimony played a part in whether jurors believed Manahan or not.

"Defendant," Laughlin reasoned, "was entitled to have the benefit of such explanation of the purchase and possession of this suspiciously large quantity of beer as he could make" (*People v. Manahan* 1901, 113).

With that, the appellate panel reversed Manahan's conviction and ordered a new trial. It took time for word to reach him in Auburn and for his lawyers to file the necessary papers permitting his release on bail. Ida and his daughters thanked God and the lawyers. For his fellow Forestport inmates, the news was a more complicated bit of business. They were certainly happy for Manahan; an injustice had been done him, and now he would get another, third, chance. But Manahan was also the only Forestport defendant to have appealed his conviction, and so the appellate panel's decision only directly affected him. While Walt Bynon's one-year sentence was already set to end in June, Clark still had two years remaining and John Conley had another seven months.

Manahan walked out of Auburn State Prison and returned to Forestport just as the unpromising 1901 canal season opened up. His old friends, customers, and drinking companions greeted him warmly. But after the muted celebrations, he had work to do in reclaiming authority over his hotel. The lawyers' bills had stacked up, largely unpaid, and while the Forestport sawmills were running again, the town could sense a diminishing. Total canal tonnage had continued to drop during 1900, a decline of nearly 10 percent to 3.3 million tons, and everyone knew it was going to get worse.

As it developed, New York officials had little interest in returning Manahan to court for a third go-around. He and his cohorts had already been punished sufficiently for the state's purposes. A year's hard time in Auburn was message enough for anyone else contemplating abuse of the Erie Canal. The political environment, besides, had changed. The original Forestport investigation had been pressed when Colonel Partridge was new in office, eager to cleanse the canal of corruption. But by 1901, Partridge's attention had moved on and his original investigators had scattered. Manahan would be allowed to reclaim his life. His criminal trials were done.

By August 1901 Walt Bynon had completed his Auburn sentence and returned home to Rose, his children, and his saloon. Physically, Bynon seemed to have changed little. He was still heavy, enough so that he joined the Forestport "fat men" in a mid-August baseball game against the "lean men." His fellow conspirators Conny Breen and Charley O'Connor, who each had paid off their fines for their parts in the Forestport Feeder affair, teamed up with him for a rambunctious game where, the amused *Boonville Herald* reported on 15 August 1901, their head-first slides were "spectacular enough for the Pan-American, and the concussion caused by their striking the earth is supposed to be the cause of the earthquake shocks experienced in some parts of the world."

On such casual summer days, Forestport seemed not much different than in the time before the breaks and the Pinkertons. Piece by piece, though, the town was changing. Next to Manahan's hotel on River Street, the liveryman Charley Denslow had moved in as proprietor of the newly repainted Hotel Doyle. Charley was a big, garrulous man, politically minded, and a long-time acquaintance and neighbor of Michael and Jenny Doyle. He had never been charged with being a part of the breaks conspiracy, but he had been, by the accounting of Howard Fordham and others, in the room when Manahan, Doyle, and the others talked loudly about the merits of another break. His own wife had passed away years before, following childbirth, and after Michael Doyle died in July 1899 he had begun paying more attention to Jenny. Jenny had her two children to tend to, and a hotel and saloon to keep up. She accepted Charley Denslow's help, and soon enough was keeping company with him.

. . .

Tom Wheeler dallied as superintendent of the Erie Canal's Middle Division. More than just a survivor, Wheeler was a perennial political combatant. He outlasted several more governors and public works chiefs, until he opted in September 1907 to run for a second term as Utica mayor. Three decades since he had brawled his way to the top of the local Republican organization, the sixty-two-year-old Wheeler remained wily and strong enough to win. The city he took over seemed to be prospering. Optimistic engineers were straightening the Mohawk River and plotting the new Barge Canal construction. The new Trenton Falls hydroelectric plant on the West Canada Creek was giving the city electricity. The booming textile mills were attracting workers, and the city's population increased 29 percent between the time the Forestport conspirators went to prison and the end of Wheeler's two-year term in 1909.

Still not through, he then wrangled an appointment to the patronage post of Utica postmaster. On Halloween 1916, following an extended illness, he died. Uticans honored him with a lavish funeral. Even the traditionally Democratic *Utica Observer*, which had harshly chronicled his maneuverings for three decades, gave him a sentimental send-off as a man of "strength and determination . . . fearlessness and boldness," though the paper delicately hinted at his involvement in "transactions which would not be tolerated at the present time." Six months after his death, the first boat carrying politicians and top-hatted dignitaries passed through Utica on the newly opened Barge Canal.

. . .

Campbell Adams, the Erie Canal engineer, abandoned upstate New York with its unhappy memories of scandal. He made his way to England, where no one knew of Forestport or the full depth of the canal controversies, and then he proceeded on to the west coast of Norway near the Arctic Circle. It might have been penance, it was so unforgivingly cold, except that Adams had too many new responsibilities to fret about his past public works sins. He capably superintended the construction of a railway and harbor for a London-based iron ore company. By 1905, he had become general manager of a facility shipping out 2,500 tons of ore daily under conditions far harsher than anything found in canal country.

. . .

Partridge, too, was still keen on advancement into his sixties. When his old ally Seth Low became mayor of New York City, Partridge put himself forward as a candidate for police commissioner. It seemed a natural fit. Partridge and Low had previously worked together when Low was mayor of Brooklyn, and they shared an interest in upright administration. With

The first lock on the Forestport Feeder, ca. 1920. Photographer unknown. *Courtesy of Dorothy Mooney.*

his military bearing, stern demeanor, and success in cases like the Forestport breaks, Partridge appeared tailor-made for the police job.

Soon enough, though, Partridge encountered intractable problems. Within a year, having frustrated potential allies and antagonized the men under his command, the weakened Partridge was forced to resign (Kurland 1971, 157). That was the end of his public career, though he remained active in local businesses and athletic clubs. He remained, as well, known for his part in pressing the prosecution of the Forestport conspirators. On his death at the age of eighty-two, the *New York Times* of 9 April 1920 misremembered Partridge's achievement in having "rooted out a gang of politicians that kept the Erie Canal in a constant state of leakage, to enable them to do the repair work."

. . .

Partridge's predecessor, George W. Aldridge Jr., remained a force to be reckoned with in western New York. Men bound to him by past favors were scattered throughout the state's political ranks, and he cultivated his role as backstage adviser and Republican State Committee member. He felt sufficiently restored that by 1910 he made his last big political miscalculation.

When Rochester's congressman James Perkins died in office, Aldridge saw an opportunity to regain his public stature. His compliant party organization dutifully nominated him, and for the first time in nearly three decades he put himself before the voters. He was weighted. Half-a-dozen Rochester clergymen came out publicly against him, with the *Times* of 8 April 1910 fervently sermonizing that "the worst features of Oriental despotism and of Russian bureaucracy . . . poverty, discouragement, bitterness and death" were all bound up in machine politics as practiced by Aldridge. The Democrat hired a detective agency to investigate rampant charges that Aldridge's operatives were importing squatters—so-called "colonizers" or "floaters"—who would vote from their temporary boarding houses before melting away.

Aldridge's maneuverings did not avail, and he was beaten soundly. Back to the backstage Aldridge went, keeping his eye out for likely allies, and in 1920 he found one in Republican presidential candidate Warren G. Harding. Aldridge was among the first New Yorkers to back Harding, and in 1921 he got his reward with an appointment as Collector of the Port of New York. The prime patronage position gave Aldridge renewed authority and an important role in overseeing the enforcement of Prohibition laws. On 13 June 1922, while setting up to drive his golf ball on hole 3 of the Westchester-Biltmore Country Club, Aldridge paled and keeled over, dead of a heart attack. His subsequent funeral in Rochester was a lush business, fitting for a boss of the old school, with platoons of policemen and city workers, an honor guard from the Knights Templar, and a lying-in-state in the rotunda of the county courthouse.

During the same summer of Aldridge's death, the dismantling of the Erie Canal that he once oversaw continued apace. By 1920 the old, abandoned Erie Canal channel through Utica had become a muddy sink, stinking and full of garbage. Several weeks after Aldridge's death Utica officials began planning to fill in the old canal for construction of a new road (Walsh 1982, 391).

. . .

The reversal of Dick Manahan's conviction did not hurt Timothy Curtin's career. By then Curtin had already won reelection to another term as Oneida County district attorney. The Forestport cases, in any event, were no longer news. Curtin was remembered vaguely for having broken a corrupt ring, and he left office in 1905 a public success. He then went into private practice in Utica and built himself a large home overlooking the Mohawk River. He died in 1936 at the age of seventy-eight. John Davies, too, had been reelected to his position as attorney general in November 1900. The Forestport breaks case was accounted a signal accomplishment, and he followed up with high-profile antitrust prosecutions against New York ice and beef interests. When his close ally Roosevelt ascended to the White House, Davies had an offer to take a lifetime seat as a federal judge, but Davies cultivated other plans. In 1902 he ran for an upstate seat on the New York Supreme Court, opposed by some familiar faces. One was Watson Dunmore, the Oneida County trial judge now seeking bigger game as what one skeptical newspaper termed the "syndicate" candidate.

Neither Dunmore nor Davies won that race, and both settled back into private practice for the remainder of their lives.

. . .

The Forestport conspirators aged and faded, the breaks and their part in them becoming just one more of the yarns spun about the way the town used to be. In polite society, the breaks were not mentioned at all. As the men began dying, their obituaries discreetly omitted any reference to the crimes.

Walt Bynon was the first to go. He had been sickly for years, rheumatic ever since he had been hauled back to Forestport from a winter's logging venture, and was too heavy for his heart to handle. Only a decade after he returned from Auburn, still relatively young at forty and with his wife, mother, and eight children still alive to mourn him, Bynon died in 1911. His death was reported in the 11 May 1911 issue of the *Boonville Herald* and was certified by Dr. Kilborn, the same physician who had been subjected to harsh questioning during the Forestport trials. Kilborn's local reputation, however, had survived the trials, and he kept practicing for years.

Five years after Bynon passed away, Kilborn certified the sudden death of hotelkeeper Charley O'Connor. O'Connor, fifty, had been plagued by an ulcerous stomach for several years, but he seemed outwardly to be in robust health. Few guessed what was eating away at him inside, and only the historically insistent might read into his obituary a glancing reference to his part in the Forestport breaks conspiracy.

"He was," the *Boonville Herald* recorded on 12 October 1916, "a public-spirited man, and ready to cooperate with others in anything resulting in the benefit and welfare of his village."

John Conley, the allegedly hard-drinking former hotelkeeper, had run a small Forestport lunchroom since his return from Auburn. His son remained in town, his daughter in Utica, and his wife, Elnora, nursed him through his decline. In 1930, when he was sixty-nine years old, he injured one foot and had to have it amputated. Three years later, having never really regained his full health, he died. Frank Bassett outlived Conley, but not easily. Bassett's quiet wife, May, passed away in October 1932, and Frank lived on for several years longer.

William Clark got out of prison and took over the livery that his wife, Mary, had run in his absence. His business was like the Erie Canal, more quaint and less practical with every passing year. The North Country lumbermen kept using horses to haul cut logs to the riverbanks, and the remaining boatmen on the Forestport Feeder needed horses, but his work was an anachronism. Clark himself hung on until he was Forestport's oldest resident, a leathery eighty-six-year-old man with stories to tell and few peers to tell them to. In 1950, his wife, Mary, gone and his final confessions made to the good priest of St. Patrick's Catholic Church, Clark died.

Dick Manahan, the only Forestport conspirator to have his conviction reversed, did his utmost to regain his place in town. He kept ordering the ale and whiskey for his saloon through Utica's West End Brewing Company, the Gulf Brewing Company, and the Utica Malt Company, and kept ordering general supplies from Herb Helmer's rebuilt River Street store. Short on cash, the hotel business seasonally unreliable, Manahan began rolling up a tab at his various suppliers. It was standard business practice, and besides, his fellow Forestport businessmen were sympathetic to his special case. The debts accumulated, to Denton & Waterbury for lumber and supplies, to storeowner and volunteer firefighter Charley Bingham, to the overworked Dr. Kilborn. Manahan's lawyer, Thomas Jones, let a $127 debt ride for two years.

The debts kept growing until they were too large for Manahan to erase. His suppliers, sympathetic to his effort to rebuilt his life, nonetheless began pressing him for repayment. His options disappeared one by one. He could not walk down River Street without running into a creditor. By June 1903, about two years after he had returned from Auburn, the *Boonville Herald* reported that Manahan saw no choice but to declare personal bankruptcy. He owed $2,167, court records showed, and claimed assets of only $25. The bankruptcy protected him from his creditors, but ended his time in Forestport. He and Ida moved on to Alder Creek, to keep another small hotel. Once a big man in Forestport, Dick Manahan faded from view.

. . .

The story of the Forestport breaks faded after a different fashion. The criminal plotting of thirteen prominent men was far too traumatic for the memory to slide beneath the waters, especially when events occurred to resurrect the old stories. The Forestport conspirators had only been back from Auburn a few years, restoring their lives, when on the morning of 13 March 1906 the town was electrified by the news that the feeder had broken out again. Astonishingly, the break resembled the three that preceded it, and "with only about two and one half feet of water in the feeder when the break occurred, suspicion was necessarily aroused as to the cause," Tom Wheeler subsequently wrote with some understatement. Wheeler was then in his last year as Middle Division superintendent; following a "thorough investigation," Wheeler concluded there was no evidence the 1906 break was deliberately caused (New York State Department of Public Works 1906). It was simply another snapping of the canal's brittle bones. It was of a piece with the overall collapse of the Black River Canal, which in all of 1906 saw only four boats travel north of Boonville.

As the canals closed and the breakers died, and their children moved away, the Forestport breaks assumed the sentimentalized status of the quaint. The facts of the matter, too, became enmeshed in selective retellings and elaborations. In Forestport, the adornments included a rumor that a secret tunnel had been built connecting Jimmy Rudolph's saloon with Michael Doyle's hotel on the other side of River Street. Through this tunnel, it was said, the Forestport conspirators would travel in the course of their plottings. Curious and hopeful boys in decades of sporadic searching never found it, though in the mid-1930s a man named Harold Larkin probed around Jimmy Rudolph's old saloon and pool hall. The building once home to plotting and rigged games of chance had since become a modest restaurant. The *Boonville Herald* of 11 July 1940 recalled that Larkin, in knocking around the place, insisted that he had discovered a block of cement that rang hollow when struck. It was evidence, he believed, of the secret Forestport tunnel. Larkin asked for a chance to roll back the stone and reveal what was hidden, but a restaurant owner refused him permission. The questionable cement block remained in place, and the tunnel was never found.

Other missing places riddled Forestport. The lumber mills clustered around the state pond had been closing one by one, after the final frenzy of Adirondack timber cutting subsided following 1910. In 1921, citing a lack of need, state officials had abolished the job of superintendent of the Black River Canal, and the *Syracuse Herald* was denouncing the Black River Canal itself as a "joke" whose continued funding was "the most ridiculous, most inexcusable waste imaginable." By 1922, the last canal boat, loaded with potatoes, had traveled the Forestport Feeder. The Literary and Social Union closed, its ambitions depleted, and in 1926 the building itself burned in the latest of the Forestport fires. River Street hotels shut down, merchants relocated, and families moved on to Utica or Rome or anyplace where there might be opportunity. By the eve of World War II, the state was finishing a new bridge over the Black River and a bypass to route cars around the village altogether, prompting the *Utica Observer-Dispatch Magazine* of 4 June 1939 to observe of Forestport: "Once a Bustling, Lively Lumber Town, Even the Road Passes It By Now."

. . .

It is still possible to leave the main road and reach Forestport, for those with motives. It is even possible to rustle up a drink in a building whose foundations were built a century ago by my great-grandfather, the man I followed.

The old town remains, in scattered parts. A mile down a gravel road, past Williams Hill where Al Schoonmaker once spied the Forestport Feeder bursting out, is the town's St. Patrick's cemetery. There are Donovans and Gallaghers and their kind buried at St. Patrick's; somewhere in this cemetery, too, is meant to be the grave of Michael Doyle, the particular man I came in search of. But time has had its way with the place, and the gravesite cannot be found. Like the past, though, it can be envisioned.

I am standing at his grave in my imagining; I am addressing the stone face. It is quiet in Forestport. It is, I think, fall. I have brought an offering. It is everything I have uncovered, all I had never known. I lay my report, with its facts, envisionings, and inevitable misapprehensions, at Michael Doyle's place. I pray it does justice.

REFERENCES

INDEX

References

Aldridge, George Washington. Papers. Rochester Public Library, Rochester, N.Y.

Alexander, DeAlva Stanwood. 1923. *Four Famous New Yorkers.* New York: Henry Holt and Company.

Archdeacon, Thomas J. 1978. "The Erie Canal Ring, Samuel J. Tilden and the Democratic Party." *New York History* 39 (October): 409–29.

Barnes v. Roosevelt. 1915. Albany County Supreme Court, Appellate Division, Fourth Department. New York: The Reporter Co.

Bethke, Robert D. 1994. *Adirondack Voices: Woodsmen and Woods Lore.* Syracuse, N.Y.: Syracuse Univ. Press.

Bielby, Isaac. 1890a. *District Attorneys of Oneida County.* Utica, N.Y.: P. E. Kelly.

———. 1890b. *Sheriffs of Oneida County.* Utica, N.Y.: P. E. Kelly.

Chessman, G. Wallace. 1965. *Governor Theodore Roosevelt: The Albany Apprenticeship, 1898–1900.* Cambridge, Mass.: Harvard Univ. Press.

Clarke, T. Wood. 1952. *Utica: For a Century and a Half.* Utica, N.Y.: Widtman Press.

Cookinham, Henry J. 1912. *History of Oneida County.* Vol. 1. Utica, N.Y.: S. J. Clarke Publishing Co.

Davies, John C. Papers. Cornell Univ. Library, Ithaca, N.Y.

Depew, Chauncey. 1922. *My Memories of Eighty Years.* New York: Charles Scribner's Sons.

Ellis, David Maldwyn. 1948. "Rivalry Between the New York Central and the Erie Canal." *New York History* 29: 268–300.

Flick, Alexander Clarence. 1939. *Samuel Jones Tilden: A Study in Political Sagacity.* New York: Dodd, Mead and Co.

Garrity, Richard. 1977. *Canal Boatman: My Life on Upstate Waterways.* Syracuse, N.Y.: Syracuse Univ. Press.

Good Government. 1896. Vol. 15.

Gosnell, Harold. 1924. *Boss Platt and His New York Machine.* Chicago: Univ. of Chicago Press.

Harter, Henry A. 1979. *Fairy Tale Railroad.* Utica, N.Y.: North Country Books.

Hogg, J. Bernard. 1944. "Public Reaction to Pinkertonism and the Labor Question." *Pennsylvania History* 11, no. 3 (July): 171–99.

Horan, James D. 1967. *The Pinkertons: The Detective Dynasty That Made History.* New York: Crown Publishers.

House Committee on the Judiciary. 1892. *Employment of Pinkerton Detectives,* 52d Congress, 2d. sess. H. Rept. 2447. Washington, D.C.

Kurland, Gerald. 1971. *Seth Low: The Reformer in an Urban and Industrial Age.* New York: Twayne Publishers.

Langbein, W. B. 1976. *Hydrology and Environmental Aspects of Erie Canal (1817–1899).* Water Supply Paper 2038. Washington, D.C.: U.S. Geological Survey.

Lanni, Clement G. 1939. *George W. Aldridge: Big Boss, Small City.* Rochester, N.Y.: Rochester Alliance Press.

Larkin, F. Daniel. 1964. "A Short History of the Black River Canal." Unpublished paper. Erie Canal Museum, Syracuse, N.Y.

McBain, Howard Lee. 1967. *DeWitt Clinton and the Origin of the Spoils System in New York.* New York: AMS Press.

McCormick, Richard L. 1981. *From Realignment to Reform: Political Change in New York State, 1893–1910.* Ithaca, N.Y.: Cornell Univ. Press.

McMartin, Barbara. 1992. *Hides, Hemlocks and Adirondack History.* Utica, N.Y.: North Country Books.

———. 1994. *The Great Forest of the Adirondacks.* Utica, N.Y.: North Country Books.

Morn, Frank. 1982. *The Eye That Never Sleeps.* Bloomington: Indiana Univ. Press.

New York State Canal Appraisers. 1869. *Testimony taken before Canal Appraisers in the Matter of the Claims for Damage Done by the Breaking Away of North Lake Reservoir.* Albany, N.Y.: New York State Archives.

New York State Canal Investigating Commission. 1876. New York State Senate Document No. 48. New York State Archives, February.

———. 1898a. *Report of the Commission appointed by the Governor pursuant to*

Chapter 15 of the Laws of 1898, as amended by Chapter 327 of the Laws of 1898. New York State Archives.

———. 1898b. Proceedings. Buffalo and Erie County Historical Society, Buffalo, N.Y.

New York State Commissioners of Fisheries, Game and Forests. 1899. *Fourth Annual Report of the New York State Commissioner of Fisheries, Game and Forests.* Albany, N.Y.

New York State Department of Public Works. 1897. *Annual Report of the Superintendent of Public Works for 1897.* Albany, N.Y.: Wyenkoop Hallenbeck Crawford Co.

———. 1898. *Annual Report of the Superintendent of Public Works for 1898.* Albany, N.Y.: Wyenkoop Hallenbeck Crawford Co.

———. 1899. *Annual Report of the Superintendent of Public Works for 1899.* Albany, N.Y.: James B. Lyon.

———. 1906. *Annual Report of the Superintendent of Public Works for 1906.* Albany, N.Y.: N.p.

New York State Engineer and Surveyor. 1896. *Annual Report of the State Engineer and Surveyor for Fiscal 1896.* Albany: Wyenkoop Hallenbeck Crawford Co.

———. 1898. *Annual Report of the State Engineer and Surveyor for Fiscal 1898.* Albany, N.Y.: Wyenkoop Hallenbeck Crawford Co.

New York State Legislature. 1847. *Report of the Select Committee of the Assembly of 1846 Appointed to Investigate Certain Frauds Committed on the Canals of this State.* Albany, N.Y.: C. Van Benthuysen and Co.

New York State Superintendent of Prisons. 1899. *Annual Report of the Superintendent of State Prisons for the Fiscal Year Ending Sept. 30, 1899.* Albany, New York.

———. 1900. *Annual Report of the Superintendent of State Prisons for the Fiscal Year Ending Sept. 30, 1900.* Albany, N.Y.

O'Donnell, Thomas. 1948. *The Sapbush Run: An Informal History of the Black River and Utica Railroad.* Boonville, N.Y.: Black River Books.

———. 1949. *Snubbing Posts: An Informal History of the Black River Canal.* Boonville, N.Y.: Black River Books.

———. 1952. *Birth of a River: An Informal History of the Headwaters of the Black River.* Boonville, N.Y.: Black River Books.

People v. Manahan. 1900. Transcript. Oneida County Supreme Court, Utica, N.Y.

People v. Manahan. 1901. New York Supreme Court, Fourth Department, 70 New York Supplement 108.

Pinkerton Archives. Library of Congress, Washington, D.C.

Pinkerton National Police Agency. 1867. *General Principles and Rules of Pinkerton's National Police Agency.* Chicago: Geo. H. Fergus.

Platt, Thomas Collier. Papers. Yale Univ. Library, New Haven, Conn.

Report of Counsel Appointed by Governor to Prosecute Certain State Officials for Alleged Criminal Practices in Carrying Out The Canal Improvement. 1899. New York State Archives, Albany, New York.

Roosevelt, Theodore. 1973. *The Autobiography of Theodore Roosevelt,* edited by Wayne Andrews. New York: Charles Scribner's Sons.

———. Papers. Library of Congress, Washington, D.C.

Schiro, George. 1940. *Americans by Choice.* Utica, N.Y.: N.p.

Shaw, Ronald E. 1966. *Erie Water West: A History of the Erie Canal 1792–1854.* Lexington: Univ. Press of Kentucky.

Sheriff, Carol. 1996. *The Artificial River: The Erie Canal and the Paradox of Progress, 1817–1862.* New York: Hill and Wang.

Thomas, Howard. 1958. *Folklore from the Adirondack Foothills.* Prospect, N.Y.: Prospect Books.

———. 1985. *Black River in the North Country.* 1963; Reprint; Utica, N.Y.: North Country Books.

U.S. Bureau of the Census. 1900. *Census of Population. Entry for Forestport, New York.* National Archives, Washington, D.C.

Wager, Daniel, ed. 1896a. *Our City and Its People: A Descriptive Work on the City of Rome, New York.* Boston: Boston Historical Co.

———. 1896b. *Our County and Its People: A Descriptive Work on Oneida County.* Boston: Boston Historical Co.

Walsh, John J. 1982. *Vignettes of Old Utica.* Utica, N.Y.: Utica Public Library.

Welsh, Peter C. 1995. *Jacks, Jobbers and Kings: Logging in the Adirondacks 1850–1950.* Utica, N.Y.: North Country Books.

Whitford, David. 1897. Unpublished Diary. Erie Canal Museum, Syracuse, N.Y.

Whitford, Noble E. 1906. *History of the Canal System of the State of New York.* 2 vols. Albany, N.Y.: Brandow Printing Co.

Index

Adams, Campbell W.: after trials, 215; background of, 71–72; conference with Gere, 73; investigation of, 75; as State Engineer/Surveyor, 13–14
Adirondack Park Enabling Act, 84–85
Ainsworth, George, 134, 138, 179
Aldridge, George Washington, Jr.: after trials, 216–17; bid for gubernatorial nomination of, 58; break in 1897 and, 63–64; campaign of 2000 and, 172; on canal boats, 30, 33; commission report on, 74–76; investigation of Forestport and, 116; patronage appointments of, 30–31, 51–58, 71, 74–75; profits from canal system, 48–50; reforms under, 9; release of, 79; Roosevelt's view of, 94; safety issues and, 59; and use of canals for political reasons, 30–31
American, The. *See* New American hotel
Andrews, Charles, 44
Andrews (Utica judge), 128–29, 132
Auburn prison, 189–90, 211
Barber, George, 70
Barlow, William, 20–21
Bassett, Frank: arrest of, 133–34; confession of, 137–38; death of, 219; prison experience of, 211; released on bail, 179; sentence of, 209
Bassett, May, 133
Bateman, Sam, 111
Bearce, Herbert W.: and arrest of Forestport men, 128; background of, 108; chats with prisoners, 139; confessions told to, 147; on injustices in system, 134; investigation of Forestport and, 109–12, 117, 118–20, 130; investigation of Larrivey shooting and, 202; Manahan's first trial and, 150; orders canal inspection, 135; reward for, 209
Bingham, Charles, 129
Black, Frank, 58, 72, 75–77
Black River: Forestport Feeder break of 1898 and, 10; Forestport Feeder break of 1899 and, 99–100; Forestport's dependence on, 3–4; North Lake Dam failure and, 40–41

Black River Canal: construction of, 36–37; deterioration of, 4–6, 13, 33, 220; effect of Forestport Feeder breaks on, 5, 66, 67, 102; function of, 34–36
boats, 4, 10–11, 29, 33
Boonville, 5
Boyce, Charles, 92
Boyce, Harvey, 92, 99–100, 102
Breen, Cornelius (Conny): 1898 break and, 141; arrest of, 138; at Bynon's release, 214; plea bargain of, 208; plea for change of venue for, 206–7
Brown, D. Bryan, 70
Brown, Harry, 44
Burke, John, 65
Bynon, Rose, 89
Bynon, Walt: 1898 break and, 141, 156–57, 159, 160, 177; business of, 7, 26; death of, 218; fire of 1899 and, 89, 90–91; flight to Utica/arrest of, 127–29; guilty plea of, 205; illness of, 85, 136, 181; Manahan's testimony about, 181; prison experience of, 211, 213, 214; trial of, 170–71; as witness for Root, 122

Canal Investigating Commission, 45–46, 72–75
Canal Ring, 42–50
Carnahan, Sol, 138
Carnegie, Andrew, 60, 104–5
Carnegie Steel Works strike, 60, 104–5
Casbacker, Joseph, 158–59
Cascum, Henry, 12
Case, Horace B., 185
Charboneau, Herbert, 99
Chemung Canal feeder break, 44, 45
Choate, Joseph, 51–52
Christian, James, 87
Clark, Fred, 169–70
Clark, L. R., 41
Clark, W. C., 51
Clark, William: 1898 break and, 141, 154, 156–57, 159, 160, 177; break in 1897 and, 64; business of, 7; death of, 219; flight to Utica/arrest of, 127–29; Pinkerton men and, 110; prison experience of, 211; profits from canal repairs, 20; re-arrest of, 136–37; testimony of, 197; at transfer of Manahan to Auburn, 191; transferred to Auburn prison, 205; trial of, 170–200, 202–4; view of trial of, 203; visits canal break, 12
Clinton, DeWitt, 42–43
Collins, Lawrence, 65
Conley, John: 1898 break and, 156–57, 177; arrest of, 128; death of, 219; fails to appear in court, 206; and payment for canal breaking, 160; plea bargain of, 207–8; re-arrest of, 136–37; release from jail of, 138; and request for indictment papers/bail, 132–33; trial of, 170–71; as witness for Root, 122
Connors, Frank, 130
Constitutional Convention, 51–52
contractors: benefit from canal breaks, 5, 17–18, 71; improvement of canal system and, 53–54; investigation of, 72–75, 92–93; spoils system and, 43, 44–46. *See also* T. J. Dwyer & Company
Cool, Byron, 118, 182
corruption: in Aldridge management of canal system, 54–58; in Erie Canal administration, 30–31, 43–50; results

of, 204–5. *See also* contractors; politician(s); politics
cost of repairs: for 1897–1899 breaks, 103; of 1897 break, 14, 67; appropriations for, 51–52; done by Dwyers, 72–73; padding of, 45–46
Countryman, Edwin, 76
Crandall, Enos, 28, 175
crime: during repairs, 20–21; against talkative Forestport citizens, 97–98, 130; theft of canal supplies, 36–37
Culver, Abner, 56
Curtin, Timothy: after trials, 218; and arrest of Clark/Bynon, 128–29; at Clark's trial, 191–200; closing arguments of, 168–69; and final arrests, 138; Fordham's arrest and, 124–25; investigation of Forestport and, 112, 113, 115–17; and Manahan's appeal, 211–12; at Manahan's first trial, 149–54, 158–71; on plea bargains, 208–9; questions raised by confessions, 147; and retrial of Manahan, 172–87; and revelation of charges, 133; and reward for Forestport trials, 209; sealed indictments and, 132, 135–36

Daily, Joseph, 67–68
dam. *See* Forestport dam
Daniels, Ike, 24
Davies, John, 92, 103, 112, 168, 218
Dawes, Charles, 185
Dawson (reservoir manager), 42
Day, James R., 8–9
Dayton (telegrapher), 11
Denison, Henry D., 46
Denslow, Charley, 78, 214
Denton, Alonzo, 162–63, 179
Denton & Waterbury mill, 4, 8
Depew, Chauncey, 53, 76–77
DePuy, M., 49
Diehl (assistant to Gere), 73
Doe, John (pseud.): arrest of, 118–21; charges against, 130; as Pinkerton operative, 135–36; rumors about, 122–23, 126
Donovan, Catherine, 27
Donovan, Jenny. *See* Doyle, Jenny Donovan
Donovan, Margaret, 27
Donovan, Michael, Jr., 27, 102, 136–37, 208–9
Donovan, Michael, Sr., 27
Donovan, William, 27, 137
Doxtater, R. H., 187
Doyle, Cornelius, 26
Doyle, Edward Vincent, 27
Doyle, Ellen, 26
Doyle, Grace, 27, 89, 96
Doyle, Jenny Donovan: break of 1899 and, 102; children of, 26–27; and death of Michael, 96; fire of 1899 and, 89, 91; marriage of, 26; relationship with Denslow of, 214
Doyle, Jimmy Curtis, 89, 96
Doyle, Michael: 1898 break and, 141, 156–57, 159, 177; background of, 26–27; break in 1897 and, 64; business of, 8; death of, 96; events during youth of, 83–84; and events in birth year, 29, 31, 83; fire of 1899 and, 89, 91; July 4th celebration in 1897, 59; testimony implicating, 176; view of Pinkerton Detective Agency of, 104–5
Driscoll, D. D., 118–20
drownings, 59, 67–68

Dunmore, Watson T.: after trials, 218; background of, 148; and bail for Forestport men, 137; on Bynon guilty plea, 206; election of, 129; explanation of charges/ responsibilities of jury, 186–87; at Manahan's first trial, 149–50, 156, 158, 169–71; and retrial of Manahan, 173–87; and ruling on delay of further trials, 170–71; and ruling on secret indictments, 135; and sentencing of Conley/ O'Connor/Donovan, 208–9; and sentencing of Manahan, 189, 190; and trial of Clark, 172, 191–92, 196, 199–200, 204
Dutch Hill, 10
Dwyer, James J.: break in 1897 and, 64, 67; break of 1899 and, 101; dealings with Wheeler of, 56; as repair contractor, 17, 53–54
Dwyer, Thomas J.: break in 1897 and, 64; dealings with Wheeler of, 159; investigation of, 72–73, 75; as repair contractor, 17. *See also* T. J. Dwyer & Company

Erie Canal system: Aldridge supervision of, 52–58; and break in 1897, 67; deterioration of, 4–6, 13–14, 29–30, 32–35, 51, 59, 62, 64; dismantling of, 217; impact of feeder breaks of, 5–6, 66; under Partridge, 92–95; political mismanagement of, 30–31, 42–50; railroads as competition for, 31–33; and Roosevelt advisory commission, 92, 121
Evans, Albert A., 150
Evans, William, 138, 176

Fardette, John: 1897 break and, 176; 1898 break and, 140–44, 151–53, 177; arrest of, 126, 127; Curtin on, 184; Jones's accusations, 167, 168; and payment for canal breaking, 194; relationship with Clark of, 197; release of, 209; testimony against, 163–64; testimony of, 159–60, 176–77
Farley, George, 111–12, 129
Fenton, Reuben E., 48–49
Fincke, Fred, 82
fires: of 1899, 87–92, 98; in 1926, 221; as necessity/danger, 60–62
Fitzgerald, J. L., 33–34
Fleury, Sebastian, 86
Fordham, Howard M.: 1898 break and, 141; attempted arrest of, 123–25, 163, 164, 169, 179, 182–83; background of, 113–14; Clark's refutation of testimony of, 197; and complaint before 1898 break, 196–97; as informant, 98, 117–18; and Jones's accusations, 167; at Manahan's first trial, 153–54, 175; Manahan's testimony about, 181–82; Perry's attack on, 161–62; on talk about Schoonmaker, 28; and testimony about unpaid bills, 126–27; testimony against Marshall of, 114–15; visits canal break, 12–13
Forestport: after the trials, 214, 220–22; break in 1897 and, 64–67; break in 1898 and, 20–23, 27–28, 70–71; break of 1899 and, 102; dam construction and, 38–39; dependence on Black River, 3–5; destructive fires in, 61–62, 87–92, 98, 221; effect of investigation, 118, 121, 130; morning of 1898 break, 3–8, 10–11; North

Lake Dam failure and, 40–42; Partridge investigation of, 95–97; reputation of, 7; in summer of 1900, 207; support of Manahan, 191; view of Aldridge appointments, 52–53; vote for Roosevelt, 79; waning industries, 82–84
Forestport dam, 8, 37–39, 41
Forestport Feeder canal: break of 1897, 62–68, 69, 176; break of 1898, 11–15; break of 1899, 98–103; break of 1906, 220–21; construction of, 36; deterioration of, 4–6, 33; effect of breaks in, 5, 14–15; function of, 35–36; investigation of breaks/repairs in, 72–73, 103, 109–39; legacy of breaks in, 220–21; repair of, 17–20, 63–64, 101; story of 1897 break in, 176; story of 1898 break in, 140–55; transportation on, 10–11. *See also* trials
Forestport Literary and Social Union, 60, 110, 221
Forestport Lumber Company, 4, 8, 86
Forestport state pond, 8, 40–41
Forestport Water Company, 153, 154, 175
Fox, Austen, 92–93
Fox, William, 84
freeze of 1899, 87

Gallagher, James, 134, 137
Gardiner, D. S. V., 173
Gere, William H. H., 30, 73, 80, 100
Getman House hotel: 1898 break and, 141; fire of 1899 and, 87–88, 90; owner of, 8; purchase of, 25–26
Gorman, William, 66, 111, 141, 162
Gosnell, Harold, 48–49
Gray, Milton C., 57
Grinno, Al, 10
Grinno, Dan, 10
Gubbins (justice of peace), 113, 121, 125

Hannan, Edward J., 47, 51
Harding, Warren G., 217
Hawkins, W. M., 117
Helfert, George, 91
Helmer, Herb, 89, 91
Helmer, John, 89–90
Hewitt, Abe, 29
Hill, Jonathan, 40, 84
Hoban, Arthur, 85–86
Hotel Doyle, 96, 102, 214
hotels: closing of, 221; feeder break in 1897 and, 64, 67; fire of 1899 and, 87–92; and profit from canal repairs, 20, 22–25; and profit from dam construction, 39. *See also* Getman House hotel; Hotel Doyle; New American hotel
Hughes, Edgar: break in 1897 and, 62–63; resignation of, 93; as superintendent of Black River Canal, 52; visits canal break, 13, 14
Hughes, Henry, 65

Inglehart, Edward, 75
investigations: of canal system management, 36, 71–75, 92–94, 120–21; of Forestport breaks, 72–73, 103, 109–39; of North Lake Dam rupture, 42, 44–46; of water shortfalls, 38
Italian laborers, 21–22, 65

James, Darwin, 17
James, William, 138
Jones, Thomas S.: and appeal of Manahan conviction, 211–12; background of, 131; at Clark's trial, 191–92, 195; final arguments of, 166–67; legal fees of, 220; at Manahan's first trial, 148–49, 151, 152, 154, 158–61; as Manahan's lawyer, 136; on Manahan's verdict, 188; and request for indictment papers, 132; and retrial of Manahan, 172–78, 181–84
July 4th celebration in 1897, 59
jury: deliberation in Clark's trial, 200, 202–3; deliberations in Manahan's first trial, 169–70; retrial deliberations, 187; selection for Clark's trial, 191–92; selection at Manahan's trials, 149, 172–74

Keating (police officer), 119
Kelts, C. K., 88
Kernan, John, 110
Keyer, D. D., 117
Kilborn, George, 136, 181, 218–19
Klinck, George, 9–11, 155
Klock, E. A., 52
Kneeland, Andrew Delos, 207, 208

Laquay, Dennis, 85
Larkin, Harold, 220
Larrivey, Adelbert, 193–94, 201
Larrivey, George "Forest," 201–2, 207
Larrivey, Joseph, 201
Laughlin, Judge Frank C., 212–13
library building, 60
liverymen: break of 1897 and, 64, 67; profit from canal repairs, 20. *See also* Clark, William
Lockport, 9
lock tenders, 8–9, 30
Lord, George D., 45, 46, 116
Lord, Jarvis, 44, 116
Lord family, 5, 45
Low, Seth, 215–16
lumber industry: break in 1897 and, 66; closing of, 221; dangers of, 85; downhill slide of, 82–85; fire of 1899 and, 91; need for water of, 38; production in 1897, 59

MacFarlane, Wallace, 93
Manahan, Dick: appeal of, 211–13; arrest of, 128; and attempted arrest of Fordham, 124–25; background of, 24–26; bankruptcy of, 219–20; business of, 8; business with Fordham, 153, 154; contribution to library of, 60; death of children of, 27; fire of 1899 and, 87–88, 91, 92; first trial of, 148–71; and 1898 break, 141, 152–54, 156–57, 160, 177–78, 193; and payment for canal breaking, 161; prison experience of, 211; re-arrest of, 136–37; relationship with Clark of, 197; and requests for indictment papers/bail, 132–33; retrial of, 172–87; sentencing of, 189; testimony of, 164–65, 181–82; view of canal breaks of, 159; view of investigation of, 188; view of Pinkerton Detective Agency of, 104–5
Manahan, Ida: background of, 25; death of children of, 27; at Dick's first trial,

148; encourages Dick, 191; fire of 1899 and, 87–88, 92; and hiring of Jones, 131; at retrial of Dick, 183, 187; visits Dick in prison, 188; as witness for Clark, 196–97; and work on hotel, 141
Marrone, Vincenzo, 65
Marshall, Edward: arrest/trial of, 113–15, 117; background of, 86; charges dropped against, 129–30; Cool's letter concerning, 118; John Doe and, 119–21, 126; fire of 1899 and, 89–90; lawyer's visit to, 134; testimony of, 162, 166, 180; as witness for Clark, 198
Mason, John E., 149
McBeth, John, 53
McCarthy, Tom, 173
McClusky, Eli, 151
McDonald, Hugh: background of, 23–24; on Forestport's character, 7; on Pinkerton investigation, 111; and profit from canal repairs, 20; testimony of, 151–52, 174, 192
McGuire, Phil, 61
McGuire (restaurant owner), 111
McMahon, Teddy, 25
McMartin, Barbara, 84
McMullen, John, 65
McParland, James, 107
Mead, W. W., 65
Minders, Peter, 16–17, 20
Morrell, William, 91, 134–35, 160
Morris, George, 14, 15, 62, 72, 73
Morton, Levi Parson, 49–50
Murray, Frank: 1898 break and, 140–47, 151–53, 157, 177; arrest of, 121–22; background of, 23–24; jail experience of, 138–39; Jones's accusations, 167, 168; profit from canal repairs, 20; testimony against, 163–64; testimony of, 159, 192

Neejer, John, 78, 88
Nelson, Norman, 53
New American hotel, 8, 26, 89, 90
New York Civil Service Reform Association, 54, 57–58
Nichols, Garrett, 8–11, 60, 86
Nichols, Henry, 196
Nichols and Curran mill fire, 61–62
Nightingale, Tom, 124–25, 126–27, 180
North Lake Dam failure, 40–43

O'Brien, Arthur, 55
O'Connor, Blanche, 91
O'Connor, Charles: 1898 break and, 141, 152–54, 156–57, 177; business of, 26; and business with Fordham, 154; at Bynon's release, 214; death of, 219; fire of 1899 and, 89, 91; Pinkerton men and, 111; plea bargain of, 208; and plea for change of venue, 207; and profit from canal repairs, 193; and rumors of squealing, 160–61; testimony of, 163–64; as witness for Clark, 196
Owens, Hugh, 65, 128, 139, 191

Parkhurst, George, 174
Partridge, John: after trials, 209–10, 215–16; background of, 81; at Clark's trial, 203; on Farley, 112; Forestport Feeder break of 1899 and, 100–101, 103; and investigation of Forestport, 95–97, 109, 131–32; Manahan appeal and, 213; at Manahan's first trial, 150;

Partridge, John (*cont.*)
Powers's accusation against, 207; reaction to Larrivey shooting, 202; reforms under, 92, 94–95; at retrial of Manahan, 174; view of Manahan's sentence of, 190–91
patronage: Aldridge appointments, 30–31, 52–58, 71, 74–75; break in 1897 and, 64–65; building of canal system and, 42–50; canal maintenance and, 17–18; North Lake Dam rupture and, 42; under Partridge, 92; under Roosevelt, 82; in twentieth century, 214–17. *See also* politician(s); politics
Pender, John J., 110–12, 117, 158
Perkins, James, 217
Perry, Josiah: and appeal of Manahan conviction, 211; background of, 128–29; as Clark/Bynon lawyer, 136–37, 170; at Clark's trial, 191–93, 198–99, 202–4; at Manahan's first trial, 148, 161–66; at Manahan's retrial, 178–80; and plea for Bynon, 206
Pierce, J. D., 173
Pinkerton, Allan, 104
Pinkerton, Robert A., 104
Pinkerton, William, 104, 106
Pinkerton National Detective Agency: Carnegie Steel Works strike and, 60, 104–6; Curtin on, 184; Dunmore's defense of, 186; investigation of Forestport by, 103, 109–39, 179–80, 181; investigation of Larrivey shooting by, 202; Jones's use of public opinion about, 183; Powers's accusation against, 207; rumors about, 23, 106, 112
Plantz, M. A., 121
Platt, Thomas Collier: Aldridge and, 48–49; campaign of 2000 and, 172; fund-raising of, 79; guidance for Roosevelt, 81; on Roosevelt nomination, 76; Waterloo retaining wall and, 43–44
politician(s): benefitting from canal breaks, 5, 17–18; Doyle as, 27; as examples of corruption, 204–5; investigation of, 72–75, 92–93. *See also* Aldridge, George Washington, Jr.; corruption; Hannan, Edward J.; Partridge, John; patronage; Platt, Thomas Collier; Roosevelt, Theodore; Wheeler, Thomas
politics: of canal men under Partridge, 94; control of water rights and, 43–44; Erie Canal administration and, 52–58; impact of canal investigation on, 75–80; impact on canal system of, 30–31, 39, 42–50; investigation of Forestport and, 116; North Lake Dam rupture and, 42; railroad rate changes and, 31–32. *See also* corruption; patronage
Potter, John, 124–25, 163, 179–90
Powers, M. H., 206–7
Pratt, Charley, 12
Prendergast, Reverend, 59
prison. *See* Auburn prison
Proctor, Thomas E., 84

railroads, 6, 29, 31–33, 61
Raymond, G. H., 31
Reese (Oneida sheriff), 112–13, 115
repair plans, 17–20, 63–64, 101
Rome: arrest of Forestport breakers in, 121–22, 134–35; arrest of John Doe

in, 118–21; arrest/trial of Marshall in, 112–15; attempted arrest of Fordham in, 124–25, 126–27; first trial of Manahan in, 148–71; impact of canal breaks on, 5, 15, 66, 100; investigation of Forestport and, 112; jail experiences in, 138–39; retrial of Manahan in, 172–87; trial of Clark in, 170–200
Roosevelt, Theodore: accusation against, 205; advisory commission on Erie Canal and, 92; on Aldridge's patronage, 30–31; appointed superintendent of public works, 79, 81; campaign of 2000 and, 172; desire for second term of, 135; as gubernatorial candidate, 76–80; investigation of canal management by, 92–94, 120; investigation of Forestport and, 112
Root, John T.: 1898 break and, 140–46, 151–53, 156–57, 177; arrest of, 121–22; confession of, 128; Curtin on, 184; dealings with Ainsworth of, 179–80; jail experience of, 139; and Jones's accusations, 167, 168; Manahan's testimony about, 181; and payment for canal breaking, 160; release of, 209; testimony against, 163–64; testimony of, 160–61, 177–78, 194–95
Rudolph, Jimmy: 1897 break and, 176; 1898 break and, 140–47, 151–53, 156–57, 177; arrest of, 121–22; business of, 8; as card shark, 23–24; Curtin on, 184; fire of 1899 and, 90; and housing of workers, 20; jail experience of, 138–39; Jones's accusations about, 167, 168; testimony against, 162–64; testimony of, 156–58, 175, 192; Wells's revelations about, 195
rumors of war/spying, 23

saloons: as definition of Forestport, 7; feeder break in 1897 and, 67; fire of 1899 and, 87–92; profit from canal repairs, 22–24; profit from dam construction, 39
sawmills: contribution to library from, 60; dangers of, 85–86; fires at, 61–62; injuries at, 9; need for water of, 38; production of, 4
Sayles, Joseph, 137
Scanlon, John, 12
Scatto, Joe, 65
Schmelsle, F. X., 179
Schoonmaker, Al: Forestport men's view of, 178; as hero, 15; Manahan's testimony about, 181; reporting of canal break, 3–11; testimony of, 155; views of, 27–28, 154
Scripture, William, 137, 138
Seaboard (newspaper), 54
Shanahan, James, 47
Shanks (deputy), 67
Smith, George W., 85, 91, 110
Snell, David I., 75
Snell, Jacob, 75
spoils system. *See* patronage
Spring, Alfred, 76
Stanburgh, Bill, 61–62
state commerce convention, 110
Strong, Charles, 117, 139

Tammany Hall, 57
tanneries, 84
Tilden, Samuel Jones, 44–46

T. J. Dwyer & Company: and escape from prosecution, 93; investigation of, 72–73, 75; investigation of Forestport and, 116. *See also* Dwyer, Thomas J.
Townsend, William, 132, 133–34
towpath: 1898 wound in, 11–15, 16; bicycle trouble on, 33; man digging in, 70; patrols along, 70, 95; repair of, 17–20, 63–64, 101. *See also* Forestport Feeder canal
trials: appeal of Manahan's conviction, 211–13; of Clark, 191–200, 202–4; of Manahan, 148–71; retrial of Manahan, 172–87; sentencing of Manahan, 189
Tubbs, J. Nelson, 151
Tuttle, Charles, 17, 101

Utica: arrest of Forestport men in, 128; commerce convention in, 110; construction of canal wall in, 46, 75; dismantling of canal in, 217; in twentieth century, 214–15; Van Wyck campaign in, 78–79; and view of Pinkerton Detective Agency, 106
Utley, Henri, 90

Van Wyck, Augustus, 78–80

Waite (deputy sheriff), 134–35
Wallace, George, 76
waste weir, 10
Waterloo, 43–44
water users, 38, 43–44
Webster, J. H., 9
Weigert (hotel manager), 202
Wells, John, 195–96
West (steamboat captain), 32–33
Wetmore (deputy sheriff), 133
Wheeler, Thomas: administration of repairs by, 20–22; after trials, 214–15; background of, 13–14, 15, 55–58; on condition of canal system, 33; and dealings with Dwyer brothers, 17; Forestport break in 1897 and, 62–64; Forestport break of 1899 and, 100; on Forestport break of 1906 and, 220; and Grand Jury investigation, 57; investigation of Forestport breaks and, 103, 116; and political life under Partridge, 94–95; retention during reform of, 82; as target of Sayles, 137; testimony of, 159, 192; Waterloo retaining wall and, 43–44
Whiter, Hiram, 60, 88, 91
Whitford, David, 62–63, 64, 66
Whitford, Noble E., 32
Williams, George, 67
Williams, Gordon, 99

Yates, John, 46
Yeomans, Elmer, 90
Yeomans, Warner, 11